Companion to the
Revised Common Lectionary

8. Mining the Meaning

Year

Sandy Williams

Companion to the Revised Common Lectionary

8. Mining the Meaning

Help in Sermon Preparation

Year C

EPWORTH PRESS

Copyright © Sandy Williams 2003

British Library Cataloguing in Publication data

A catalogue record of this book is available
from the British Library

0 7162 0565 3

First published in 2003
by Epworth Press
4 John Wesley Road
Peterborough, PE4 6ZP

Typeset by Regent Typesetting, London
Printed and bound in Great Britain by
Biddles Ltd, www.biddles.co.uk

Contents

General Introduction to *Mining the Meaning: help in sermon preparation, Year C*

For almost twenty years Epworth Press has offered *Companions to the Lectionary* as an aid to preachers and worship leaders. The majority of the material has been prayers in various styles and for different purposes.

The *Companion to the Lectionary* (from 1998) has already broken new ground with material for All Age Worship for Years A, B and C, but now Epworth offers aids to reflection and thought for those who will be preaching on appointed lections.

The three volumes in the *Mining the Meaning* series, of which this is the third, will follow the Lectionary for the Principal Service for the day, as it is set out in the *Methodist Worship Book* (1999). This is virtually identical to the ecumenical *Revised Common Lectionary*, authorized for use in a number of major denominations. We offer this series, like its predecessors, to all who are called and appointed to preach.

Gerald M. Burt
Editorial Secretary

Introduction

One of the ways in which God reveals himself is through Scripture, yet what a difficult book the Bible can be! It is often helpful when biblical stories are introduced to us by someone whose understanding is greater than our own. This is the task of the preacher for whom this book has been written.

Biblical study and the task of preaching go hand in hand. For Christians, the Bible is first and foremost a book to aid both personal and public devotional life. This means that the Bible must be read prayerfully. No text can have any meaning unless it is read, and in this case meaning lies in the relationship between God, the writer (collators and editors, scribes and translators) and the community out of which the writing arose, and also every subsequent reader. However, the context of writing must be taken seriously and it has always been the Church's task to be a community of interpreters. Interpretation begins within the Bible itself as New Testament writers quote and interpret Old Testament Scripture. Today there is a great body of scholarly writing available about every biblical book and such scholarship offers many valuable insights.

The first part of my task involved examining lectionary passages in the light of contemporary scholarship, attempting to set each in its original context (the exegetical task). It was important to highlight any particular insights or difficulties that might affect its interpretation taking into consideration, for example, whether a particular passage was a piece of poetry or liturgical material, Gospel or letter and considering its historical base. This is inevitably a highly selective and personal enterprise and other writers might have made different points. The second part of my task has been to consider how a preacher might find 'touching points' between the passage in its original context and issues affecting Christian discipleship today (the hermeneutical task). I have deliberately kept the two parts of the task separate to make a clear distinction between them. A glance at the text will show that an exegetical paragraph is usually followed by a few hermeneutical starting points.

There are many different ways of reading and studying the Bible:

disciplines such as literary criticism and psychology, for example, have offered new insights. In recent years liberation theologians, including black and feminist theologians, have shown how people who are oppressed have rediscovered the Bible's relevance in their own struggles. Although I have referred constantly to the historical context of writing, I have also attempted to approach each passage from a multidisciplinary perspective and, where appropriate, have offered insights from a wide range of biblical scholarship.

It is clear that a short paragraph about each lectionary passage can only serve as an introduction for the preacher. I hope that this book will whet the appetites of those who wish to take the task of preaching seriously. Perhaps those preachers who have not yet begun to assemble their own library of commentaries may be encouraged to start purchasing their own. The choice of commentaries is bewilderingly large, but I would like to recommend the Epworth Commentaries, which have been written especially for preachers, and offer excellent introductions. During the preparation of this book many commentaries have been consulted. However, in Year C of the Lectionary most of the Gospel passages come from Luke and the commentary I have found most helpful is that by Judith Lieu (*The Gospel of Luke*, Epworth Press 1997).

One difficulty I faced related to dating. Many people use the terms BC (Before Christ) and AD (Anno Domini, The Year of the Lord), but today most biblical scholars prefer the respective terms BCE (before the Common Era) and CE (Common Era). The use of BCE and CE has become a way of showing respect to people of other faiths. While some may feel that this is politically correct language taken to an extreme, I feel that such courtesy is more likely to facilitate discussion than prevent it! It is also helpful to preachers to use the terms that they will find in their own commentaries.

Like my colleague, Michael Townsend, the author of the second book in this series, I struggled with the challenge of using inclusive language about God. I agree with him that God is beyond gender and that to refer to God solely by the male pronoun (he, him) can be misleading. I also rejected the option of using both he and she when referring to God and, for the same reasons as Michael Townsend, decided to use the male pronoun (see *Mining the Meaning: Year B*, p. xv). Nevertheless, I wish to signal here that this is an issue that all preachers must take seriously.

This book offers introductions to the lectionary passages in Year C of the *Revised Common Lectionary*. Following Trinity Sunday two Old Testament readings are offered each week. These are

Continuous Readings and *Related Readings*. As the title would suggest, *Continuous Readings* provide an opportunity for sections of the Old Testament to be read as a 'serial story', one week's reading following on from the previous week's reading. *Related Readings* have been chosen because their subject matter is more directly related to the content of the epistle and the Gospel. The preacher will need to decide which Old Testament reading to choose. In addition, there are a number of days when lectionary passages are common to all three years, for example the readings for Christmas Day, Mothering Sunday, Ascension Day, etc. The writers for Years A and B, Henry McKeating and Michael Townsend, have offered their own thoughts about these passages. As the third writer in the series, it has not always been easy for me to find something 'new' to say! In addition, Michael Townsend has also offered comments on the additional lections for a number of special services (Church Anniversary, Covenant, Harvest Thanksgiving, John and Charles Wesley, New Year: Watchnight and Remembrance Sunday) and these can be found at the back of *Mining the Meaning: Year B*. I commend the first two books in this series and the work of my colleagues to the readers.

Finally, I would like to thank Gerald Burt for reading this script and for his perceptive and helpful comments and constant encouragement. I must also acknowledge a huge debt of gratitude to my husband, Gil, who not only acted as my first reader, making Gerald's job easier than it might have been, but who also took on most of the 'domestic duties' for twelve months, enabling me to sit at the computer. Without him, this book would never have been written. Lastly, I thank Rosie, my collie-cross dog, who helped me to relax and reminded me that there was a world outside!

Sandy Williams

YEAR C

FIRST SUNDAY OF ADVENT

Jeremiah 33.14–16; 1 Thessalonians 3.9–13; Luke 21.25–36

Jeremiah 33.14–16

This passage comes at the end of 'The Book of Consolation' (Chapters 30–33) in which Jeremiah addresses the people during the final siege and destruction of Jerusalem by the Babylonians. However, there are two reasons why the words of hope in these particular verses were probably written by a later hand: firstly, because they express a more distant future hope and secondly, because that hope is expressed in messianic terms more familiar to Isaiah's thought than Jeremiah's. It was the task of the king, God's earthly representative, to bring justice and peace to Jerusalem and to protect the city from her enemies, but recent kings had failed and the Babylonians had triumphed. The writer of these messianic verses assured the people that their future well-being still lay with the Davidic dynasty. The expected Messiah is described as a 'righteous Branch'. David himself was described as a shoot from the tree of Jesse and this idea seems to have been taken up by Zechariah who describes the one who was the focus of his messianic hopes as 'my servant the Branch' (Zech. 3.8).

When Judah is ruled by God's Messiah she will be given a new name, 'The Lord is our righteousness'. God will deliver his people from destruction and devastation through the one who rules justly. Under such a rule, Judah and Jerusalem will also reflect the righteousness that comes only from God.

In a world where oppression is rife and rich nations thrive at the expense of poorer nations, Christians are called to live as people who serve a just God. The Church must speak and act for those whose voices are not heard because the sound of coins clattering into the coffers of the wealthy deafens ears!

1 Thessalonians 3.9–13

Paul and Silvanus had been expelled from Thessalonica and were concerned about the faith of this young congregation left without their guidance. Timothy was sent to visit the church and came back with the good news that the people had not wavered in their faith. In the face of opposition, with God's grace and in the power of the Spirit, they were standing firm. Their conversion had not been a 'five-minute wonder' but a life-changing experience.

When Paul heard the news from Timothy his relief and joy overflowed in thankfulness. Letters are all very well, but Paul wanted to be with them in person, so that he could encourage them and nourish their faith.

Paul prays for the Thessalonians asking that their love for each other will extend to all. Does this mean everyone in the church, or does 'all' refer to those who are not Christians? Paul seems to be saying that the love which they experience within their own fellowship cannot be contained, but will overflow to extend beyond the church to everyone. Paul also asks God to strengthen their hearts and the heart was the seat of the will, not the emotions. We all have hidden motives which affect our conduct, and Paul prays that their wills may be conformed to God's 'in holiness'. Implicit is the idea that Jesus' will was at one with God's will and they are to be like him. Thus, when Jesus returns, they need not fear the outcome. This is true for us too, though we do not share their expectation of Jesus' imminent return to judge and bring in God's new age.

Luke 21.25–36

Luke offers an apocalyptic description of the collapse of the created order, painted in dramatic and disturbing imagery, which provides a 'poetic' rather than a literal picture, but what other way is there of visualizing the end of existence as we know it? This is the moment when divisions between heaven and earth are ended and all creation becomes one under God. The climax is heralded by imagery drawn from Daniel 7.13–14 in which 'one like a human being' ('one like a son of man') represents the righteous people who had experienced suffering and oppression and pleads for them before God. These are those who will be vindicated at the final judgement. Now Jesus is identified as *The* Son of Man. Luke changes the clouds of Daniel (and Mark 13.26) into a cloud presumably because Jesus will ascend to heaven in a cloud (Acts 1.9) and presumably this is how he will return.

Just as the fig tree's leaves indicate the coming of summer, so the cataclysmic events indicate the coming of God's kingdom, which is expected in the lifetime of Luke's own readers. Apocalyptic passages balance judgement with liberation. Those who are ready to meet the Son of Man are no longer caught up in the temptations of ordinary life, but are free to live in this world in the light of the next.

When difficult days come, like the first Christians, we are called to remain faithful and trust in Jesus, the Son of Man, who suffered on the cross and continues to take the pain of the world to himself.

SECOND SUNDAY OF ADVENT

Baruch 5.1–9 or Malachi 3.1–4; Philippians 1.3–11; Luke 3.1–6

Baruch 5.1–9

Baruch is to be found in the Apocrypha, a collection of writings from the intertestamental period. This was a period stretching from about 200 BCE to 100 CE and corresponds roughly to the time between the writing of the Old and New Testaments. One reason for including passages from the Apocrypha in the lectionary is that these writings are part of the contemporary 'thought world' at the time when the early Christian church was being established. Baruch is a pseudepigraphal book, that is, a book written under the pseudonym of a famous figure from the past, in this case by Jeremiah's friend and scribe, Baruch. The setting is the troubled time of the Exile, following the fall of Jerusalem to the Babylonians, and the people are being reassured that God's splendour will be restored to the city and that he still has a purpose for it. It is likely that the actual time of writing followed the destruction of Jerusalem by the Romans in 70 CE. If this is so, then the people had recently experienced the destruction wreaked by war and must have been overwhelmed by misery and a sense of hopelessness and futility. Once again, despairing people were being reminded of God's faithfulness in the past and were being assured that God had not abandoned his city.

The imagery in the passage is of Jerusalem personified, taking off garments of sorrow and putting on the clothing of righteousness. God's splendour is only seen where righteousness and peace flourish. To such a city, exiles will return, led home by God. In language reminiscent of Isaiah 40.4, obstacles will be removed as the ground is made level so that people can walk in safety. This is a joyous homecoming because God in his mercy acts with and for his people.

Today, many displaced people long to return home and others feel that they have no roots. The Church is called to become a welcoming community so that those who enter will feel that they have 'come home' and have found a place where they belong. How can we become such a community?

Malachi 3.1–4

Following the period of the Exile and the restoration of the Temple, the hope that the people had learned from past mistakes seemed to be in vain. Corruption was still rife even among the priesthood. The people had continued to act unfaithfully. The question Malachi responds to in these verses is, 'Where is the God of justice?'

A messenger (an angel) is coming who will speak the truth in order to prepare the way for God's arrival. This is the messenger of the covenant, who will remind the people that God's faithfulness requires a response of willing obedience. The implication is that this relationship has once again been broken. Judgement will begin in God's house. The Temple was thought of as the place of God's dwelling and yet paradoxically it is also the place to which God will come. When God comes to judge, his arrival is like that of fire – the fire of purification, which both refines and cleanses. This purification will begin with the priests who stand at the heart of religious life. Then true worship will be like it was in days of old, in the ideal age of obedience. Once again, a prophet looks back to a time of perfect relationship, when God and his people were one. Was there ever such a time? Yet how important it is to feel that this is about restoration of relationship.

This Advent season is a good time to remember that the God we encounter in worship expects our lives to reflect the divine life. Do we hear the words of the messenger, challenging us to recognize our own need for purification so that we are ready to stand before the God whom we already know, but for whose coming we prepare? We must not forget that 'purification' is about not only our relationship with God, but also our relationships with each other. By caring for others and welcoming them, we are worshipping God.

Philippians 1.3–11

Paul is in prison when he writes to the church at Philippi. He prays to the one he calls 'my God'. Paul does not mean that his God is not also the God of the Philippians, rather he is reminding them that this is the God who is the Father of Jesus to whom his people can pray with confidence. Paul thinks about his friends in Philippi and to 'remember people before God' is to pray for them, just as they 'remember' Paul and pray for him. Paul's personal situation may be devoid of hope, yet he is strengthened and encouraged both because he is certain that, through Jesus, God's loving purposes will be completed (v.6) and because the Philippian Christians remain faithful. The overwhelming emotion of these verses is one of thanksgiving and joy because in God's grace they join with Paul in their commitment to the gospel. What is clear is that Paul and the Philippian Christians are partners and their relationship is one of mutual support. Paul expresses his longings for their spiritual well-being, asking that God will continue working in their lives until 'the day of Christ', the time of Jesus' expected return, the same Jesus who has helped to produce 'the harvest of righteousness' in their lives. Here the Advent tension is expressed: that the Jesus for whom we wait is the same Jesus who works in our lives helping us to reach out both to God and to others, especially those in need.

When we find it difficult to offer time and service, when we avoid approaching someone because we are afraid of where an encounter will lead, it is good to know that we are not alone. The wonderful paradox of the gospel is that Jesus, for whom we wait, is also the one who is closer to us than our own breathing! He is with us whenever we approach friend or stranger with love in our hearts, whenever we are ready to go where he leads and whenever we offer our help with openhearted generosity.

Luke 3.1–6

Luke makes a new start to the story of Jesus. The early chapters, with their birth narratives, have raised our expectations about the one we are about to meet as an adult. Now Luke sets the scene for what is to follow. The action takes place on a universal stage with Rome as its goal (Acts 28.14). Luke's Gospel is the first act of a two-part drama, Luke-Acts, written by the same author. As the drama unfolds it will take place within the Roman Empire. Pontius Pilate will play his part as will the ruler of Galilee, Herod Antipas (one of the four 'puppet kings', the tetrarchs), along with the Jerusalem priesthood who saw Jesus as a threat.

Into this world John appears, centre stage. It is no surprise that his voice is heard in the wilderness, the place where God led his people and dwelt with them following the Exodus from Egypt. The wilderness became synonymous with God's saving act and the time of covenant relationship when people lived in obedience to God's will. The wilderness would be the place of the new salvation. John was baptizing people who were ready to repent and hoped to be forgiven so that right relationships between God and his people would be restored. The prophecy from Isaiah, which was also referred to in this week's passage from Baruch, speaks of levelling ground. In Isaiah, this is about the smooth path which God makes for his people's return. In Luke, the levelling also has resonances with Mary's song, the Magnificat (1.51–53) when the injustices of this world are also removed. This is what it means to repent: that people must share in God's concern and act on behalf of the lowly, the hungry and those who are most in need, overturning the accepted way in which society is structured. Those who repent in this way will be ready for what is to come when Jesus steps onto the stage.

All four readings bring us face to face with our own selfishness and complacency. It is human nature to wish to be safe, warm, clothed, fed and comforted. However, we must remember that this is what God wants for all his people. It cannot be right that we have so much when others have so little. Yet, guilt is often debilitating! We must not act out of a sense of guilt, but out of a sense of gratitude. When we rejoice because we belong to God's people, then we will discover how to share our plenty as we turn towards those who need us to speak and act for them.

THIRD SUNDAY OF ADVENT

Zephaniah 3.14–20; Philippians 4.4–7; Luke 3.7–18

Zephaniah 3.14–20

These last verses in the book of Zephaniah depict the glorious future when God will reign as King in Jerusalem. This was the hope of God's people during the years of exile. God would no longer judge them for what was past, but would vanquish their enemies. The poetry of this passage reads like an enthronement psalm, but here God is the warrior king in their midst. When God reigns those who were despised in society, represented here by the lame and the outcast, will be restored within the community of praise. Verse 20 is probably a post-exilic addition promising the return of the exiles. Once again, here is a prophecy which offers encouragement to later generations living in challenging circumstances. Today, we may find it difficult to read passages which speak of God 'taking sides' and defeating enemies. However, prophecies which describe the restoration of Jerusalem's fortunes signal the time when God will draw all nations together under the divine rule bringing universal peace for all people who wish to become citizens.

This reading enables us to acknowledge feelings that often remain hidden, for we too would like God to 'vanquish our enemies' whose actions cause immeasurable hurt and destruction. Yet we know that God's judgement and mercy are found on a cross where God in Christ takes the pain and anger of the world to himself.

Philippians 4.4–7

Towards the end of his letter Paul offers the Philippians instructions about living a Christian life. He tells them to rejoice and that the source of their rejoicing is Christ. Knowing everything that Christ has done for them and the relationship they have with him, the only possible response is one of joy. Paul continues by reminding them that 'gentleness' should characterize their relationships with each other. Perhaps the best translation would be 'magnanimity', the ability to treat even the most irritating people courteously and reasonably. It may be that there were some divisions in the church and that joy and mutual consideration were lacking, but 'everyone' might well refer to those outside the church who were making life difficult for the Christian community. If so, this might explain why Paul goes on to tell them not to be anxious but to pray in every situation. Requests should be made with thanksgiving, for remembering with gratitude what God has already done is an expression of confidence in his faithfulness and love. Praying in this way brings God's peace, the sense of wholeness and 'at-one-ness' with God, grounded in the relationship with Christ which nothing can shake.

It is easy to pay lip-service to the idea of placing all our anxieties in God's keeping when we pray, but less easy to 'let go' of our worries. Perhaps we forget that prayer, like anything else that is worthwhile, requires practice!

Luke 3.7–18

John preaches to the people who have come to be baptized and speaks in the context of the last days before God's final judgement, 'the wrath to come'. His opening words are harsh in the extreme as he addresses the crowd as 'You brood of vipers'. These are Israelites who have assumed that because they are members of God's chosen people they will not be judged severely and their salvation is already assured. John insists that there is an urgency about their repentance and they need to change their ways immediately because there is no time left.

The fruits of repentance have practical expression as those who have more are confronted with the imperative to share with those who have less. Two groups are singled out: tax collectors and soldiers. The tax collector's job was offered to the highest bidder and extortion was rife. Tax collectors had to fraternize with Roman authorities and handle Roman coinage, and were shunned because of their greed and their religious impurity. The soldiers mentioned here might well have been Jews in Herod Antipas' army and their task may have been to support the tax collectors in their duties. John's requirements reflect not practical reality but an ideal, yet they are rooted in real concern for those despised by society.

John's baptism is with water, but the Messiah's baptism is with the Holy Spirit. Does this reflect a later Christian understanding of baptism? The Messiah is the one whose coming brings the final judgement, for fire both refines and purifies. People will be sifted like wheat from chaff and it is clear that those who fail to repent share the fate of the chaff! The image of being burned in 'unquenchable fire' is not likely to appeal to today's congregations. However, the outcome of people's greed and the unequal sharing of the earth's resources is that many people live in appalling conditions. Luke's Gospel is always concerned with the overturning of the existing order and with God's concern for those despised or forgotten by society. What should be the fate of those of us who refuse to listen to the voice calling us to change our ways?

FOURTH SUNDAY OF ADVENT

Micah 5.2–5a; Hebrews 10.5–10; Luke 1.39–45 (46–55)

Micah 5.2–5a

God promises that from Bethlehem will come a ruler whose power will extend over all the earth. The double name, Bethlehem Ephratha, seems to represent two different family groups whose history had long since merged. Both names were associated with Jesse, the father of David. In Bethlehem, God once again chose the smallest and most unlikely place just as in the past he had chosen the youngest of Jesse's sons, the last to be considered, to become king.

The description of the woman in childbirth is unlikely to refer to the birth of the new ruler. More likely, the labour pangs mirror the experience of the people in exile who were suffering under the power of their enemies. The moment of birth is the moment of their liberation and their return to Jerusalem. Their future hope is in a ruler who will be the ideal king, the shepherd who guides, protects and provides for the needs of his people. Such an earthly rule is an expression of God's rule, which brings peace.

A suffering world still experiences pain as people suffer under unjust regimes. The Advent hope is also a challenge to Christians who understand Christ's coming to be the fulfilment of this prophecy. Jesus' coming can only make a difference in each generation if his followers continue his ministry of liberation in today's world. How can the Church protect and provide for those in need now?

Hebrews 10.5–10

The idea of animal sacrifice tends to be a 'turn off' for today's congregations. However, for the writer of Hebrews, animal sacrifice was still an accepted part of Jewish religious practice. Here he quotes verses from Psalm 40 but the voice speaking them is Christ's. The quotation is taken from the Greek Old Testament, which unlike the Hebrew version speaks of 'a body you have prepared for me', and although the crucifixion is not mentioned directly, most readers would make this connection. Sacrifice was intended to both express and build up the relationship between people and God, whether the offering was one of thanksgiving or repentance. Psalm 40 echoes a recurring strand in the Old Testament which questions the worth of sacrifice, especially when the worshippers continue to live in disobedience to God's will. Now God's will for humanity finds expression in Christ, whose perfect obedience leads him to the cross, and whose will is at one with the divine will. It is time for God to abolish the old order because Christ becomes a 'once-for-all offering' and never again will there be need for any other sacrifice. For the writer of Hebrews, Christ's death is the offering which provides the means of access to God for all time.

On the cross, God in Christ has shown that there is nothing he will not suffer for us. He knows our pain and takes it to himself, even when it is caused by our disobedience. Often we find it difficult to be honest with ourselves, let alone with God, but we can be sure that when we turn to him nothing will stand in the way.

Luke 1.39–45 (46–55)

The birth narratives as told by Luke introduce themes which will be explored further as the story unfolds. Here, the angel speaks God's message, and Mary hears that she is to have a baby and is told the names already prepared for her unborn child. He is to be called Jesus (and Luke's readers would have known that Jesus meant 'Saviour'). He is the 'Son of the Most High', the heir to the throne of David whose rule will have no end and so he will be the fulfilment of messianic promise and hope. Mary expresses her amazement because she is a virgin. The part played by the Holy Spirit in the child's conception is one of the mysteries of Christian faith and has been the subject of much theological speculation and debate. Yet, its significance for Luke is clear – the baby will be holy, the Son of God from the beginning. In later years, the Christian Church would use the title Son of God to speak of Christ's sharing in the divine nature. In Luke, this idea is not yet formulated, but the power of the Holy Spirit in Jesus, present at his birth, will be seen in his life, death and resurrection as the story unfolds.

The narrative continues with Mary's visit to Elizabeth whose unborn baby 'leaps in her womb' in recognition of Jesus' status. In adult life, John will acknowledge Jesus' precedence. Elizabeth inspired by the Holy Spirit rejoices and blesses Mary and her child.

The preacher is offered the option of continuing the reading to include Mary's song of joy, 'The Magnificat'. Again, Jesus and the focus of his ministry – the reversal of the established order – are the subject of these verses. In Luke's Gospel, Jesus demonstrates the constant outpouring of God's loving-kindness towards those whom society too often despises or ignores. Luke challenges his readers to follow Jesus' example.

CHRISTMAS DAY: SET I

Isaiah 9.2–7; Titus 2.11–14; Luke 2.1–14 (15–20)

Isaiah 9.2–7

Isaiah, who prophesied in Judah, was aware that in the north people were suffering at the hands of the Assyrians. Light signifies life and darkness points to death. The light of God is so great that, when it shines in the midst of death and destruction, suffering is ended. Is the land of deep darkness Sheol, the abode of the dead? Sheol was a tomb-like place of decay, where worms crawled. There the dead eked out a pitiful, mindless, 'subhuman' existence. Such an existence was literally 'no life'. It is a dreadful fact that in every age some people live a 'Sheol-like' existence because of human cruelty and greed. When God's light penetrates, people live in peace and flourish. Hope meant that children would be born and the growing nation would once again give thanks to God, just as they did at harvest time or when dividing spoils after a victory. The extent of the people's suffering is described in three ways: as yoke, bar and rod (v.4). This is how it felt to be oppressed. To be released from such tyranny would be as great and unlikely an event as the day when Gideon, with a handful of men, defeated the Midianites (Judges 7). Yet, however glorious a victory may seem, bloodshed is always a messy, distasteful and horrific experience and the bloodstained clothing of returning warriors has to be burnt.

Who will save the people? When there is a royal birth people look to the future, hoping that the child will grow to be a strong and just king. Kings were 'sons' of God, God's representatives on earth. Whether or not Isaiah was referring to the birth of Hezekiah, the names given to the child are signs both of hope and of prophetic promise, and epitomize the qualities people long to see in their ruler. Isaiah's hope was in a Davidic king, the inheritor of the promises God made to David's line. God will enable him to rule justly and right-eously and the future welfare of a kingdom built on such principles will endure. The prophet is sure that God's vigorous involvement with his people will ensure the fulfilment of the prophecy. Although the northern kingdom was destroyed, Judah survived.

There is no doubt that Isaiah's prophecy related to the contemporary situation. However, it is not surprising that Christians have read these verses in the light of Jesus' birth. The poem speaks of light and life instead of darkness and destruction, of a growing nation of thankful people and of hope embodied in the birth of a baby who, when grown, will rule the kingdom justly. On Christmas Day, the imperative for all who rejoice in Jesus' birth is to share the vision of Isaiah: of a people whose well-being depends on justice and selflessness, not on power-seeking and greed.

Titus 2.11–14

Christians are to live within God's grace, the divine outpouring of loving-kindness and generosity, offered to everyone and seen supremely in Jesus. Yet those who receive God's grace must live their lives accordingly, not in order to save themselves, but as a response to the gift accepted. This means living a disciplined lifestyle that consciously rejects all that was destructive of goodness in people's old way of living. Impiety was one of the most damaging things, in other words the failure to honour God or, at worst, the dishonouring of God, led to people being ruled by their own selfish needs. Those who honour God must live in the present as if the end time has arrived; they must live as people with their feet on the earth and their eyes on heaven! The Christian hope and expectation is that eventually all people will live under God's rule. This is the moment when the splendour or 'manifestation of glory' of God and Christ will be seen (v.13). In the meantime, Christians must share the divine eagerness for all people to live faithfully. This involves total commitment to a way of life, characterized by good deeds, that seeks the welfare of all. This is why Jesus gave himself for us. The payment of a ransom brings freedom instead of captivity. War-captives and slaves were ransomed; their freedom was bought, so that they could take their places as responsible members of the community. True purity was seen in Jesus' self-giving and is to be seen in the lives of Christians who, with God's grace, follow him.

When a child is born, most parents commit themselves both to nurturing their child and to becoming the best parents they can be. However, most parents would admit that they are far from perfect. What is important is that their intentions remain steadfast and that they keep trying. This, I think, is what Christian purity is about!

Luke 2.1–14 (15–20)

This passage is examined in Christmas: Set II (see p.15). Here the division is between verses 14 and 15, suggesting that the emphasis is on the angels' song of God-given peace, the wholeness of life described in the passages above.

CHRISTMAS DAY: SET II

Isaiah 62.6–12; Titus 3.4–7; Luke 2.(1–7) 8–20

Isaiah 62.6–12

Although the Exile is over, Jerusalem remains in a sorry state as the rebuilding of the city gets underway. Sentinels stand on the city walls and it is not clear whether the walls of Jerusalem have already been rebuilt, or are in ruins. Either way, the sentinels cry out to God to restore their city and they will continue to cry out until God responds! That response comes in verse 5 as God answers them: he has made a solemn oath to protect them with his mighty arm, the symbol of his strength. Is God to protect the people from raiders who make incursions across the border of Judah, or from the greedy leaders who, for personal gain, levy heavy taxes and bring the population to a state of poverty? God will act and Jerusalem will prosper. Once again, a thankful people will worship wholeheartedly, their gratitude spilling over as they bring offerings of grain and wine to their festival celebrations. Now everyone will be able to enter Jerusalem, and come and go in peace. Both the people and the city will be given new names (v.12) that ring with joy and affirm that God dwells in the midst of his people.

Sometimes we feel that we are standing on 'shaky ground' as all that once seemed solid and secure crumbles around us. At such times we may call on God and wonder whether he will ever answer. This passage reassures us that not only will God answer but he will bring us through times of trial to a time of rejoicing when we will know God is with us always.

Titus 3.4–7

God is intimately involved in his world and this is evident in the goodness and loving-kindness seen in Jesus. These are saving attributes of God. Human beings can't save themselves no matter how many good deeds they do, they are dependent upon God's mercy. Now, through Christ, that same goodness and loving-kindness is poured out in the gift of the Holy Spirit. The Spirit is characterized by the compassion shown by Jesus: just as Jesus' compassion reached out and brought people into full fellowship with God and with each other, in other words into eternal life, so the Holy Spirit continues that task. To be the recipient of such an outpouring of mercy washes away everything else and people emerge from such an experience 'reborn' and 'renewed'.

This is what it means to enter into eternal life and to share in the inheritance of Christ. (Although 'washing' may bring baptism to mind, it is unlikely that this passage is referring to baptism.)

This passage evoked an image of someone standing under a hot shower, the water cascading down, and then emerging clean and tingling. We stand under the 'shower' of God's goodness and loving-kindness made known to us in Jesus.

Luke 2.(1–7) 8–20

Augustus Caesar was the most powerful ruler in the known world of Jesus' day. One of Augustus' titles was 'saviour'. At the beginning of the story of Jesus' birth Luke offers a contrast between the power of Augustus and the seeming powerlessness of the baby Jesus through whom God would offer universal salvation. By means of the census, the story moves from the world map to Bethlehem, the 'city of David'. Mary was carrying a baby before Joseph, who came from the line of David, had a sexual relationship with her. This underlines the involvement of the Holy Spirit from the moment of conception: Jesus would be no ordinary baby, but the expected Messiah who would bring salvation for the world. In a hot country, it was usual for mangers to be carved out of the bedrock and they would often be in the open. Luke makes no mention of a stable, and states only that Jesus was placed in a manger. 'No room in the inn' (v.7) meant exactly that. A nativity scene that takes place within a timber-framed stable comes from a western interpretation of Luke's narrative. From the outset Luke shows that Jesus is the one who will reverse the usual world order of rich and poor, powerful and powerless: the child who was born without shelter, shelters others.

Verses 8–20 tell the story of the shepherds. The angels' song is of glory and peace. Peace has to do with the well-being of those whom Jesus will restore to full relationship with God, who will then accord God honour (glory). It is interesting that David was a 'shepherd boy' and here angels come to shepherds in David's town. Mary 'ponders' these things – there is more to come!

Christians already know the end of the story, this is why we celebrate its beginning!

CHRISTMAS DAY: SET III

Isaiah 52.7–10; Hebrews 1.1–4 (5–12); John 1.1–14

Isaiah 52.7–10

The time of restoration has arrived and a herald runs swiftly from Babylon to Jerusalem with the good news that the exiles have been released and are returning. How many marathons would that be? (These days we are used to instant communication by telephone or email and the old postal service has become 'snail mail'.) It is his feet that bring the thrilling message, no wonder they are described as 'beautiful'! God has brought an end to the dark days of uncertainty, when people must have felt he had abandoned them. Those who hear the news first are the watchmen who 'see' God, pictured as a person, return to Zion (Jerusalem). Around the ruined city, battered by enemies and not yet rebuilt, the shout of joy echoes as first the watchmen and then the people, take up the cry of the herald. God 'rolls up his sleeves', he bares his arm ready to fight anyone who opposes his return to the city. No longer will any enemies vanquish the people because God is their protector.

In days of trouble people often ask, 'Where is God?' Perhaps it is comforting to realize that this is not a new question! The experience of God's people from the beginning is that dark days come to an end and the time arrives when God's light shines out. For us to imagine the dirty, blistered and bloody state of the herald's 'beautiful feet' may show how literal and unpoetical our minds can be, but at the same time this is a reminder that the good news of God's saving acts is worth proclaiming no matter what effort and cost is involved.

Hebrews 1.1–4 (5–12)

Hebrews begins with affirmation of God's self-revelation in Christ. Clearly, God has always enabled people to glimpse the divine nature, but often God's relationship with humanity had been marred by human disobedience. Now, through his Son, God acts to restore a broken relationship for all time. The Son inherits the Father's nature and shares in his creative purposes. This is why Christians affirm that when they look at Jesus they see God. Before Jesus, the law required people to atone for their sins and receive forgiveness through the sacrificial system. Jewish tradition spoke of the law being given to Moses by angels, God's messengers, at Sinai (Acts 7.38, 53; Gal. 3.19). This is why the comparison is made between the Son and the angels: with the coming of God's Son, people would no longer rely on the law to put them right with God. The writer will argue that only through Jesus are people restored to right relationship with God. The emphasis on Jesus' status as the one who shares God's throne seems at odds with the Gospel picture of Jesus the servant who ate with the outcasts of society. Yet it is this same Jesus, with his concern to restore a broken relationship, who has the authority of God.

God continues to reveal himself in many different ways, yet Christians would wish to affirm that supremely, in Jesus the Son, we discover that the purpose of the loving creator is that our relationship with him should be restored.

John 1.1–14

No short paragraph can do justice to this wonderful passage. The Gospel writer speaks of the outpouring of God's own nature in creation. When God spoke things happened! These verses resonate with the account of creation in Genesis 1: 'Let there be light', God said, 'and there was light!' (Gen. 1.3). It is not surprising that the evangelist says, 'In the beginning was the Word' (1.1). Yet this Word is more than God's words. Even the human enterprise of creation involves self-giving, how much more did God give of himself in the divine act of creation? The Word is both the means by which God created and the essence of the divine nature that we see reflected in creation. It is this Word, present from the beginning, that in Jesus, became embodied in a human person. This is the good news, the Gospel according to John. From the outset, readers are required to choose between light and darkness. John the Baptist was the one who 'testified to the light' (v.7) and he was put to death. The cost of discipleship is spelt out from the beginning. 'The world' (v.10) represents all who refuse to accept the light or actively oppose it. Many of Jesus' own people refused to accept him, and the shadow of the cross, although not mentioned explicitly, is present from the beginning. Yet, just as the cross did not have the last word, so those who believed Jesus and recognized God's Word in him would also become sons and daughters of God.

All three passages on Christmas Day speak of God's initiative paving the way to a renewed relationship. Hebrews and John show that relationship being restored through Christ. However, those who choose the light will have to face the cost of discipleship, but, as God's children, that relationship will never again be broken.

FIRST SUNDAY OF CHRISTMAS

1 Samuel 2.18–20, 26; Colossians 3.12–17; Luke 2.41–52

1 Samuel 2.18–20, 26

Samuel's mother, Hannah, was barren and had prayed for a child, promising that if she did have a son she would dedicate him to God.

In his boyhood, Samuel performed priestly service in the Temple. He was clothed in a linen ephod (a kind of loincloth), the garment worn by priests who deal with sacred things. Hannah's practice was to visit the Temple with her husband annually to offer an animal sacrifice and to bring Samuel a robe for outerwear. Eli, as a sign of God's approval, blessed Samuel's parents, praying that they would receive the gift of more children. If we look at v.21 we discover that Hannah did have three more sons and two daughters. Samuel and his family are the focus of these verses, which are set within the contrasting story of Eli's sons' disobedience. Verse 26 emphasizes that Samuel grew in stature both physically and spiritually, meriting the favour of God and the people.

The biblical message is clear: Samuel and his family put God first and received God's blessing and people's respect. However, faithful living does not always result in blessing. What of those who, for example, care for an elderly relative, or are involved in Christian service in a war-torn or famine-struck area of the world? Caring is a costly business! Obedience to God can involve facing financial hardship or ridicule when a Christian refuses to accept, for example, questionable business methods.

Colossians 3.12–17

The teaching in this passage may have taken place within the context of preparation for baptism. The past age was characterized by sin, but in baptism believers share in Christ's death by 'dying to sin', and rising from the water they leave their old ways behind. This is described by the metaphor of taking off old clothes and putting on new.

In the ancient world, moral teaching often took the form of lists of virtues and vices. Here the five virtues in v.12 contrast with the list of five vices in v.8. Perhaps the most significant virtue is humility, the unselfishness, or lowliness of heart and mind, which was a characteristic of Christ. Taken with the other virtues the list points to how members of the new covenant people should act towards each other. Forgiveness is offered in baptism and makes new life possible, thus those who follow Christ's example should be tolerant and forgiving. Love is like the top-coat which protects the other clothes from the elements and is also the underlying motivation that makes perfection possible.

To live a Christian life is to allow Christ to 'rule' our hearts. The life of peace is found when we let Christ judge our actions and this peace will be expressed in thanksgiving in worship. Does the church's worship today express heartfelt thankfulness that we belong together as Christ's people?

Luke 2.41–52

Was Jesus always obedient and when did his sense of vocation begin? The story of Jesus' visit to the Temple when he was twelve years old is found only in Luke's Gospel and introduces themes which will be developed as the action unfolds. There are incipient tensions between Jesus, the teachers in the Temple and his own family as Jesus begins to experience what it means to fulfil his vocation as the Son of God.

All male Jews were required to travel to Jerusalem for the Passover Festival, and Jesus and his family were faithful to the Temple. The Temple held a central place in Luke's infancy narratives. Jesus will teach in the Temple, the earliest Christians will meet there at the end of the Gospel (24.53) and in the early days of the church (Acts 2.46). It is easy to forget that Jesus remained a faithful Jew and that Christianity's roots are in Judaism. Jesus' wisdom (v.40) is demonstrated as he listens to the teachers in the Temple and both questions and answers them. In later years, Jesus will challenge the teachers and they will seek to kill him (19.47). When his anxious parents find Jesus he tells them he was *bound* to be 'in his Father's house'. Here the obedience of Jesus as God's Son is a prelude to the obedience which moves the story to its climax. His parents' bewilderment is strange when considered in the light of the Annunciation (1.35), yet as Mary continues to ponder the significance of this event, Luke invites his readers to join Mary in her task.

Jesus lived as a faithful Jew, yet challenged his own tradition. Perhaps Christians too need to recognize the tension of living faithfully, while being prepared to challenge those aspects of Christian tradition which prevent the Church from living and proclaiming the gospel. Perhaps the greatest challenge facing today's Church has to do with unity. Every denomination will need to 'let go' of some traditions that are held dear while being ready to receive treasures from the traditions of others (see *Hymns and Psalms* 765 v.4).

SECOND SUNDAY OF CHRISTMAS

Jeremiah 31.7–14; Ephesians 1.3–14; John 1 (1–9) 10–18

Jeremiah 31.7–14

This passage is made up of two poems sharing the theme of rejoicing at the return of the exiles from Babylon. Shouts of joy welcome home a remnant, purified by their experience, who will form a restored covenant community. People will be gathered from the farthest horizons and unlike the first Exodus their march will be easy, for God will lead them by flowing streams to their homeland. Even the disabled and those who are pregnant and give birth on the way will arrive safely – guided, guarded and gathered in by God's fatherly love.

The second poem begins at v. 10. Now nations and people from distant islands witness the return. The symbolism of a shepherd and his flock is followed by the image of redeemer. The redeemer would 'buy' a family member out of trouble by 'paying the price', either as a ransom or by redeeming debts, thus securing their relations' freedom from slavery. The liberated people arrive singing and with glowing faces to find that God has provided for them out of his bounty. Listed are the ingredients of a staple diet with a plentiful water supply to ensure continuing abundance. Priests will receive 'their fill of fatness', probably indicating a return both to prosperity and to a life in which worship has a central place.

As God's people today, it is our task to real-ize (make real) our worship by bringing our offerings, that those who seek freedom from war, oppression, cold and hunger may also discover what it is to experience the joy of homecoming and plenty.

Ephesians 1.3–14

Here we are offered a kaleidoscope of images in the form of a eulogy or possibly a hymn of praise rejoicing that spiritual blessings of Christ in heaven are available to his people now. They live in the time between the two advents of Christ, but while they wait on earth they also share the life of heaven. Perhaps the most difficult idea in this passage is that of a love which foreordains the inclusion of a select group among those chosen by God 'before the world's foundation'. Our response might well be to ask about the fate of those who were not chosen. Yet, this is to ignore the emphasis on God's grace made known in Christ which has two outcomes: firstly, people are forgiven, their relationship with God restored and secondly, they are offered insights into the mystery of God's loving will and purpose for themselves and for all creation. God's love is not exclusive, rather it is the task of those he has chosen to 'live to praise his glory', in other words to share in those loving purposes. The good news is that those who believe the gospel are promised the help of the Holy Spirit. The experience of the Spirit in this life is described as a 'pledge' or 'guarantee' of the heavenly life that is yet to come. This is rather like the engagement ring that is a promise of the married life that is assured, although it remains a future hope.

The outworking of the eternal will and purpose of God is rooted in the response of those who have faith in Jesus Christ. Although those who respond to God's love may be few amongst many, we are called to live in the light of God's Spirit. Perhaps we could think of ourselves as bearers of the 'heavenly engagement ring'! How can we live the life of heaven now and help others to recognize God's loving purposes for his world?

John 1 (1–9) 10–18

In verses 1–9, John introduces the idea of God's Word that spoke creation into existence in Genesis 1. The world to which the Word came is the social world that people inhabit and yet they did not recognize the divine light that enabled society to function. The Word came to God's chosen people who had experienced God's faithfulness throughout their history and were the very people who should have recognized and welcomed the light that came from God – but this is a story of rejection. Yet some people were given the ability to trust and respond and they became God's children. It seems that the mystery of God's purpose, then and now, is to be unfolded through people of faith.

Then the Word becomes a human being in whom God's light is clearly seen as Jesus offers God's love in his ministry. He is full of grace, God's generous goodness and truth and the integrity which contrasts with the lying words of his opponents. John, who represents the prophets, testifies that Jesus supersedes the Mosaic law because in him we receive 'grace upon grace', the reality of God's loving-kindness that the law signalled. In Jesus, we see divine love in action.

Are we amongst those who have been given the capacity to trust and respond to the love of God in Christ? If so, then we are part of the unfolding story of God's love. What a privilege!

THE EPIPHANY

Isaiah 60.1–6; Ephesians 3.1–12; Matthew 2.1–12

Isaiah 60.1–6

Zion is pictured as a woman in mourning for her scattered children. She wakes to the cry, 'Arise!' (v.1). Those who mourn do not want to get out of bed in the morning, because there is nothing to get up for. The 'wake-up call' is that Zion's light has come: God returns to the city and the divine light throws the lands of other nations into shadow. Attracted by God's light, strangers from other nations bring home the dispersed Jews, Zion's sons and daughters. In an image of infinite tenderness, they carry her daughters whom they have nursed. No wonder Zion trembles with joy and is able to respond to the imperative not only to arise, but to 'shine'! The nations bring their wealth, in fleets of ships by sea and in numerous caravans by land, and all enter the city. Their gifts, including gold and frankincense, are brought joyfully to God who deserves their offerings. This is echoed in the Gospel passage.

It is the nature of joy to give. What greater cause for celebration can there be than God dwelling among us? Is our response to offer all that we have and all that we are?

Ephesians 3.1–12

These verses are written, as if by Paul, in the first person. True followers of Christ are willing to give up anything, even personal freedom, and there is no doubt that Paul was imprisoned on more than one occasion. He risked his own freedom in order to preach the gospel to the Gentiles. God had revealed his hidden purpose to Paul: that salvation, through Christ, was for all people. This would have contrasted with contemporary philosophies that suggested divine salvation was only for an elect group. Instead, the writer asserts that God's purposes are for everyone. Within the church God's promises are given to those from both Jewish and pagan backgrounds. All converts to Christianity enter the community of God's people on an equal footing. Paul is a servant of the gospel not because of his own abilities, but through God's grace. Today's reader might feel that the writer is overstating the case when he says he is the 'least of all the saints', but this is a rhetorical device to compare his own unworthiness with the 'boundless riches of Christ. (v.8) This is always what it feels like to meet God, because in the presence of God's purity and goodness people discover their own unworthiness. God's creative purpose, his 'wisdom' is multifaceted and infinite in its variety, and differing ethnicities and cultures are to be valued and celebrated. The Church must reflect this to 'rulers and authorities in heavenly places'. (v.10) This is about ultimate salvation being available to everyone. The Church as 'the body' reflects God's 'heavenly' purpose in its 'earthly' life.

Once again, the Church is challenged to become more inclusive. This is not merely about making strangers welcome, but recognizing that those different from ourselves are people from whom we can learn.

Matthew 2.1–12

It is only too easy to read this passage without giving a thought to the community for whom it was written. It is probable that Matthew's community included new converts from the pagan Roman world. How they would have enjoyed the story of the Magi! The tale begins before the death of Herod the Great in 4 BCE. Messianic expectation looked for the appearance of a star or comet from the East (Num. 24.17). The Magi are mystical figures who study the stars. It is not surprising that they are spoken about today as 'wise men' because not only does God communicate with them through stars and dreams, but also their wisdom lies in understanding and acting on that divine message. The journey they undertook was no small enterprise! The Magi were looking for the Jewish Messiah. Matthew affirms both ethnic groups in the Christian community: Jews from whose country and culture Jesus belonged and Gentiles who 'journeyed', both literally and metaphorically, to worship him.

The contrast between Herod and the Magi is between false and true worship (homage). True worship is about the response of joy and humility. When the Magi saw the child, they knelt down (v.11). Their gifts represent the offerings the Gentile Christians brought to Christ, which, while pointing to the child's identity (think of the sermons preached on 'Gold for a King, frankincense for a Priest and myrrh to anoint the body of the one who died on the cross'!), primarily affirm the valued status of the Gentiles within Matthew's church.

Those who are wise worship in humility and joy alongside other Christians, irrespective of ethnic and cultural differences. We belong to a worldwide Church. Let us rejoice in our diversity as we kneel before Christ.

SUNDAY BETWEEN 7 AND 13 JANUARY INCLUSIVE

Sunday after Epiphany

First Sunday in Ordinary Time

Isaiah 43.1–7; Acts 8.14–17; Luke 3.15–17, 21–22

Isaiah 43.1–7

The prophet of the Exile, known as Second or Deutero-Isaiah, responsible for Isaiah 40–55, wrote this oracle of salvation to a people who needed to hear a word of hope. They are told that they are 'precious in God's sight' (v.4). These words form the heart of the message and how much they must have meant to this tiny group of miserable, uprooted, displaced people! The passage is in two parts, each beginning with the words 'Fear not', more accurately translated 'I have set you free': the change in their circumstances has already happened and so their journey home is assured. A note of exultation is present in the reminder that God 'called', 'created' and 'formed' them as his people. This happened when God led them out of Egypt, through the wilderness and into the Promised Land. Last week's reading from Jeremiah introduced the idea of a redeemer as the one who buys the freedom of someone who has fallen into debt. The language of redemption, which usually meets a private need, is here a word of release to the nation. The words, 'You are mine', 'I am your God' and 'I am with you' are more than a recurring reassurance; they are a recognized legal formula that promises protection. God is able to save them, because he has sovereign authority over all nations and was at work in the political changes that were taking place.

The second part echoes the promise of the return. Yet this is not the end of the story, for this nation has been created 'for God's glory' (v.7), they are part of God's saving work. The Christian Church throughout the world, often made up of small, seemingly insignificant groups, needs to hear that all her people, without exception, are both embraced by and invited to share in that same saving work. God speaks to us all when he says, 'I have called you by my name, you are mine!'

Names say something about identity. These days, when women no longer automatically take their husband's name, double-barrelled names are becoming more usual. Whether we like or dislike this fashion, such names indicate the new identity of people who belong to each other. As Christians, we carry God's name and are called to reflect his loving-kindness.

Acts 8. 14–17

Philip had been to Samaria and many people had been baptized. The apostles at Jerusalem accepted the news, seemingly without surprise, but as the story unfolds we realize that there was a real concern. They send John and Peter back to Samaria because although the gift of the Holy Spirit was usually part of baptismal experience, this had not been witnessed. The shared experience of the Spirit was needed to break down barriers between Samaritans and Jews in order to unite a divided people. The Spirit came when the apostles laid their hands on the Samaritans. Perhaps this action served to emphasize the continuity between the Jerusalem church and its new members, who came from a group with whom relations had been not merely strained, but broken to the point of enmity.

One insight we may take from this passage is that the Holy Spirit's work includes that of reconciliation. As a baptized people, we are invited to share in that task. With the guidance of the Holy Spirit, the Church needs to consider how Christians may become a healing presence in personal relationships, in society and between nations.

Luke 3.15–17, 21–22

People wonder whether John is the expected Messiah. Those who recall the meeting between Elizabeth and Mary in the infancy narratives already know the answer! John confirms Jesus' superior status. In words found in all four Gospels, he speaks of the contrast between a baptism by water and by the Spirit and also about not being fit to untie Jesus' sandals. The early church's experience was that baptism and the gift of the Spirit went hand in hand. Christians believed that they were living in the last days before Jesus' return, which would herald the last judgement. Both Luke and Matthew reflect this understanding as they portray fire as a purifying agent and winnowing as a symbol of judgement. Surprisingly, Luke is quite clear that this is good news!

Jesus was baptized along with others. However, for Luke the key feature was not Jesus' baptism but rather that Jesus was praying when the Holy Spirit came. The picture is of heaven opening to reveal the coming of the Spirit. God's voice acclaims Jesus both as Son and as beloved. Equipped with the Spirit Jesus is to fulfil his task as God's Son, that is, as the one whose will is conformed to God's and in whose loving obedience God takes pleasure and delight.

Unlike Jesus, we often waver in our obedience, but when we ask the help of the Spirit, we too bring joy to the heart of God.

SUNDAY BETWEEN 14 AND 20 JANUARY INCLUSIVE

Second Sunday in Ordinary Time

Isaiah 62.1–5; 1 Corinthians 12.1–11; John 2.1–11

Isaiah 62.1–5

These verses are written by the third prophet whose words are found in the book of Isaiah. The time of exile is past and those who have returned to Jerusalem cling to God's promise of faithfulness. For many years, the people felt that God had forsaken them. Now, for the sake of Jerusalem, the prophet assures them that God will remain silent no longer and that Israel's salvation will be seen by the whole world. The nations will know that Jerusalem is like the jewel in the crown that adorns God and in which he delights. The contrast between the old and new names for Jerusalem is a reminder that God who had turned away from his people turns towards them once more. The land that lay desolate and forsaken is no longer forgotten. Trito-Isaiah, like prophets before him, speaks of Jerusalem as God's bride. The nature of the divine promise is utterly personal and just as a bridegroom rejoices over a bride, so God rejoices over Jerusalem. Whenever the metaphor of marriage is used in the Old Testament, God's partner is always a community and never an individual. This image of Jerusalem as God's bride is picked up by New Testament writers. For example, the culmination of God's purposes are described in the book of Revelation by the metaphor of the heavenly Jerusalem 'prepared as a bride adorned for her husband' (Rev. 21.2). The preparation involves the purification of God's people.

The images of Jerusalem as jewel and bride both point to God's choosing of and delight in his people. However, the jewel can become clouded and the bride unfaithful. God is also the builder who restores the walls of the city. The good news is that God helps to build up his people that they may live justly and lovingly as bright jewel and faithful bride.

1 Corinthians 12.1–11

In worship what matters is whether a person is inspired by God or by something other than God. 'Charismata' is the Greek word which is translated 'spiritual gifts' or 'gifts of grace', bestowed freely by God. Paul writes to the Corinthian Christians to correct misconceptions about the nature of spiritual gifts. There were three kinds of misunderstanding: firstly that spiritual gifts were for Christians' personal benefit, secondly that this was the primary way in which the Spirit's presence was to be experienced and thirdly, that some gifts were more highly prized than others, for example speaking in tongues. This would have led to the formation of an elite group. Paul emphasizes that gifts should be used in ministry and service. The value of spiritual gifts lies in building others up, not in their spectacular nature. The ability to help others is as important as apostleship and to be an able administrator is as important as possessing the gift of healing. Paul insists that no one is without any gift and all gifts come from the same divine source.

It is easy to give lip-service to the idea of valuing all gifts. For example, do we really believe that unassuming assistance and quiet encouragement are to be valued as highly as gifts of leadership and preaching? Too often, we fail to affirm those who serve 'behind the scenes' and leave them feeling that their contribution is not appreciated.

John 2.1–11

The account of the wedding at Cana is the first 'sign' in John's Gospel. A sign always points to a reality beyond itself and this story offers insights about Jesus' identity. The setting is a wedding feast at which the wine runs out. Jesus' mother prompts him to perform this sign and he responds with the words, 'My hour has not yet come' (v.4). As the Gospel narrative unfolds it becomes clear that 'Jesus' hour' refers to his arrest and subsequent crucifixion, the supreme act of self-giving love. The amount of water used for purification far exceeded the amount of wine the wedding guests could possibly drink; yet, Jesus turned it all to wine – 120 gallons! Jesus provided both quantity and quality. Wine in both Greek and Jewish culture was often used as a symbol of divinely given well-being and happiness. This sign revealed Jesus' glory (v.11) and yet the abundance of divine generosity would not be fully revealed until Jesus hung on a cross. Glory and honour are synonymous terms: Jesus, who acts with God's authority, is accorded honour that is due to God. What a contrast with the social humiliation that would have resulted had there been insufficient wine to offer the wedding guests!

As the disciples recognized the superabundance of divine generosity they honoured Jesus and believed in him. This sign anticipates the glory of self-giving love yet to be revealed. Do we, who know the end of the story, join Jesus' disciples throughout the ages by affirming our belief in him?

SUNDAY BETWEEN 21 AND 27 JANUARY INCLUSIVE

Third Sunday in Ordinary Time

Nehemiah 8.1–3, 5–6, 8–10; 1 Corinthians 12.12–31a; Luke 4.14–21

Nehemiah 8.1–3, 5–6, 8–10

Ezra, described as both scribe and priest, has brought the book of the law of Moses back from Babylon. A large crowd gathered by the water-gate in Jerusalem for a public reading. This did not happen in the Temple, but in a place where no one would be excluded; even those who were ritually unclean could attend. Ezra seemed to be at pains not to impose this reading on the people and waited until the representatives of the people asked him to bring the book. In the form of scrolls, its content probably corresponded to the first five books of the Old Testament. Ezra unrolled the scroll and the people stood up to hear the Scripture read. It was first light and the reading went on for five or six hours, until midday, and the people listened attentively! Ezra began with a blessing, a brief thanksgiving for the law, to which the people responded with a double 'Amen', strongly affirming their assent. Then they prostrated themselves in worship. The actual reading was done by Levites and may have taken place as a choral reading to ensure that the sound carried. How impressive that would have been! The people wept, presumably in sorrow and regret that the law had not been kept in the past. Nehemiah, the governor, told them not to weep, for a day holy to the Lord was not about grief but joy.

How can we make sure that everyone has access to Scripture? Christians in a country such as North Korea put their lives at risk if they are found with Bibles, yet Bibles are still being smuggled into the country. When we hear Scripture being read do we listen attentively, realizing how privileged we are to have access to the Bible and recognizing its importance for our lives? How often do we grieve because of our failure to live out God's will and rejoice because we are the recipients of God's mercy and grace?

1 Corinthians 12.12–31a

Christians in Corinth seem to have valued those who possessed more sensational spiritual gifts, such as speaking in tongues, more highly than others. This was contrary to the gospel that proclaimed Jews or Greeks, slaves or free, were of equal status. Paul reminded them that the Church, in its unity and diversity, is like a body with different limbs and organs. God gives as he wills and calls people to serve him accordingly. There is no place for envy or arrogance because everyone has some gifts, and no one has too many gifts but all gifts are necessary and are to be used. Even those organs which seem more frail are needed if the body is to function properly. Similarly, even those Christians who are not perceived to have special gifts are worthy of respect and have a part to play. Members of the community will suffer together or flourish together because the life and mission of the church depends on mutuality in which all gifts are used and valued. Paul stresses that the value of spiritual gifts lies not in their spectacular nature, but in how much they contribute to building up the church. All Christians must walk in the way of love and so gifts must be used to benefit everyone.

This reading challenges the individualism that characterizes our own society. The importance of community and mutual responsibility is something to which the Church pays lip-service, but too rarely embodies. In our congregations there are, for example, hospital porters, bankers, classroom assistants and business managers. How rarely we discuss what it means to be Christian in the workplace and help one another to live out our faith within the wider community.

Luke 4.14–21

Luke begins his account of Jesus' ministry with a visit to the synagogue in his home town. The early Christian community would have recognized the practice of any male adult being asked to read from the Scriptures appointed for the day. The quotation, adapted by Luke, comes from Isaiah 61.1–2 and emphasizes the promise of salvation which Jesus will fulfil. Jesus is the one on whom the Spirit already rests and his task is one of liberation. The year of the Lord's favour is an allusion to a year of jubilee: for the land when soil would lie fallow and for people when debts would be rescinded (Leviticus 25). The theme is one of reversal of fortunes grounded in political reality. People will receive physical healing and release. The congregation would have been shocked by Jesus' assertion that in him, that very day, this text had come true. Jesus took to himself the prophet's vocation and this was good news for those who would no longer be excluded through physical disability or social and economic status.

Jesus challenged poverty and oppression in his ministry. He calls his followers to do the same. All three readings remind us that God's community is inclusive.

SUNDAY BETWEEN 28 JANUARY AND 3 FEBRUARY INCLUSIVE

Fourth Sunday in Ordinary Time

Jeremiah 1.4–10; 1 Corinthians 13.1–13; Luke 4.21–30

Jeremiah 1.4–10

Jeremiah tells how he received God's call when he was still a boy or a young teenager. He was convinced that God had chosen him, even before he was born, for a task so great it seemed impossible. How could a youngster begin to imagine being God's mouthpiece to the nations? Yet, when Jeremiah demurred, God's word came to him again, assuring him that God would be with him and that he would speak for God in the places God would send him. The words of Jeremiah's prophecy will not be his own, but God's. It is God who 'touches his mouth' (v.9) and gives him the words to say. The message will be twofold: that of judgement and redemption (v.10). Prior to the Exile, Jeremiah will warn the people and be despised and rejected by them, but once destruction has come to Jerusalem his message will be one of certain hope and renewal because God has not abandoned them.

Many congregations would like to see more young people in their midst, yet they rarely include youngsters in decision-making. It is essential that we are ready to learn from those younger than ourselves and listen to what they have to say. They have skills and insights to share.

When does the Church feel compelled to speak out in today's world? Perhaps it would be easier if God 'touched our lips' and gave us the right words at a time when ethical decision-making has never been so complex. How do we discover God's word now?

1 Corinthians 13.1–13

Paul's great 'hymn of love' is one of the best-known passages in the New Testament and is often read at weddings. However, Paul is writing to a church that has failed to demonstrate love in Christians' dealings with each other and these verses were first heard in the context of chastisement! The first three verses set the scene. The Corinthian Christians prized gifts such as speaking in tongues, which they believed were indications that they had already entered the life of heaven of which they had special knowledge. Paul begins by warning them that these gifts are nothing without love. Verses 4–7 describe the nature of love. It can not always be assumed that what Paul says counteracts the way Christians were actually behaving. Nevertheless it seems likely that conceit and arrogance, along with a perverse pleasure in other people's misdeeds, were characteristics of some members of the church. 'Rudeness' may relate to the practice of the rich starting to eat before others arrived at celebrations of the Lord's Supper (11.20–22). Paul goes on to contrast the temporal and the eternal, for in this world we can never experience or enter fully into the divine life. Just as a child's awareness and behaviour changes with maturity, so must that of the Corinthian Christians. In the present, experience of God is partial, like looking at a mirror image. The reality of God's presence is not yet fully known, but is always characterized by faith, hope and love (v.13), for love is the essence of God's nature and activity. Is it ours?

When we realize that Paul is giving the congregation in Corinth a 'dressing down', we respond to his words in a different way. Perhaps we should ask whether our behaviour in any way mirrors that of the Corinthian Christians!

Luke 4.21–30

This is the response of the congregation in Nazareth to Jesus' 'sermon'. To begin with the people approved of him; the boy they had seen grow up was 'doing them proud'. Yet, there was a sudden swing of mood as Jesus challenged them. Perhaps Luke is preparing the reader for what is to come when Jesus performed so many miracles in Capernaum, but none in Nazareth. Jesus goes on to give two examples: the widow (1 Kings 17), a foreigner, who received help from Elijah during a time of famine; and the healing of Naaman the Syrian general, also a foreigner, whose leprosy was healed by Elisha. In both cases, Israelites were also suffering but were neither fed nor healed. Not surprisingly, these examples inflamed the congregation. What is more, they were so angry that they were ready to hurl Jesus off the cliff! As Luke's Gospel progresses into Acts, we see this pattern continuing to unfold. Jesus, like the prophets of old, experiences rejection and so do his followers, who also risk their lives. As Luke looks back to the start of Jesus' ministry, he is aware how many people in the synagogues refused to accept Jesus as Messiah, and by the time these words were written he knew that many Gentiles would become the backbone of the new Christian Church.

It is not always the 'religious' people who follow Jesus. Do we ever consider those people outside the Church who reflect 'Christlikeness' and so enter into the divine life more fully than we may have imagined?

SUNDAY BETWEEN 4 AND 10 FEBRUARY INCLUSIVE

Fifth Sunday in Ordinary Time

Isaiah 6.1–8 (9–13); 1 Corinthians 15.1–11; Luke 5.1–11

Isaiah 6.1–8 (9–13)

In 742 BCE God called the prophet known as Isaiah of Jerusalem. The incident probably took place in the Temple and, from where he stood, Isaiah could see the screen that covered the Holy of Holies. In his vision, Isaiah sees beyond the screen to the mystery and majesty of God. Isaiah is offered a glimpse of God's holiness: his train, a symbol of his high status, fills the Temple; he is attended by seraphim, heavenly beings who sing of God's separateness and purity in the words, 'Holy, holy, holy' (v.3). In the presence of such holiness, Isaiah recognizes that he and all humanity are 'unclean', unfit to worship such a God. Isaiah's awareness of his own sinfulness prepares him for cleansing. A seraph touches his lips with a burning coal from the altar where a perpetual fire burned, the place where people's relationship with God was restored. At the moment of forgiveness Isaiah hears God's word, 'Who will go for me?' and his response is to say, 'Send me' even though he does not know the nature of the task (v.9).

Verses 9–13 are a reminder that the prophet goes into a troubled world to a people who do not listen. Yet his task is to remain faithful in word and deed.

Is Isaiah's experience a paradigm for our worship? Are we awe-struck by the mystery and majesty of God? We confess our sins, but do we realize just how far we fall short? Do the words of absolution release us so that we are ready to hear and respond to God's word?

1 Corinthians 15.1–11

Paul reminds the Corinthians about the content of the gospel and its significance for their salvation. This is a life and death matter! They have to 'hold on' to what they first believed (v.2): in other words, their belief must be reflected in their lives. What were they to hold on to? Almost certainly, the gospel Paul had preached was that God's grace in Christ was available to Jews and Gentiles alike and probably his opponents were trying to keep Christianity under the umbrella of Judaism. Verses 3–5 contain what is probably an early credal statement about the death and resurrection of Christ. Paul follows the tradition that Peter (Cephas – the rock) was the first person to see the risen Lord. (Paul seems to ignore traditions that suggest women were the first witnesses as their testimony would count for little within Judaism.) He then goes on to speak about appearances to the twelve, and to more than five hundred people. While the latter could refer to the coming of the Spirit in Acts 2, the allusion is uncertain, as are the incidents of Christ's appearing to James and to the apostles.

Most significantly, Paul speaks of his own encounter with Christ in order to demonstrate his authority as an apostle before pressing home his argument. He describes himself as one 'untimely born'. These words have been interpreted in various ways, but Paul is probably referring to the circumstances that prevented him, unlike the other apostles, knowing Jesus during his lifetime. Paul's credentials as an apostle lie in his being commissioned by the risen Christ, even though he had been an enemy of Christianity. Paul had worked harder than any, but his value as an apostle did not lie in his efforts but in God's grace.

These days we seem to have lost the sense of urgency in matters of faith. We rarely think that our response to the gospel is a 'life and death matter' that affects our relationships in the present! Our belief must be reflected in our lives, not to 'earn' God's favour, but to reflect his grace to us and to all.

Luke 5.1–11

This is Luke's account of Simon Peter's call. From Simon's boat, Jesus taught the crowd and afterwards enabled Simon to pull from the lake a miraculous catch of fish. Luke is not concerned with questions about what actually happened, but invites the reader to recognize that Jesus' authority and power come from God. Simon, like Isaiah and Paul in the readings above, when aware of the divine presence, is overcome by a sense of his own sinfulness. The contrast between the response of sinners, aware of their own need, and self-sufficient 'righteous' people is a continuing theme for Luke. Simon's declaration of his own unworthiness leads to his commission to follow Jesus and 'catch' people. In v.8 Simon is called Simon Peter (the rock). Luke, knowing the end of the story, is looking back from the perspective of the early church for Simon became the rock on which the Church was founded.

All three readings this week are about call and commissioning. Are we, like Isaiah, Paul and Simon, aware of our own inadequacy? If so we can be assured of God's mercy and grace as we seek to become the people he would have us be.

SUNDAY BETWEEN 11 AND 17 FEBRUARY INCLUSIVE

Sixth Sunday in Ordinary Time

Jeremiah 17.5–10; 1 Corinthians 15.12–20; Luke 6.17–26

Jeremiah 17.5–10

Jeremiah offers two contrasting images to express his understanding that human sinfulness begins when people believe they are self-sufficient. The first picture describes those who fail to put their trust in God. They are like a shrub in a barren land; its chance of survival is negligible. The second is of those who put their trust in God. They are like a tree planted by a stream, its roots drinking from a never-failing water supply even in times of drought.

At a time when Jeremiah's words seemed to be falling on deaf ears, it is not surprising that he goes on to speak about the perverseness of the human heart. It is worth remembering that in Hebrew thought the heart was the seat of the will, not the emotions. The people are determined to go their own way. Only God can understand people's motives for their behaviour and so God alone is able to judge fairly.

How apt these words seem today when we are encouraged to 'look after number one' both as individuals and nations. A sense of mutual dependency, reflecting our trust in God who loves us all, would alter the conduct of family members and national leaders alike.

1 Corinthians 15.12–20

Some of the Corinthians seem to have been denying that there would be a resurrection of the dead, a belief common in Judaism but not in the Gentile world. This denial seems to have led to a refusal to accept that Christ was raised from the dead. Paul turns the argument around to show that it is precisely because God has raised Christ that people can trust that they too will be raised.

Paul may have been trying to counteract the view that soul and body reflected good and bad aspects of human nature respectively, thus only the soul could continue beyond death. The doctrine of resurrection denies such dualism and affirms that the whole person is known and valued both in this life and beyond death. This is the truth which can be lost if the questions about the nature of a resurrection body expect too literal answers. We recognize people as we look at their faces. None of us can know what life after death is like, but we can be sure that we will be both recognized and welcomed. What is more, Christ died *for our sins* (v.17) and God's raising of Christ restores the relationship damaged by sin, a relationship that transcends death.

Holistic approaches in medicine encourage us to recognize that we are both physical and spiritual beings, and it is important that we nurture both ourselves and others physically and spiritually. People strive to become healthier by working out at the gym and search for spiritual well-being by means of many diverse paths, including that offered by Christianity. Yet we do well to remember that we are created by God and that, ultimately, God alone can make us 'whole' as we enter into resurrection life.

Luke 6.17–26

Luke describes people coming from great distances to see Jesus. Jesus teaches them and heals them and they are aware of God's power. At a point in the Gospel when opposition from the religious leaders is rising, Jesus is portrayed as a charismatic figure who speaks and acts with divine authority. It is this Jesus who addresses his disciples, both those present and the wider group of Luke's readers then and now. Mirroring the Sermon on the Mount (Matt. 5–7), Jesus teaches in what is known as 'the sermon on the plain' (v.17). The Beatitudes, a series of promised blessings, are spoken to those who really are poor, hungry, weeping and despised for their faith, for God's concern and blessing is for them. Unlike Matthew, Luke does not allow any possibility of spiritualizing Jesus' words; in socio-economic terms, these people have little or no status. The contrasting woes are a warning to those who are enjoying life in the present, presumably without doing anything to help those who suffer.

The theme of reversal of fortunes is a constant thread running through this Gospel and is a challenge to all who wish to follow Jesus. Were the disciples amongst the poor and hungry, or amongst the wealthy and well fed? History's answer is that they were in both groups. God's blessing promises future well-being in the life of heaven to those who suffer. The challenge is to make the life of heaven possible in the present. This can only happen when the existing world order is overturned. Jesus' disciples must respond to the divine imperative to ensure that those in need feel blessed! This may involve both sharing what we have and challenging worldly authorities. It is human nature to give first priority to our personal security and comfort, but we do not face the task alone, but with God's grace and as members of the community of faith.

SUNDAY BETWEEN 18 AND 24 FEBRUARY INCLUSIVE

Seventh Sunday in Ordinary Time

Genesis 45.3–11, 15; 1 Corinthians 15.35–38, 42–50; Luke 6.27–38

Genesis 45.3–11, 15

Joseph received the brothers who had sold him to traders many years ago (Gen. 37.28) and there was a moment of recognition. It was a time when emotions would have been running high and Joseph sent everyone else away so that he and his brothers could meet privately. Joseph, who is portrayed as the archetypal wise man, asserts that past events were guided by God. This is the most important feature of the Joseph story: that God 'sent' Joseph to Egypt (rather than the brothers selling him into slavery); that through God's action, in the face of human sinfulness, hate was redeemed and the brothers' guilt was taken away. Joseph's father, brothers and their dependants were offered land and life, instead of famine and death. The rescue of this family becomes the motif of the saved remnant who have survived universal disaster. Joseph is described as 'father to Pharaoh' (v.8), the title of a high court official authorized to make and carry out political decisions in all Egypt! The irony is that the brothers whose envy could have had destructive consequences have to accept Joseph's high position.

Joseph's willingness to forgive and help his brothers mirrors God's generous goodness that offers the possibility of new beginnings to all who are willing to acknowledge guilt and accept loving forgiveness. How often stubborn pride prevents reconciliation at every level of human life.

1 Corinthians 15.35–38, 42–50

People who believed that the physical body was part of the corrupt material world, with no ultimate future, would find the concept of a resurrection body offensive. Paul seems to be opposing the view that physical and spiritual represent 'good' and 'bad' respectively. He uses the analogy of the necessary 'death' of the seed before a new plant can grow, the new life being radically different from the old. Just as someone looking at a bare field cannot imagine the wheat that will grow, so humanity cannot envisage the resurrection body. God alone will choose the appropriate body for the new life he offers.

Paul uses the term 'spiritual body' (v.44), an expression bound to shock those who understood spiritual and physical as antithetical. Yet this language was appropriate for Christians who had experienced the gift of the Spirit, the source of divine life and power, already present in the risen Christ and in believers. The contrast is between two ways of being human: that of sinful humanity (Adam, 'the man of dust') and 'heavenly' humanity (Christ). For now the life of the Spirit is experienced in the finite physical world, but beyond death the mode of human existence must change for people to enter the imperishable life of heaven.

What happens after we die? This is a question most people ask when faced with their own mortality, or the mortality of someone they love. Yet it is a seemingly unanswerable question. Nevertheless, Christians can respond positively because Paul assures us that the creator God, whose great love is seen in the risen Christ, has our future in his keeping. If we trust God for what is to come, we are freed from anxiety and are able to live faithfully in today's world.

Luke 6.27–38

Jesus' teaching goes beyond what might be expected in the 'golden rule' (v.31). By using the language of opposites, Jesus has already drawn a contrast between opposing attitudes: love instead of hate, blessing instead of cursing. To fail to love and bless is to condone and even participate in their opposite. Jesus places stringent demands upon his followers when he urges them not only to accept abuse, but also to offer the other cheek and to give generously to those who have stolen from them! The term 'sinners' is used to denigrate attitudes based on mutual care and love that would usually be perfectly accept-able. Jesus' enormous expectations of right behaviour go far beyond this. Is Jesus exaggerating to make his point? What possible grounds are there for such teaching? Only that this is how God acts towards humanity. God's mercy must be reflected in the lives of Christians and it is not their task to judge, but to forgive, exemplifying God's abundant generosity in the way they treat others. Jesus' followers will then discover the overflowing abundance of God's goodness poured out for them.

To take this teaching seriously challenges us at every level of our lives. We must not condone injustice by silence or sit secure in our plenty while others are in need. A lifestyle of radical self-giving in the way of Christ counters prevailing cultures in today's world. How else can the recurring pattern of human violence and greed be brought to an end? Do our attitudes reflect the compassion of God?

SUNDAY BETWEEN 25 AND 29 FEBRUARY INCLUSIVE

Eighth Sunday in Ordinary Time

Sirach/Ecclesiasticus 27.4–7 or Isaiah 55.10–13;
1 Corinthians 15.51–58; Luke 6.39–49

Sirach/Ecclesiasticus 27.4–7

Jesus Ben Sira was a Jewish Scribe who wrote in about 190 BCE to encourage Jews to hold fast to their own code of ethics at a time when Hellenistic (Greek) values were prevalent. His book contains teaching and a collection of wisdom sayings. In this short poem he considers the relationship between a person's integrity and the spoken word. He offers three images by way of illustration: rubbish left in a sieve, flaws found in a fired pot and the quality of fruit on a tree.

Firstly, he pictures wheat, which after the first threshing is placed in a sieve so that the grain falls through. What is left behind can be translated as 'refuse' or even 'dung'! Perhaps the oxen have trampled their own dung into the straw and this remains in the sieve along with husks and other rubbish. Ben Sira does not 'pull his punches' as he makes the analogy with the 'filth' (a literal translation) that a person who speaks with no integrity leaves in the minds of those who listen. Secondly, he pictures a flawed pot. Just as flaws show up when the pot is taken out of the kiln, so a person's lack of integrity becomes obvious during conversation. Thirdly, he pictures a fruit tree. The quality of fruit will show how well the tree has been cultivated and tended. In the same way, Ben Sira suggests, a person's words show how well the mind (literally heart) has been trained and disciplined. Lack of integrity is a stumbling-block to trusting friendship. The poem finishes with the suggestion that it is unwise to praise anyone before hearing them speak.

Today, when integrity is not always highly prized and the actions of politicians and public figures too rarely match their promises, we might wonder whether speech is a good indicator of a person's integrity! Nevertheless, we all know people who will never speak a bad word about anyone and these people command our respect. Does our speech mirror right actions as we seek to live as God's faithful people?

Isaiah 55.10–13

These verses form the conclusion to Deutero-Isaiah's book (Chapters 40–55). Here, the prophet of the Exile pictures the joyful return of the exiles to Babylon. God's word of promised salvation is certain and can be relied upon absolutely. It is like rain and snow that water the ground and result in a harvest that feeds the people. In the same way, God's purpose will not fail. For God to speak is for God to act and when he speaks something happens! It is no accident that Deutero-Isaiah describes the salvation of the exiled people, the climax of his prophecy, in terms of God's word, the instrument of their rescue. However, this raises a question: 'Would salvation have come about if the people had not listened and responded to God's word?' There is always tension between the conviction that God's loving purposes will not fail and the necessity for people to respond in faith if their salvation is to be assured. In this context the people have already responded to God; the prophecy comes at the end of the story of the Exile when reconciliation brings about the joyful return.

A sense of overwhelming joy pervades the final verses. Creation itself sings as the people set out on their journey home and in a memorable and evocative picture even the trees 'clap their hands'! The return of the exiles has significance for all peoples and also for the whole created order. They left during a time of war and return in peace. The blossoming of the earth is a constant reminder that God's creation will never be cut off from the creator. The song is a shout of praise!

Nowadays there are many displaced people who can hardly dare to dream of a peaceful journey home. Land is laid bare by the destruction and devastation of war and made dangerous by unexploded mines. Where is the joyful return for the exiled people of today? The problem of increasing numbers of asylum seekers raises difficulties for governments and local communities alike. Many of those who flood into our country have experienced hardship beyond our imagining. Do Christians leave the task of the world's salvation to God and sit back in apathy, or are they called to do their part that warfare may end and earth be reclaimed so that land and food may be shared at the time of harvest and wanderers may return home in safety?

1 Corinthians 15.51–58

Paul uses the language of metaphor to speak about the moment of transition from this world to the next, from mortality to immortality. He begins by affirming what everyone knows: that this is a mystery.

Nevertheless, Paul tries to 'unfold' that mystery, which becomes an open secret in the light of his belief that the time is coming when Christ will return and God will transform human history. Both those who live and those who have already died will belong to the coming new age. Paul seems to include himself among the living and so expects these events to happen very soon. This poses a difficulty for today's readers who do not share this immediate expectation. Yet, Paul's conviction that those who have already died are not beyond God's reach is one Christians still share. Paul uses conventional images of the day to offer a picture of the moment of transition. He says that all those who belong to Christ's people will be changed and the transformation will happen quickly. Paul uses words which stay in the memory: 'at the sound of a trumpet', 'in the twinkling of an eye' echoing language used in Jewish apocalyptic writings about the end time. Transformation will be like putting on a new garment, that of immortality. Thus, there will be continuity with what has gone before: people who change their clothes are still recognizable, however, the different garment enables personality to be expressed in a new way.

The quotations from Isaiah 25.8 and Hosea 13.14 are linked by the idea of victory over death. Paul picks up the thought from Hosea and equates the sting of death with sin. Obedience to the Jewish law was supposed to prevent sin, but often the law was so detailed that it was virtually impossible to keep it in its entirety and its effect was to highlight people's failure to live obediently. Human sinfulness led to Jesus' death on the cross but was vanquished at the resurrection. In the closing doxology Paul gives thanks that those who believe in Christ share his resurrection life. For Paul, sharing in the resurrection life of Christ must always result in right attitudes and behaviour. The Corinthian Christians who had questioned his authority had failed in a number of ways, but Paul still calls them 'his beloved' (v.58).

When we take issue with people who criticize us and whose ideas we find offensive are we able to address them as 'beloved'? Perhaps, when our feelings are far from loving, it is helpful to remember that those we find hard to like are beloved by God. If our attitudes are to embody those of Christ, then we must treat them lovingly, no matter how difficult that may be. Paul did not turn his back on those who criticized him, but continued to minister to them while continuing to use persuasive argument as he proclaimed the gospel.

Luke 6.39–49

In these verses Luke has collected a number of independent units of teaching and has placed them in an order of associated thoughts. Beginning with the well-known saying about the inevitable outcome when the blind leads the blind, Luke's thought moves to the teacher whose task is also to guide, until students are ready, in their turn, to become teachers. Perhaps the saying about the 'plank in your own eye' is a reminder that those who rate their own learning too highly are at risk of becoming arrogant and judgemental. In ancient thought, the eye was 'the window to the soul'; in other words, the eye reflected the essence of the person, so this saying about clear sight is also about honesty, integrity and the avoidance of prejudice. In contrast, in an image from the theatre, a hypocrite was a person who wore a mask to hide his own personality (actors would be male) and take on another. The only possibility for right relationship is when eyes meet in trusting acceptance.

The saying about trees being known by their fruit is concerned with the nature and essence of goodness. For Luke and his contemporaries the heart was the seat of the will, not the emotions. People's conscious intentions can be turned towards or against goodness and their words will reflect this. (Note the connection with the first lectionary passage above.) The character of the good student (or disciple) should reflect that of the teacher. When Jesus' disciples address him as 'Lord', their relationship with their teacher should be evident, both inwardly in their intentions and outwardly in their behaviour.

Luke concludes this series of sayings with the parable of the house built on rock. It is left to the readers to make connections between this parable, the teaching in the previous verses and their own lives. One way of exploring the connections is to argue that just as a house with firm foundations will not fall in time of flood, so a disciple of Jesus whose character reflects that of his Lord will not flounder, either in terms of character and integrity, or in faithfulness when faced with hardship or persecution. Those who follow Jesus today are also expected to reflect the character and actions of the one they call 'Lord'.

SUNDAY BEFORE LENT

Exodus 34.29–35; 2 Corinthians 3.12–4.2; Luke 9.28–36 (37–42)

Exodus 34.29–35

After God gave Moses the Ten Commandments he descended the mountain. Moses' face was so illuminated with divine radiance that the people were afraid to approach him. His radiant appearance left the people in no doubt that he had encountered God and that the commandments he gave them were of divine origin. There is often a sense of fear and awe when the reality of God's presence seems too great for human beings to bear. This is why Moses veiled his face. (The Hebrew word for 'shone' is similar to the word for 'horn' which is why some works of art depict Moses with horns on his head!)

Moses has returned from the mountain and the encounter with God has ended, and yet he keeps returning to speak with God (v.34). This is not to imply that Moses continues to climb up and down the mountain, but more probably that he spoke with God in the 'tent of meeting' described in 33.7–11. Moses' meeting with God has implications for the life of the people who are to act in obedience to God's commands.

Mountain-top experiences often leave people feeling exhilarated, as if their faces are shining. Sometimes people live on the memory of such experiences and fail to move on in their faith. Moses reminds us that our relationship with God does not depend on one encounter but on many meetings. If we do not set time aside to spend with God, we are unlikely to be able to discern his guidance in our daily lives.

2 Corinthians 3.12–4.2

In Exodus, Moses veiled his face because of people's fear when God's splendour overwhelmed them. In contrast, Paul suggests that Moses veiled his face so that the people would not see the brightness fading. This suits Paul's argument that only Christ can remove the veil that separates people from God. Paul was struggling to understand why so many of his fellow-Jews had failed to turn to Christ. He suggests that the veil prevented those whose 'minds were hardened' from recognizing that the old covenant was only an interim measure, until it was fulfilled in Jesus. Although Christians do not have a veil in front of their eyes, nevertheless they see God's glory only as a reflection in a mirror. Is 'glory' a way of expressing the 'otherness' of God whose perfect love and purity is beyond human comprehension and before which people hide their eyes? Openness to Christ's Spirit enables the process of transformation to begin, as Christian life starts to reflect divine life. This passage begins and ends with the necessity for 'boldness' (3.12), in other words, 'not losing heart' (4.1). Christians have nothing to hide and must live in the light of their conscience, so that they will recognize whether the message and motives of others are consistent with the gospel.

Luke 9.28–36 (37–42)

Who is this Jesus? Luke's story of the transfiguration combines a number of images to enable Peter, John and James (and his readers) to answer this question. Jesus and the three disciples have gone to the mountain, the place of divine encounter, so that Jesus can pray. In Luke, whenever Jesus prays something significant follows. On this occasion Jesus' face shone, recalling Moses' experience on Sinai, and his clothes became dazzling white, an image associated with those who would enter God's kingdom. Moses and Elijah appeared beside Jesus 'in glory', a way of expressing God's encircling presence. Here two great figures from Israel's history stand shoulder to shoulder with Jesus as he turns to face Jerusalem and certain suffering. The three disciples are witnesses and Luke assures his readers that they were awake and not dreaming. Peter's response was to speak about making three shelters; this was how the wilderness years were recalled at the Feast of Tabernacles, a reminder that God had remained with his people during their time of suffering and had led them to safety. At that moment a cloud descends, also representing divine presence, and as at Jesus' baptism (3.22) God's voice is heard. Jesus is greater than Moses and Elijah, for he is God's Son, chosen by God, and Jesus' followers are to pay attention to what he says.

Verses 37–42 speak of the healing of a boy suffering from what people then would have thought to be possession by an unclean spirit, the convulsions an expression of fear as the spirit recognized Jesus. The disciples failed to heal the child; only Jesus acts with the power of God.

All three passages encourage us to ask: Does our worship reflects a sense of awe when we stand in the presence of God and are made aware of our own human frailty? What are the 'veils' that we place before our eyes today? Are we allowing Christ's Spirit to transform us and to guide us in our judgements?

ASH WEDNESDAY

Joel 2.1–2, 12–17 or Isaiah 58.1–12; 2 Corinthians 5.20b–6.10;
Matthew 6.1–6, 16–21

Joel 2.1–2, 12–17

A plague of locusts had decimated the crops wreaking as much
destruction as any army (1.4–7). Such a disaster was thought to be
divine punishment and was expected to precede the Day of the Lord,
the moment when God would finally judge his people who would
experience devastation on a scale never experienced by their ancestors. Because the people were afraid, they were receptive to Joel's
message that the time had come to repent. This was to be no outward
show of repentance simply to placate God, but had to be wholehearted, signalled by fasting and lamentation. Yet the passage brims
over with hope. Joel tells the people, 'Return to your God'. This is the
God with whom they are in covenant relationship, and past events
have disclosed his nature to them. God will not abandon them if they
turn to him but will offer pardon and blessing.

The blast of the horn will summon people to a special service that
everyone must attend. Usually, certain people would be excused from
cultic obligations, for example, the very old, or very young or a new
bridegroom. The priests were to offer prayers and begin the communal lament. When people from other lands realized that the nation was
facing disaster, they would think Israel's God was weak and so it was
imperative that God should act for the sake of his own honour. Joel's
prophetic task was to bring an end to the people's indifference
towards God. In these verses his work reaches a climax as the people
realize at last that they are entirely dependent upon God's mercy for
their salvation.

At the beginning of Lent Christians are invited to face unpalatable
truths about themselves. It is easy to be complacent, considering ourselves to be 'good' people, or at least not as 'bad' as others. However,
when we recognize the goodness of God we realize just how far we
fail him and each other and it is easy to put off any self-examination
until another day. The idea of 'The Day of the Lord' is a reminder that
we should live every day as those who are accountable to God.

Isaiah 58.1–12

Why do people fast when God doesn't seem to take any notice? God
commands the prophet to tell the people, with a voice like a trumpet,

that they have been rebellious. There is no possibility that they will not hear the message! They are living a lifestyle that is in direct opposition to God's will and yet they want God to act on their behalf. They seem to have no idea that their expectations are unreasonable and are surprised that when they fast in order to persuade God to act for them, he seems to do nothing! It is probable that fasting had become part of religious life after the catastrophic events that led to the Exile. Now that the Exile was over, people were wondering why they had to go on fasting. What kind of answer is given? Fasting should be about 'humbling themselves' (v.3). In other words, they should recognize their own failings and shortcomings before God in order to improve relationships within the community. Instead, the people continued to argue amongst themselves – perhaps about matters of business – to the point where fights break out. The prophet utterly denounces any kind of fast that is insincere. Fasting that pleases God is about abstaining from any selfish and greedy ways that undermine relationships within the community. They are to remember their days as slaves in Egypt when they were oppressed. They should know that right relationships within the community depend upon justice that releases people from all that binds them. What are the evils of society that fetter people? The examples given include those who are landless and without home or shelter. Here is a description of poverty so extreme that people are unable to clothe or feed themselves and go cold and hungry (v.7). Fasting that caters for their needs will bring blessing: the light of God. The picture offered is of a society that cares for every member. Only when all that is damaging and destructive in society is put right will God's healing be experienced. Such a fast will involve a tremendous change in attitude and behaviour, but it will be like finding water in the desert – spring water – God's free gift in a dry land. This is the only way in which the city will be rebuilt.

Traditionally, Christians have fasted on Ash Wednesday and have continued to observe a period of abstinence during Lent. The intention of such 'fasting' is to enable a period of self-examination as God's goodness and generosity are contrasted with individual and corporate failure to reflect that same loving-kindness to others. Here is the imperative to live less selfishly and to act on behalf of those who are oppressed or needy within society. How often the needs of others are placed at their own doors. The causes of homelessness, for example, are rarely addressed, as it is much easier to blame individuals for their own fate. Asylum seekers are thought of as 'spongers' who deplete the country's resources and prevent others from being housed. Too often people speak without personal knowledge of the circumstances of those they talk about. It is easy to pay lip-service to the ideal of caring for others as God cares, but far harder to make personal contact with those we prefer to avoid. Any observance of Lent that does not involve the Church in giving, to improve the lives of others, will not please God!

2 Corinthians 5.20b–6.10

Reconciliation between God and disobedient humanity is possible because God has taken the initiative in Jesus. God has allowed 'him to be sin who knew no sin' (v.21) Sometimes these words have been cited to explain that Jesus received the punishment humanity deserved. This is known as the penal substitution theory. What, however, does this say about God? It makes God out to be merciless not merciful! Another view would suggest that on the cross God's love is seen in Jesus' self-offering, demonstrating that no sin can separate people from God's love. In Judaism, worshippers identified themselves with the sacrificial animal when presenting sin offerings. Jesus, who shares God's nature, chose freely to identify himself with people's sin and to suffer in order to bring about reconciliation. Yet the people can choose whether or not to accept this act of grace. The day of deliverance described in Isaiah 49.8 is seen supremely in Jesus.

Paul is a follower of Jesus and this means that he exemplifies a 'cruciform' lifestyle. He avoided putting any obstacles in the way of faith. In other words, he did everything he could to enable people to be reconciled to God through faith in Christ even when that meant he and his companions had to face suffering and hardship. Their total commitment to the gospel culminated in beatings and imprisonment, and there were many days when they had to press on despite exhaustion and hunger. This is what missionary work involved! So where did they find their personal resources? What strengthened them and gave them the ability to endure? Their resources were the moral qualities that reflect the divine nature. Apostleship means that Paul had to face dishonour and blame rather than honour and praise. In a culture in which honour was highly prized, loss of face was to be avoided at all costs. Yet, reconciliation to God meant following in the way of a crucified Christ and the cross was the ultimate symbol of shame. It is probable that the Christians in Corinth were not reflecting this in their own relationships, but may have been vying for power and popularity within the life of the church.

Verses 9 and 10 offer a list of contrasts. For Christians the paradoxical truth is that it is possible to be dying yet alive. The picture of someone suffering from terminal illness, who is able to bring joy to family and friends, is one we all recognize. It is possible to be sorrowful but rejoicing. The task of ministry is to share the pain of others, but to hold fast to the gospel message that Good Friday became Easter Sunday. Those who are poor are able to make others rich as they offer friendship and commitment. It is a truism to speak of 'those things that money cannot buy', yet self-giving love, exemplified by Jesus, is one such commodity! This is exactly what a 'cruciform' lifestyle is about. Sharing in such a 'cross-shaped' way of life is to be reconciled to God and to discover that the cross was not the end, but a marvellous beginning!

Once again, the demands of the gospel are presented unambiguously. As Christians enter into the period of Lent, they are called to examine themselves in the light of the cross. However, no one is asked to turn their lives around in their own strength, for the cross is a promise that God's grace has broken down the barrier that sin creates. We move into Lent with the assurance that God will help us to begin again.

Matthew 6.1–6, 16–21

Charity, prayer and fasting go together. Why was it so important to give 'secretly'? Presumably to avoid any idea of reward and public display. Goodness must be its own motive. Verses 1–6 speak of the hypocrisy of people in synagogues. It is probable that this reflects the bitter tension that arose between the church and the synagogue after Christianity and Judaism parted company. Any public display was compared with the performance of actors who strutted on stage in order to receive the applause of the crowd. This is the basis of hypocrisy: to be more concerned with adulation than with helping others and pleasing God. The advice given is to pray in private.

Verses 16–21 are about 'joyful fasting'. Rather than parading personal discomfort, fasting should be done with quiet delight. This is the joy that comes from a deepening relationship with God that overflows in actions that seek to improve quality of life for others.

In today's culture, an outward parade of religious piety is hardly likely to earn respect! We all know people who give of themselves, but despite the personal cost involved radiate warmth and approachability. This is the difference between the 'do-gooders' who cause resentment in those they seek to help, and the genuinely good who are always welcome.

FIRST SUNDAY IN LENT

Deuteronomy 26.1–11; Romans 10.8b–13; Luke 4.1–13

All three passages describe worship as the expression of our commitment to live in right relationship with God and with other people. This is our response to God's generosity and goodness.

Deuteronomy 26.1–11

Confession of faith in God's goodness is accompanied by the offering of first fruits. The Deuteronomic emphasis is set out in this passage, possibly in the form of a credal statement used in worship (26.5–9). The ancestor, described as 'a wandering Aramean' may refer to Jacob who became known as Israel, the father of the nation, or it may refer to any one of the people's ancestors who wandered in the wilderness before entering the Promised Land. The Israelites experienced oppression in Egypt before God rescued and provided for them. The wilderness was the place of the covenant and as God's people they are committed to care for others as God cared for them. The offering of first fruits is accompanied by a willing sharing of the harvest feast, the celebration of God's bounty, not only with their own households, but with strangers and Levites. The context of writing is the time when hill-shrines were destroyed to prevent people from combining worship of God with worship of Canaanite fertility gods and so many of the hill-shrines' priests (Levites) became unemployed as the Temple became the only centre for worship. This passage affirms that the land and its harvest came from God's generosity and the right response is to make an offering to God and to share his bounty.

Lent is traditionally a time of self-denial, but self-denial that is the response of gratitude to a bountiful God. We, who are the recipients of so many good things, deny ourselves in order to provide for others. Although this can be the responsibility of individuals, it is also appropriate for the local church to consider how to respond to the needs of the world.

Romans 10.8b–13

Paul speaks about the nature of righteousness and salvation. To live in right relationship with God meant keeping the commandments that formed the Mosaic law. However, for Christians the preached word of faith focuses on Jesus as the fulfilment of those commandments. Faith is present whenever the preached word is received so wholeheartedly that the hearer can do no other than become the proclaimer. The title, 'Jesus is Lord' seems to have been the earliest Christian declaration of faith and as such may have been a prerequisite for baptism. To call Jesus 'Lord' was to place obedience to him above that required by any earthly authority. For Roman Christians, allegiance to Jesus could bring 'shame' within a culture that prized 'honour' (the opposite of 'shame') and where the worship of Roman gods was the norm. Yet, Paul's assurance is that God will not fail anyone who puts their trust in Jesus as Lord. Obedient Christians are all acceptable to God and should be treated as such by each other, regardless of race, ethnicity or gender.

When we can do no other than proclaim God's word in speech and actions, we are amongst those who from the earliest days of the Church have put their trust in God, rather than in the good opinion of others.

Luke 4.1–13

Jesus is not faced by doubts, but goes 'filled with the Spirit' to the deserted place where he can spend time alone as he prepares to follow his vocation. The Israelites spent forty years in the wilderness and in their trials often failed to put their trust in God. Jesus remained in the wilderness for forty days and his trust in God never wavered.

The last three temptations point to Jesus' identity as 'the Son of God'. Every time he is tempted, Jesus responds by quoting Scripture. Firstly, Jesus is tempted to appease both his own hunger and the hunger of others, but the obedient Son of God relies only on God's word which alone can satisfy (Deut. 8.3). Secondly, it follows that Jesus' total commitment is to God (Deut. 6.13). There is no suggestion that earthly authorities are led by the devil, rather that the nature of God's authority will unfold in the person of his Son. Thirdly, the final temptation takes place at the Temple, the focus of divine/human relationship. Scripture is tested against Scripture as the idea of God's protection of anyone who is faithful (Psalm 91.11–12) is balanced by Jesus' conviction that an obedient son does not try to manipulate or test God (Deut. 8.3). The passage ends with a note of menace and the shadow of the cross looms as the thwarted devil bides his time!

Jesus is the Son of God who relies only on God, he will act with God's authority and, in his person, God's loving purposes for the world will be revealed. Jesus, rather than the Temple, becomes the place where those who also turn from temptation are drawn back into right relationship with God.

SECOND SUNDAY IN LENT

Genesis 15.1–12, 17–18; Philippians 3.17–4.1; Luke 13.31–35

Genesis 15.1–12, 17–18

God's word comes to Abraham and, in a vision, he is promised a great reward. Abraham is so anxious about his childlessness that he cannot believe God has anything profitable to say to him. After listening to his troubles, God tells him to go out of the tent and Abraham the stargazer, against all reason, trusts God who promises that his descendants will be as numerous as the stars. Trust is the basis for belief and brought Abraham into proper relationship with God. This right relationship is the prerequisite of righteousness.

Verses 1–6 and 7–12 give two different accounts of Abraham's call. Verse 7 introduces God as the one who brought Abraham to the land he now possesses. The picture of ritual covenant-making may be uncongenial to today's reader: primitive practice was that animals were halved and laid opposite each other. The partners to the covenant would have walked through the pathway between the halved animals to signify their acceptance that they would be cursed if they broke the covenant. Do the birds of prey signify hindrances that will make it hard for people to fulfil their promise? In the theophany of verses 17–18, a smoking fire-pot and a flaming torch pass along the pathway, implying that God is underlining his part in the covenant. Notice that the picture is of God's willingness to ratify the covenant by entering into a human ritual! Abraham's role is simply to watch passively before God reaffirms the gift of land.

After we share our anxieties, do we move forward making trust in God the basis for our actions? If we do not expect God to be present in our religious rites then they may become blocked pipes rather than channels of grace! How much better to come with open hearts and minds expecting to meet God. Then the words of our prayers and hymns become the means by which God's grace may flow.

Philippians 3.17–4.1

It seems likely that the context of this passage lies in Paul's opposition to Christians from Jewish backgrounds who felt that converts from pagan backgrounds should conform to Jewish law. Paul fears a split within the congregation and points to others of his own persuasion as good examples. His opponents must be seen as enemies of the cross of Christ. Paul wept over them, understandably if they were his fellow-

Jews whom he felt were heading for destruction. Is Paul talking about circumcision, the outward sign of Judaism, when he speaks in such a derogatory way about opponents: 'their god is the belly' and 'their glory is in their shame'? Just as Romans lived in Philippi as if it were Rome, so Christians are called to live in this world as if it were heaven, in preparation for Christ's return when all things will be transformed. It follows that bodily matters, whether or not people are circumcised, will cease to be important. Meanwhile the Philippian Christians remain a source of joy to Paul, for they are the fruits of his missionary endeavour and are like the victor's wreath presented to the winner at the games. They should stand firm because they can trust the Lord to sustain them in the way of life Paul commends.

Here trust is based on God's will that divisions between Christians should be broken down. Is the Church ready to hear and act on that conviction?

Luke 13.31–35

The shadow of Jerusalem hangs over these verses. Surprisingly, it is the Pharisees, usually portrayed as Jesus' enemies by Luke, who warn him of his danger. Were these a group of open-minded Pharisees or, as they seem to be hand in glove with Herod, were they goading him about the danger he faced? Herod, who had already murdered John the Baptist, is described as a 'fox', an animal known for its wily and destructive character, suggesting that he would probably like to get rid of Jesus too. Danger threatens, but Jesus stays focused on his divinely appointed task of saving people by casting out demons and healing. Jesus' ministry of salvation cannot be halted by threats, but moves inexorably towards its goal – today, tomorrow and the next day (v.33). Jesus is like prophets of old who met their deaths amongst those they came to warn. He comes to Jerusalem, the temple city, the place to which Jews scattered throughout the Roman world sought to return. In an image of infinite tenderness, Luke describes Jesus' longing to protect the people (v.34) yet in 70 CE, probably by the time the Gospel was written, the Temple would be destroyed. In words that point to Palm Sunday, Jesus is described as the one who keeps coming and does not turn his back.

The good news is that Jesus not only 'kept coming' on Palm Sunday as he faced death in Jerusalem, but that he has 'kept coming' ever since. In all places and all times, the risen Christ comes to his people.

THIRD SUNDAY IN LENT

Isaiah 55.1–9; 1 Corinthians 10.1–13; Luke 13.1–9

Isaiah 55.1–9

The delivered people, on their return home from Babylon, hear the cry of the market seller ring out, 'Come, buy!' This is the land of milk (of the herders), and honey (of the agriculturalists – for honey, think of abundant fruit, including grapes for wine). Yet, God's free gifts can be purchased without money. In Old Testament Scripture, 'to hear' (vv. 2 and 3) means 'to obey' and God's imperative is for people to eat the food that satisfies and gives life, that is to enter once again into covenant relationship. Previously, the covenant blessing was understood to include God's protection of the people and victory over the nation's enemies, along with the promise of growth and prosperity. Now, people from other nations no longer pose a threat but stream to Jerusalem in their wish to become citizens and worship Israel's God, thus increasing her numbers and wealth. To 'seek the Lord' is to turn towards God who is near, in other words ready to forgive, so that worship may find its expression in faithful living. God's 'thoughts' have to do with his purposes for creation and his 'ways' with their outworking. No wonder humanity is unable to fathom them!

Britain seems like 'a land of milk and honey'. At a time when people from other nations stream to our country, how do we understand Deutero-Isaiah's message: 'Seek the Lord'? Historically, Britain has not always helped people from other nations, but has grown rich at their expense. Do we resent the presence of shopkeepers, doctors or bus drivers who have come to this country and have become citizens, or do we rejoice in the diversity of today's society?

1 Corinthians 10.1–13

It seems that the Corinthian Christians had been participating in pagan meals and were arguing that because they also participated in the Lord's Supper they were remaining faithful. Paul refutes this by reminding them of the wilderness wanderings when spiritual food and drink (manna and water from the rock) did not avert God's displeasure and many died in the desert (v.5). In the past, people ate before the golden calf, just as in Corinth they ate in the presence of idols; and there is a suggestion that their revelry both in the past and present included sexual activity. Paul warns them that by attending pagan meals they are putting Christ to the test just like their ancestors who were destroyed by snakes in the wilderness. They must not think that because the new age has begun in Christ they are already saved and can do as they like, rather they must take note of the wilderness warning. Paul is aware of the pastoral necessity to follow his admonishment with encouragement. Instead of relying on the sacraments in an inappropriate way, they can have complete confidence in God's faithfulness, because they will never be tested to the point where they will be overwhelmed.

The idea that God never tests us beyond our endurance raises difficulties for Christians who suffer to the point of physical or mental breakdown. Verse 13 must be read in the context of the first-century pagan world, when Paul is encouraging the Christian community to remain faithful in the assurance that the Church will not be destroyed.

Luke 13.1–9

Luke is the only Gospel to record two appalling and catastrophic events resulting in loss of life. For Pilate to commit murder (whether or not in the name of the law) and mix the blood of the dead with the blood of sacrificed animals would have defiled the Temple in a horrific act. In contrast, a tower at the water source at Siloam collapsed killing eighteen people. Whether or not these two incidents have any historical basis, they represent the kind of disasters with which humanity is only too familiar and explore the kind of theological responses such events often elicit! Jesus refutes the idea that there is any link between these catastrophes and divine punishment of the worst sinners. Nevertheless, these events provide a warning to disobedient Israel, which is like the fig tree that fails to bear fruit and so deserves to be cut down. If Luke was writing after the destruction of the Temple in 70 CE this parable would have special significance.

Death-dealing disasters occur both through deliberate human cruelty and by accident. Jesus, while refuting the idea that divine punishment led to such catastrophic events, nevertheless took the opportunity to face humanity with the unpalatable truth that if we fail to 'produce fruit' (in other words, live faithfully), we may deserve no less. Sometimes, it is only when disaster strikes that people are receptive to God who calls us to live in harmony with each other and with him. In the aftermath of destruction caused by flood, earthquake or bomb people often rush to the aid of strangers, ready to brave cold or heat, exhaustion and hunger to save those in need. How sad it is that such self-giving does not always characterize our everyday lives.

FOURTH SUNDAY IN LENT

Joshua 5.9–12; 2 Corinthians 5.16–21; Luke 15.1–3, 11b–32

Joshua 5.9–12

It would be only too easy to look at this passage from Joshua without considering the preceding or following verses, however these are important to 'set the scene'. Joshua has led his people across the dried-up River Jordan and the years of the wilderness wanderings have come to an end. Their first act was to circumcise all males, perhaps because those who entered the land were a mixed community, perhaps because the practice of circumcision had not been adhered to during the wilderness years, but its purpose would have been to provide an outward sign that this motley crew were one people committed to God's law.

Now the people are ready to celebrate the Passover meal, and verses 9–12 begin with God's assurance that the 'disgrace' or 'shame' of bondage in Egypt has been rolled away and God's promises are fulfilled as the people become landowners. Here is a community committed to God, whose first act in the land they will occupy is to celebrate their release from bondage in Egypt and give thanks to God. No longer will they eat manna, the provision of God during the desert years. The food at the Passover meal was the produce of the land, 'parched grain' being a staple part of the diet. The mention of unleavened bread is interesting, as in the early years the feast of unleavened bread began as a separate feast day that followed the Passover, so it is likely that an editor's hand can be discerned reflecting later practice. However, the story does not end with our passage. The people are now prepared for action. Today's reader may recoil from the idea that what they are prepared for is warfare, for this is a story of a nation which believes that God is on their side as they seek to occupy Canaan. Yet, this is part of a larger story, that of a people's relationship with the God who rescues them from what binds them, a people who recommit themselves to God in thanksgiving and who move on – sometimes to make more mistakes, sometimes to faithful living – but in the certainty that God is always faithful.

Lent is a time of preparation for the events of Holy Week. In Jesus, the greatest rescue operation of all took place. This is what we mean when we say 'God is on our side'. God has always saved his people from whatever binds them and prevents them from flourishing. God rescues humanity because he longs for us to grow to become the children, women and men he would like us to be. We are not left to struggle alone, for God offers his help. However, we must seek the help that God offers to all who turn to him. Sometimes athletes prepare themselves for a race by crossing themselves and murmuring a prayer. Do we always dedicate our efforts to God and seek to do our best in his service?

2 Corinthians 5.16–21

In the preceding verses, Paul has emphasized that one man has died for all. No longer are people to be valued superficially, perhaps by their race, age or appearance, but as those whose worth is measured by Christ's willingness to die for them. Now Christ too can be known, not partially as in his earthly life, but fully because he is revealed as the one who loved enough to face the cross. In his death, Christ reflected the love of God who raised him to a resurrection life that has transformed creation. How has this happened? It can only be through the transforming power of divine love. When human beings love, whether a place, person, or any other created thing, it is transformed in their eyes; how much more when God loves! Those who believe in Christ belong to this 'new creation', for this is not just about individuals, or even about the Church, but about a whole new world order! Nevertheless, it is still the time of 'now' and 'not yet', because although those who believe in Christ are already transformed (because God refuses to hold their wrongdoing against them) and their relationship with God is secure, however there is work for them to do. They are to act as Christ's authorized representatives, his ambassadors, so that others may also be drawn into that same transforming, divine relationship. Such a relationship has been made possible because Christ identified himself so completely with sinful humanity that he was prepared to die to show people that their wrongdoing could not put them beyond God's love. Christ's sacrifice, unlike temple sacrifices, provided the one offering that demolished the barrier that sin presented to entering into full and right relationship with God.

Do we believe that God looks on us with such love that we are transformed or do we have a sneaking suspicion that our sin prevents us from being loveable? If we know that Christ would die for each one of us to bring us into that perfect relationship with God, how do we respond? Only by learning to love as God loves! What implications that has for Christian living!

Luke 15.1–3, 11b–32

The theme of God's love that will not allow sin to be a barrier is portrayed supremely by the parable of the prodigal (or lost) son. For those who first listened to this story its shocking nature would be evident. While sons would work on the land they would inherit, that land would not become fully theirs during their father's lifetime. For the youngest son to ask for his inheritance was to act as if his father was already dead! The father allows the son to take the value of what had been promised to him and make his own mistakes – and he does! What is more he moves outside his own Jewish culture to 'foreign parts' where he can indulge himself with prostitutes (v.30). Already horrified by his behaviour, Jesus' listeners are told that the son was reduced to circumstances that would have been repulsive to them: starving, he is forced to eat the food of pigs, unclean animals, thereby becoming unclean himself and beyond God's love and mercy. Even then, he does not repent but is still concerned with 'looking after number one'. He intends to return and ask for a position as a hired servant. In other words, he was going to ask for a wage from the father he had treated so abysmally! What would have been even more shocking was the father's response. In a culture that prized dignity and honour, the picture of a father who not only waited for his son, not only ran to meet him but flung his arms around him and kissed him would disgust those listening to the story. The shocking nature of the story would only be compounded by the father's actions when he interrupts his son's rehearsed speech and receives him again as an honoured member of the family. He places a ring on his finger – the seal of the ring that may have been pressed into wax to ratify business deals. If so, the son, who had spent all his inheritance, was being given authority to act once again as his father's agent! The nearest parallel today, would be to give his son the use of his credit card! A cloak was placed around his shoulders; servants wore tunics, only sons wore cloaks and this was the best cloak kept only for honoured guests! Sandals were placed on his feet; only sons wore sandals, servants went barefoot!

This isn't a story about a real family. How many earthly fathers would act with such generosity? Yet Jesus seems to be saying that this is how God treats people irrespective of their selfishness and gross insensitivity to the needs of the whole family! It is not surprising that the elder son was angry. He had continued to work on the property, serving his father (and his own interests) and there had never been a celebration in his honour. However, at the end of the story he is reminded that he is still his father's heir and his father is always with him (v.30) *and* he still has a brother! The celebration is about the restoration of family relationships irrespective of the younger son's actions, but simply because this is what the father wills for his family.

Have we heard this parable so often that we have lost our sense of shock? How do we respond to an undignified God who runs to meet a child who has behaved so reprehensibly, a God who not only celebrates his arrival and restores him to his place within the family but also restores him to a position of trust and responsibility? Of course, we could say that Jesus often exaggerates to make his point and the use of hyperbole should not be taken too literally! Another way of looking at the story is to see ourselves in the characters depicted. There are times when we are selfish, both as individuals and communally, and when we think it time to return to God, we want to do so on our own terms – as hired servants – not offering all we have and are. It is easy to see ourselves in the elder brother, but do we hear God's loving word that he is always with us and all that is God's is ours? Yet, surely we are also called to see ourselves in the picture of the Father, ready to put aside our own dignity and the good opinion of others in order to welcome those of God's children, who like us need to discover the generous welcome of God who will never let our sin become an insurmountable barrier.

MOTHERING SUNDAY

Exodus 2.1–10 or 1 Samuel 1.20–28; 2 Corinthians 1.3–7 or
Colossians 3.12–17; Luke 2.33–35 or John 19.25–27

Exodus 2.1–10

The story of Moses' birth is reminiscent of other Ancient Near
Eastern legends, for example, that of Sargon (a Mesopotamian king)
who was also placed in a rush basket and drawn out of the river. Such
stories were told to legitimate the claims of great leaders who came
from humble beginnings. It is easier to understand the story's significance for Israel if it is read as story rather than history.

The baby is born to a family from the tribe of Levi. The names of
his parents and sister are not given until 6.18–20 and to begin with
they remain anonymous. Is this to emphasize that their baby is like all
the others whose lives are threatened? The baby shares the fate of all
the Israelite male children when he is put into the Nile but, unlike
those who are drowned, Moses lives. He is saved from death because
he was placed in a waterproofed, rush basket, a tiny version of the ark
that protected Noah and his family from the floodwaters. The basket
was placed amongst the reeds and it is no coincidence that the 'sea of
reeds' (Red Sea) would be the scene of the people's deliverance in the
future. When Pharaoh's daughter opened the basket, this was like the
moment when Noah and his family came out of the ark. It is surprising that one of the hated Egyptian oppressors is portrayed as compassionate, especially as she acted in the full knowledge that this was
an Israelite child. It is the women who enable the child to survive.
Much ink has been spilt on the subject of the baby's name. It has often
been said that the Hebrew word 'to draw out' (of the water) is similar
to Moses. However, names such as Ra-meses were made up of an
Egyptian god's name, in this case 'Ra' and the root of the word meaning 'to give birth'. Ra-meses, therefore, means 'Ra gave birth'. Was
'Moses' the second half of such a name? Could the deliverer of Israel
ever have been known by the name of an Egyptian god? Names
matter because they point to a person's identity. Moses' deliverance
and the deliverance of the Israelites came from the God of Israel alone
and the name of Moses has ever since been associated with that of the
archetypal deliverer of God's people.

This story, like that of Cinderella, is a portrayal 'from rags to
riches'. Moses was offered 'fame and fortune' as an adopted member
of the royal family! Yet he will turn his back on his Egyptian inheritance and, with God's help, save an oppressed people. Those who

carry the name 'Christian' are also called to reject the lure of wealth and status and to act as deliverers in ways either great or small.

1 Samuel 1.20–28

A woman who could not bear children was disgraced within Hannah's society. (In those days infertility was never thought of as a male problem!) It was assumed that childlessness was a punishment by God. How desperate Hannah must have felt! Her delight and relief when she became pregnant was heartfelt! Now she could hold up her head again. It seems that the decision to take her son to the shrine at Shiloh was Hannah's own; yet how hard it must have been, even though she was giving him back to God. Her offerings came from a heart spilling over with gratitude, for a three-year old bull was a costly gift.

Mothering Sunday can be a painful day for women and men who have longed in vain for their own children. As one of them, I am sure that it is important for pain to be acknowledged in worship and for the preacher to state unequivocally that childlessness is never a punishment. Hannah's desperation reminds us that our worship should never generate a sense of isolation in others. God 'mothers' us all, shares our pain and leads us through our distress to a time when thanksgiving will spill over into grateful giving.

2 Corinthians 1.3–7

Paul gives thanks that God is the one who comforts those in trouble. Those who receive consolation are, in their turn, able to offer that same comfort to others. God's names (v.3) indicate that he is the comforter par excellence and the reader may find it interesting to count how many times words about comfort and consolation are used in this short passage. Comfort and deliverance go hand in hand: comfort enables people to stand up and move on, therefore those who have received comfort must also give it. Paradoxically, suffering and consolation are opposite sides of the same coin. Christian life involves sharing in Christ's sufferings, yet Christ is also the one who offers comfort to those who suffer. This is about a lifestyle that reflects a pattern of dying and rising as Christians discover a way of living that mirrors the experience of both cross and resurrection. To put this colloquially, Christ and Christians are 'in this together'! To be in solidarity with Christ means that distress is inevitable. For believers in the early church, faith in Christ led to opposition and division in families as well as persecution from pagan society. Yet, the assurance of consolation, combined with a commitment to comfort others, produces a response that brims over with confidence and hope.

To be a parent is to become a comforter. It is the parents' task to stand their children back on their feet after a fall and to set them on their way again. Yet parents also need comforting when children hurt themselves or others, or put themselves at risk.

Colossians 3.12–17

Those who are both chosen and beloved by God must reflect his moral nature, represented here in a list of five virtues, aspects of God's character. The list ends with humility, a quality despised by a society that valued honour and pride. In his portrayal of Uriah Heep, Charles Dickens also dealt humility a body blow as 'being humble' is frowned on just as much today! Yet true humility is about placing the welfare of others before personal pride. Christians are to take on the characteristics of Christ who was willing both to serve and to forgive others. This is why Christians must forgive. If each virtue is like a garment, then the overcoat for a Christian is love: the longing for health and wholeness for another. Christ's peace stems from a life in which Christ is allowed to be the arbiter, or umpire. The gospel, the good news of Christ's involvement in Christian life, can only lead to thanksgiving. And it is in a spirit of thankfulness that members of the community teach others. Such glad thanksgiving spills over into joyful worship.

The best teachers lead by example! How many of our skills have been developed by teachers whose enthusiasm we caught? Are we filled with joyful thanksgiving because Jesus 'humbled himself' to show us God's love? Is this the moment when we 'catch the vision' and discover the true meaning of humility that builds up others?

Luke 2.33–35

From the outset, Jesus is portrayed as no ordinary child! Simeon has expressed his conviction that the child he held in his arms would bring light not only to his own people – and that in itself was a large enough claim – but to other nations! Parenthood is always a surprise! The amazement of Jesus' parents echoes the wonder they felt when the shepherds told their story (2.17). Simeon blesses both Mary and Joseph, but his words of prophecy are addressed to Mary. The child she has borne will bring both judgement and salvation as he fulfils the task appointed to him by God. The words, 'falling' and 'rising' remind the reader of the constant theme of reversal of fortunes that runs through Luke's Gospel. As the story of Jesus unfolds, it will be seen that those who 'rise' will be people despised and forgotten by society, and those who 'fall' the ones who have ignored their plight. Jesus will become a 'sign', warning the nations that God is about to judge the world; as such, he will face inevitable opposition. People will choose either to obey or to disobey Jesus' teaching and in their choices their thinking will be exposed. As Jesus is held in Simeon's arms the shadow of the cross is already present. Mary's soul, all that she is, her whole self, will be pierced with a sword (v.35). This powerful allusion pictures the extent of the agony she will feel as Jesus leaves home and family behind, and begins his ministry with new companions as he commences the journey that will lead inevitably and inexorably to the cross.

No matter how well a parent prepares for a birth, the child cannot be known until she or he is encountered as a person. Parenthood brings both joy and pain and involves both loving and letting go. This reading is bitter-sweet as Mary faces the loss of Jesus, in his ministry as he finds other companions, and in his death.

John 19.25–27

The scene is the crucifixion. Jesus hangs on the cross and before him stand four women including Jesus' mother. From the cross, in the moment of his agony, Jesus provides for her and for the disciple he loves. The identity of this disciple is never revealed but he becomes the representative of all faithful disciples down the ages. This is not about material provision for Mary, as she had other children to care for her, not least her son James, who would become an important leader in the Jerusalem church when it was formed. Instead, this is about the creation of a new family unit as the disciple becomes a member of Jesus' own family with its customs and traditions. At the wedding at Cana, Mary had told people to obey Jesus (2.5). Here, the obedient disciple, beloved by Jesus, takes his place within the family.

What makes up a family? Today, there are many step-families and adoptive families. What holds families together is a sense of belonging and mutual commitment. Family traditions develop over the years as people share experiences and pore over photographs or watch family videos. Those who belong to Jesus' family are also 'beloved' disciples who share the family tradition of mutual care that spills over into care for others.

FIFTH SUNDAY IN LENT

First Sunday of the Passion

Isaiah 43.16–21; Philippians 3.4b–14; John 12.1–8

Isaiah 43.16–21

God reminds the exiled people that he saved them from Egypt at the time of the first exodus by parting the sea before them and destroying their enemies. If he has saved them once, then surely he will save them again. Yet, there is no point in looking back, no matter how great their former deliverance, because it will pale into insignificance in relation to the new thing God is about to do. Rather than clinging to a past seen through 'rose-tinted spectacles', but which they never expect to experience again, the exodus story offers a surety for the future. God who led them through the wilderness then, will lead them again through a desert transformed by rivers of water. Even the wild animals will share in its abundance. As they drink, the people's thirst for their old ways will be slaked, for God's creative purpose for them has not ended. They are the people who will praise God as a witness to God's continuing saving and transforming power.

The Christian Church needs to stop clinging to the past in a negative way, but must look to the future trusting that God's purpose for his people remains: for we will always be 'a people for his praise' – praise that is reflected in our worship and in our lives!

Philippians 3.4b–14

The Philippian Christians were afraid that if they renounced their Jewish commitment to the law they would put themselves beyond God's grace. Circumcision was the outward mark of belonging to Judaism. Paul offers himself as an example. He had been so strongly rooted in his own tradition, that he persecuted Christians. Yet, all that had changed. Now his relationship with God is based on faith in Christ and not on his enthusiasm and commitment to his own religious practice even though that had been exemplary! Paul's religious standing must have seemed enviable, yet in the strongest possible language he impresses on the recipients of the letter that all he has relinquished is 'garbage' of as much value as the contents of a dustbin! (v.8) This is because for Paul righteousness was about being in right relationship with Christ and that involved entering into the experience of Christ's suffering and death in the hope of sharing in his resurrection life.

Perhaps the nearest analogy is of lovers who work together for the good of others, sharing a cross-shaped way of life, but whose relationship is enriched and deepened over the years. For the Philippian Christians, to follow Christ was to be on a collision course with pagan society. Yet, this was also to share in the life-giving, loving purposes of God that would be fully experienced in the resurrection life to come.

Those Christians we know who have spent a lifetime in loving service, offer us a glimpse of that same unity of love and purpose.

John 12.1–8

(Note that comments on John 12.1–11 can also be found under Monday in Holy Week.)

The order is out for Jesus' arrest. Nevertheless, he goes to prepare for Passover at the house of his friends. The readers of John's Gospel, like us, know that this is the prelude to Jesus' death, but Lazarus' presence is a reminder that death does not always have the last word. The story focuses on Mary who amazed everyone by her extravagance in pouring an exorbitantly costly perfume imported from India, over Jesus' feet, before wiping them with her hair. The scent filled the house and nobody could ignore what she had done. Judas' comment is a reminder of the hypocrisy of all those down the ages who have put forward the needs of others with the intention of benefiting themselves. In contrast, Jesus commends Mary's generosity with a strange saying (v.7). For she had not kept the perfume for his burial, but used it out of overflowing gratitude and love, that would support and sustain him for the ordeal that lay ahead. It is the memory of Mary's action that would remain when death came.

Few people nowadays expect death to come tomorrow, or even the next day. It is only when unexpected illness or accident happen that the need to express our love becomes an urgent necessity. For example, these days flowers are often left at the scene of a road accident. People who live in a semi-religious society are finding new ways of showing their concern. Yet church services continue to offer opportunities for such emotions to be expressed. When the gospel story touches the stories of those who suffer today, lives are changed and despair is turned into hope. The postscript (v.8) is a reminder that the task of caring for those most in need was not forgotten, or belittled by Mary's action, rather this was and is a constant commitment for Jesus' disciples – for in the light of Easter the picture has changed!

SIXTH SUNDAY IN LENT

Second Sunday of the Passion or Palm Sunday

Entry into Jerusalem: Luke 19.28–40
The Passion: Isaiah 50.4–9a; Philippians 2.5–11; Luke 22.14–23.56
or Luke 23.1–49

Gospel Reading for Palm Sunday: Luke 19.28–40

Jesus goes up to Jerusalem and this is a signal that the narrative is
reaching its climax. The story of Jesus' entry into the city is found in
all four Gospels but Luke tells it in his own way, emphasizing themes
of peace and judgement.

Jesus enters by way of the Mount of Olives, the scene of God's final
judgement (Zech. 14.4). No previous arrangement with the colt's
owners is mentioned, rather the story progresses as a sacred drama. A
colt never previously ridden is suitable for a sacred purpose and its
owners defer to Jesus' claim, for his lordship is superior to theirs. As
Jesus rides into the city cloaks are thrown down before him (Luke
makes no mention of palm branches) and his disciples, those who
have witnessed his mighty acts, begin to shout their praise in the
words of the psalmist (Ps. 118.26), recognizing that Jesus' kingship
belongs to the realm of heaven where peace will prevail. The
Pharisees demand Jesus to order his disciples to be silent, but his
response is ominous, for if the stones took up the cry, creation itself
would speak against a corrupt world (Hab. 2.11) and affirm Jesus. As
he weeps over the city, Jesus foretells its destruction by enemies.
(That destruction had already taken place by the time Luke wrote his
Gospel: the Roman invasion of 70 CE and its devastation would be
fresh in the minds of his readers.) Destruction follows the people's
failure to recognize that God has visited them in Jesus (v.44) and presumably their failure to respond to his teaching. Peace in this world
depends on the well-being of all and reflects the peace of God's realm
about which the disciples sang (v.38).

The next stage of the drama takes place in the Temple. Luke omits
details found in the other three Gospels so that the focus can be only
on Jesus' words that spell judgement to those who have failed to use
the Temple for its rightful purpose – prayer.

The disciples' song proclaimed Jesus as 'king of peace'. If the
Church today is to sing that same song, Christians must speak and act
against power that corrupts society to ensure that the world's resources benefit all people. To join in such a song is to rediscover that
prayer is an imperative for right action.

Old Testament Reading for the Second Sunday of the Passion: Isaiah 50.4–9a

This third Servant Song combines elements of lament, prayer and a song of confidence. The servant seems to take the mediator's role. He is the one who is commissioned to teach and sustain others with God's word, but to fulfil this role necessarily involves rejection and suffering. There are resonances with Jeremiah's experience, for he too was commissioned for a task that seemed too heavy and even though he was scorned he continued to affirm his trust in God.

The prophet-servant has to be aroused, woken up so that he can hear God and he is sent to those who are still weary, in other words not fully awake. If the one who is sleeping is Israel, then the nation needs to be aroused before there is any chance of the message being heard. Yet that awakening is not a one-off event, but has to happen every morning. Those who do not want to be roused resort not only to insults but strike out physically. In the prophet's culture, his willingness to accept the blows and insults would have been interpreted as tacit acceptance that God was on the side of those who struck him, justifying his opponents' behaviour! What is being offered is a picture of a prophet who must have doubted whether he had understood God's word correctly, a situation faced by most people of faith at some time in their lives. In startling contrast to this crisis of confidence v.7 is an amazing statement of assurance. Against all his cultural understanding and experience, the prophet-servant is convinced that it is God's will that he accepts his suffering and that his disgrace is not the shame it seems. The final verses take the form of a courtroom scene as he faces his opponents in a legal contest. That is where the passage ends – with a cliffhanger! Those who oppose him have not changed their views and the prophet-servant remains convinced that God will vindicate him and that ultimately his enemies will receive their just deserts. It is left for the reader to act as the jury – yet the reader is also one of those who may react badly to being roused from sleep!

Epistle for the Second Sunday of the Passion: Philippians 2.5–11

The Christian community is to reflect Christ's attitude towards others and to take to heart his example. To this end, Paul offers the 'Hymn to Christ' that follows.

The first part of the hymn (vv. 6–8) speaks about Christ who, like us, was offered a choice. That choice seems to have been between continuing to share in God's sovereign power, a position of high status, and assuming the role of a slave, a position of low status. Slaves are obedient to their masters, and Christ was obedient to God. Once he had made the choice Christ did not look over his shoulder, as it were, in order to bolster his own authority or to achieve honour. Instead, he 'emptied himself' (v.7) refusing to use his relationship with God for his own ends. Within a culture that valued honour, Christ's total obedience to God led him to the most shameful and humiliating of deaths, death on a cross. The second part of the hymn (vv. 9–11) speaks about God's response to Christ's obedience. God raised Christ from the position of humiliation to that of the highest status. Not only does Christ once again share in God's reign, but now this is publicly acknowledged as a sign of God's approval signalled by a new name, in other words by a new identity. He is the one before whom everyone will bow: the honour accorded to God is now accorded also to Christ. Ultimately, all people will praise him.

The hymn offered the Philippians a paradigm for Christian living that was counter-cultural in the extreme. They had to be prepared to face humiliation for their faith. Yet although they might face shame in society, they would be honoured by God for their faithfulness.

All people like to receive praise from their friends, but Christian living should be characterized by an attitude of humble service, offered not to receive accolades, but freely given.

Gospel Reading for the Second Sunday of the Passion: Luke 22.14–23.56 or Luke 23.1–49

If the longer reading is chosen, there is an opportunity to allow the Gospel to speak for itself. The passion narrative was almost certainly read in its entirety to the earliest Christian congregations, and to share that experience across the years is both a humbling and exciting activity. This is a long extract for one person to read, unless that person has particular gifts in reading and storytelling. It may be that the passage should be divided into smaller sections to be presented in different ways. Some parts of the story would benefit from dramatic actions, for example, a figure representing Jesus standing to lift bread and wine (22.17–23), a group seeming to argue (22.24–27), and kneeling in prayer (22.41–44) and so on. These actions would be evocative, without being an elaborate attempt to dramatize the whole reading. Some passages cry out for the use of different voices and there is an opportunity to involve the congregation in joining their voices to the shouts of the crowd (especially at 23.18, 21 and 23), but this would have to be orchestrated before the service, so that emotional involvement with the narrative was not interrupted. Between sections, it might be helpful to offer times for reflection. These might include the opportunity to listen to music, or the placing of symbols to form a display (again these might include bread and wine, a picture of people in dispute, a candle, etc. relating to what has just been heard). Whole hymns or songs, or individual verses could be sung either seated or standing. This is the preacher's opportunity to enable Scripture to be heard in a fresh way and some (but not all) of these suggestions may be helpful – the key to an effective presentation is usually to 'keep it simple'!

If the shorter passage is chosen, this is still longer than most! It is appropriate to ask how Luke interpreted the death of Jesus. It is important to remember that Luke wrote for a church trying to survive within the Roman world. While Jews had already gained acceptance within Roman society, Christians were looked on with suspicion, and this was a time when relationships with the synagogue were strained to breaking point. It was essential that Christians were not seen to blame Rome for Jesus' death and so Luke places the blame firmly on the Jewish authorities. Luke alone speaks of a trial before Herod Antipas, the tetrarch of Galilee (23.6), who reacts to the accusations of the chief priests and scribes by allowing his soldiers to amuse themselves by mocking Jesus (23.11). When Jesus is sent back to Pilate Luke tries to place the weight of blame firmly on the crowds who shout out that he should be crucified, but only Roman authorities could sentence anyone to crucifixion! It is essential for Jewish/Christian relationships that preachers explain Luke's context in their preaching to avoid sounding antisemitic.

Luke offers many other helpful themes. These include discipleship – epitomized by Simon of Cyrene, who follows Jesus and carries his cross; compassion – for the people of the city (see comment on Luke 19.28–40 above); forgiveness – of his enemies; the response of those present – of rejection or belief; salvation – that paradoxically is available at the moment of his death (v.43); confidence in God – in Jesus' last words (v.46) that contrast with the cry of dereliction in Mark 15.34.

Whichever theme is chosen, it is essential that the members of the congregation are invited to 'write themselves into the story'. We are like the women who stand at a distance, watching (v.49). Are we merely observers, or do we weep with Jesus over a world in need? Are we ready to follow him and carry the cross?

MONDAY IN HOLY WEEK

Isaiah 42.1–9; Hebrews 9.11–15; John 12.1–11

Isaiah 42.1–9

This first 'Servant Song' is found in the second part of the book of Isaiah that addresses the people at the time of the Babylonian Exile, but may not have been written within that context. For this reason, the reader is like a detective looking for clues! What can be discovered? Firstly, the servant is chosen by God who delights in him and he, like other charismatic figures, is equipped for the task because God's spirit rests on him. These words are echoed at Jesus' baptism (Mark 1.11) so it is not surprising that Christians read this passage with Jesus in mind. Perhaps the Servant Song provides a 'job description' for Jesus! Secondly, the task is to bring justice to all the earth by over-turning the expected order: unlike lamps that burn low or plants that are damaged the servant will not be extinguished or broken before the task is completed, even though he will face extreme suffering. A dispirited, frightened people would find comfort in these words and their hope would spread to all the world, beginning at the coast where traders from many nations gathered. Thirdly, the servant was called by God the creator who has a special relationship with Israel. Verse 6 implies that suffering Israel is the servant, because her covenant commitment is to remain faithful and to continue God's saving work. In solidarity with those who suffer, Israel is to relieve their suffering by bringing freedom and light.

The servant is a multilayered designation for both the individual and the community who suffer with and for others. Such suffering love, seen supremely in Jesus, calls Christians to speak and act for those most in need, whether or not that message is unpopular. Who are the people most in need of an advocate in society today?

Hebrews 9.11–15

The question being addressed is, 'By what means do people have access to God?' In Judaism, on the Day of Atonement, the high priest would enter the Holy of Holies and sprinkle sacrificial blood, symbolizing life, on the altar. Such rites tend to generate feelings of repulsion amongst many people today; however, this was the time-honoured way in which sins were acknowledged and atonement was made. Nevertheless, Jesus' death and resurrection have changed everything! Because Jesus gave himself, on the cross, willingly for others he has become the once-for-all offering and any other sacrifices have become redundant. Jesus has become the means by which people can come into God's presence. Sacrificial animals had to be perfect and Jesus is described as being 'without blemish' (v.14). What does this mean? For the writer of Hebrews, Jesus' sinlessness relates to his agony in Gethsemane (5.7) and his perfect obedience that led to death.

Through Jesus people have access to God, but like him must be obedient, even though such obedience may be costly. That is what it means to enter into a new covenant relationship!

John 12.1–11

(Note that comments on John 12.1–8 can also be found under Fifth Sunday in Lent.)

In John's Gospel, the story of Mary anointing Jesus' feet comes just six days before the events that led to his crucifixion. As usual, Martha waits on the guests, but Mary, who liked to sit and listen to Jesus, brings costly perfume and pours it over his feet, wiping it with her hair. Oil of Nard was brought by traders from India and would have cost the equivalent of a year's wages for a farm labourer! This is an act of extreme, extravagant, embarrassing devotion. Judas complained indignantly about the waste, claiming that the money should have been given to the poor. The motive attributed to him by the evangelist is that, as the dishonest treasurer to the group, he would have preferred to feather his own nest! Nevertheless, his question is also the readers' question! Whether Mary realized that Jesus was courting death can never be known, but he commends her, suggesting that her action will be remembered and, at the time of his burial, she will be honoured for having anointed him. Crowds surround the house because they have come to see Lazarus whom Jesus raised from the dead and the sense of impending doom is heightened as the religious leaders of the day plot against both Jesus and Lazarus. (The suggestion that many people were deserting Judaism and turning to Jesus seems to come from a later period when the church split from the synagogue.)

Jesus, who raised Lazarus, chose the path of obedient suffering and faced his own death. Only Mary was prepared to give all that she could to show the extent of her love for Jesus. Christians in later generations are challenged to respond with the same extravagant, generosity: but now that giving must be focused on the needs of others.

TUESDAY IN HOLY WEEK

Isaiah 49.1–7; 1 Corinthians 1.18–31; John 12.20–36

Isaiah 49.1–7

These verses come from the second 'Servant Song'. The servant feels he has been called from the womb (v.1). His sense of selfhood relates to his prophetic role as God's servant. He is to speak God's word, described as sword and arrow. The military language shows that his task is offensive and his words both strike directly like a sword and range far and wide like arrows. Although born to challenge God's people to live faithfully he has to wait for the right moment. The servant is both the individual who speaks to Israel and the faithful remnant of obedient people within Israel who take on the same role. There is a time when the servant despairs, convinced that he has failed, for Israel has refused to listen. However, he has been faithful and his seeming failure has not broken his relationship with God, for God gives him a new task. Now he is to become a light to the Gentiles. The time will come when people will change their previous view of the servant who will be honoured by other nations. This verse is easier to understand if it applies to Israel as a despised nation whose status is now restored, not least as a religious community witnessing to the faithfulness of God.

Jesus called people to live faithfully and took on the role of the servant. His followers, notably Paul, took the good news of Christ to the pagan world. Is the Christian community 'a light to the nations' as across denominational boundaries we seek to make God's love for all people a reality?

1 Corinthians 1.18–31

To preach about a crucified Christ was a hard task for the newly formed Christian Church. The cross was 'a stumbling block to Jews and foolishness to Gentiles' (v.23). Jews put their faith in a powerful God who had saved them from their enemies time after time by his mighty acts. The cross, for the Jews, was a shameful symbol of their enemies' triumph! Greeks, however, put their faith in wisdom and rationality as a way of attaining religious knowledge and becoming one with the divine. The cross, for the Greeks, symbolized folly not wisdom! Paul argues forcibly that God's power is seen here in weakness. In a series of stark contrasts (vv.27–28), he describes the gulf between human perception and God's ways. Through the cross, God overturns human understanding of reality. People's understanding of strength and weakness, wisdom and foolishness, honour and dishonour is reversed.

As people respond to the unlimited love of the cross their way of relating to the most vulnerable in society is challenged.

John 12.20–36

The Greeks who went to Jerusalem for the Passover were attracted by the Jewish religion. Their question is also the post-resurrection question of all who 'wish to see Jesus' (v.21), that is, not only to meet Jesus, but to discover his significance for themselves and for all people. This is the question Jesus himself answers. Jesus is to be encountered as the one who was lifted up on the cross. Jesus' 'hour' is the hour of crucifixion which, paradoxically, is the moment of glory. Jesus is 'the Son of Man': the representative of suffering humanity. Jesus' death is compared with the grain of wheat that has to die in order to bear fruit. To understand what follows it is necessary to recognize that 'the world' in John's Gospel signifies all that opposes God's will. Jesus' followers are to 'hate' life in this world because they, like Jesus, must stand against all destructive forces. Instead, they will enter into eternal life, that is the life of God characterized by a 'cross-shaped' way of life. Eternal life, therefore, is not simply about everlasting life but about quality of life under God that death cannot bring to an end. This is why following Christ involves service. God honours those who live obediently. Verse 27 speaks of Jesus' agony in words that recall Gethsemane (Mark 14.34–46, Matt. 26.36–39, Luke 22.41–44). This is the moment of greatest obedience and the angelic voice (v.30) reinforces the message that God's glory is most clearly seen in the mutual honouring of Father and Son. People's greatest fears are of abandonment and annihilation and therefore of death. The lifting up of Jesus on the cross was the 'hour' when death was overcome. This is the moment of enlightenment when people are liberated from their fears and are challenged to live within the eternal light and life of God.

Jesus' followers are called to a life of costly service. This goes against the present climate of self-indulgence. Yet, through service people discover the eternal life of God that brings both joy and an end to fear. Do we believe this?

WEDNESDAY IN HOLY WEEK

Isaiah 50.4–9a; Hebrews 12.1–3; John 13.21–32

Isaiah 50.4–9a

Here in the third 'Servant Song' is an individual lament reminiscent of
Jeremiah's cries to God when he was being cruelly treated by his
enemies. The servant is the one who both hears and speaks God's
word. God wakes him every morning and it is the servant's task continually to rouse a tired people and challenge them to listen. He is
God's disciple, learning from God and teaching others. We do not
know the content of the message, but we do know that his words
engendered a hostile response, ranging from verbal to physical abuse.
He was treated shamefully, yet remained faithful. Convinced that he
was doing what God required, he accepted his suffering willingly as
part of his task. He 'set his face like flint' (v.7) certain that although,
according to public opinion, he seemed to be disgraced, he was not
shamed in God's sight. Instead, he challenges his opponents to face
him in God's courtroom, sure that he will be vindicated and God's
justice will prevail.

Are we ready to hear God speaking 'every morning' as we prepare
ourselves for the day? How are we to respond to friends and colleagues in the light of media reports of domestic and international
affairs? Are we ready to face a hostile response?

Hebrews 12.1–3

Spectators at an athletic event watch the runners to see how they will
endure the pain involved in racing. For Christians, the spectators are
the 'cloud of witnesses' who have already reached the winning post;
they are the faithful people of the past. Runners are hampered by
sin that entangles or restricts them and threatens to trip them up! The
runner must keep going at all costs, keeping his eyes fixed on Jesus
and ignoring all that may cause him to stumble. Jesus is both the
pioneer, because he was the first one to reach the winning tape, and
also the perfecter of faith, because he helps people to complete the
race. Jesus suffered pain and seeming disgrace, yet instead of being
dishonoured by dying a shameful death, now 'sits at the right hand of
the throne of God' (v.2), in other words he shares the divine task of
bringing justice. The writer of Hebrews is aware that he is addressing
people who are enduring hostility and so he reminds them that Jesus
also suffered and was treated cruelly. They are to follow his example

and must not become discouraged or too weary to continue the strug-gle. It is implied that Jesus is the one who will judge their enemies.

Although few Christians in the West are badly treated for their faith there are times when we, like the first Christian congregations, need encouragement. When we remember not only what Jesus suffered for us, but that the way of suffering led to joy, we are more likely to stand firm. We also need to remember that we, like the writer of Hebrews, are called to be encouragers!

John 13.21–32

The scene is the Last Supper. In the middle of the meal Jesus startled his disciples by announcing that one of them would betray him. As Jesus reclined at table he was flanked by the two men who represent us all: the beloved disciple and Judas, the former representing the obedient disciple and the latter the disobedient disciple who damages Jesus' ministry. This is the first mention of the beloved disciple and his identity is never revealed. When Jesus dipped his piece of bread in the bowl and passed it to Judas, a usual courtesy, he made it clear that he knew Judas was about to betray him. It is important not to specu-late about Judas' motives. The passage states explicitly that Judas betrayed Jesus because 'Satan entered into him'. We could say that 'Satan' becomes shorthand for all that opposes Jesus, and Judas becomes the focus for that opposition. At that moment, 'it was night' (v.30). Here is the darkness that threatens to overwhelm humanity. Also, at that same moment, Jesus the Son of Man, who acts for all innocent sufferers, was glorified. The time of deepest darkness was also the occasion of perfect obedience when Jesus faced the worst that the world could do. He honoured God as he accepted suffering and death and was honoured by God for his obedience.

Perhaps all Christians have within them the potential to be both the beloved disciple and Judas. While we strive to be the former, we are sometimes the latter. Jesus, in the pain of the cross, took our weakness to himself and offered us a new beginning. He is the one who helps us to become faithful disciples.

MAUNDY THURSDAY

Exodus 12.1–4 (5–10) 11–14; 1 Corinthians 11.23–26;
John 13.1–17, 31b–35

Exodus 12.1–4 (5–10) 11–14

God's people came to identify themselves as 'the Exodus people'. The Passover festival was more than a re-enacting and remembering of that event, for through the religious ceremony they became part of the same story. These verses give an account of the institution of the Passover and recall God's instructions to Moses and Aaron. Even though the Passover became a pilgrim festival, the Passover meal and the retelling of the story took place within the family or household. Verses 5–10 set out the ritual requirements that mirror the experience of the first Passover. Only perfect animals were to be offered at such a time and it does not take much imagination to recognize why later Christian doctrine emphasized the perfection, or sinlessness, of Christ, who came to be seen as the archetypal Passover lamb. The most important requirements were to recapture the sense of urgency and that everything was to be consumed, although provision was made for leftovers. It is difficult for Christians to accept the idea of God as the destroyer, yet the picture is of God's victory over the Egyptian gods (v.12). Blood is a sign of life. Life was offered to those who were oppressed and life was taken away from the oppressors.

As Christians, God's story is our story helping to define us as members of the community of God's people. Do we need to tell that story in our homes so that children and adults discover their identity and a sense of belonging within individual Christian families? We also need to recapture a sense of urgency about the rescue of those who are exploited and harshly treated today.

1 Corinthians 11.23–26

Paul has condemned the behaviour of wealthy members of the church who had been celebrating the Lord's Supper by enjoying good food and good company while poorer members were sidelined and excluded. He follows this with an account of its institution, reminding them that their commitment to Christ is also a commitment to each other. Paul's is the earliest account of Jesus' words (Mark's account would have been written about fifteen years later). The bread represented all that Jesus had been to his friends, all that he would be in the future. Jesus' blood, his life, poured out for them like wine, would enable them to enter the new covenant relationship. While Jesus was with them, he had reached out to others, preaching, teaching and healing. Now they were to take on that task knowing that Jesus had given himself to them. Paul was reminding the Corinthians that every time they ate together they were to remember Christ. This would ensure that they treated each other lovingly. Christ's death enabled them to become God's new covenant people living in right relationship with God and with each other.

Those who gather round the Lord's Table today come, not only as individuals, but as members of the community. Too often, as bread and wine are placed in our hands we concentrate on our personal relationship with God and forget those who kneel beside us. Our commitment is both to God and to each other.

John 13.1–17, 31b–35

In John's Gospel the Last Supper takes place before the Passover, but follows the usual custom for the Passover meal: Jesus and the disciples recline, in Roman fashion, at a low three-sided table. Leaning on their left elbows they would have eaten with their right hands, their feet stretched out behind. Foot-washing was a usual courtesy offered by a host before the meal. Yet, on this occasion, Jesus rises from the table and washes the feet of his friends, overtly performing a symbolic action to teach them something they needed to learn. Peter's refusal to allow Jesus to wash his feet leads to a conversation about cleanness. It is Judas, who is not clean. (See yesterday's Gospel passage for Wednesday in Holy Week.) He is the one who represents all that opposes Jesus. It is the task of the disciples to be clean themselves and to clean up all that stands over against Jesus in the world.

Verses 31–35 follow Judas' departure. Jesus gives the remaining disciples their final instructions. Once again, the language of mutual glorification of the Father and Son is a reminder of God's joy that Jesus chose the way of obedient suffering for others. Although they cannot go with Jesus and will feel abandoned, the disciples remain his 'little children' (v.33), secure in his love and they must love one another.

All three readings emphasize what it means to belong to the community of God's people. Together Christians are to live obediently by seeking and acting for the good of all God's children.

GOOD FRIDAY

Isaiah 52.13–53.12; Hebrews 10.16–25 or Hebrews 4.14–16, 5.7–9;
John 18.1–19.42

Isaiah 52.13–53.12

The fourth 'Servant Song' has often been read in churches on Good
Friday. For this reason many people assume that it is a prophecy about
Jesus. However, like the other Servant Songs, the prophet is speaking
about a role rather than a person. Jesus becomes the Servant because
he fulfilled the role and because the language of 'lifting up' and 'exal-
tation' (v.13) can be read in the light of the cross. Through the servant,
God's power is revealed in weakness and this is astonishing. Beauty
was associated with God's blessing and the servant's appearance
repulsed those who saw him not only because of his disfigurement,
but also because it was assumed that God looked on him with dis-
favour. The servant was isolated from society, suffering both the pain
of infirmity and the pain of rejection and contempt. Yet in this
despised fragment of humanity God did something new, as the
servant, by accepting his own agonizing suffering, also carried the
suffering of others. What were the pains of others that he bore? In a
culture that believed all sickness was the result of human sinfulness,
the servant carried the sins that caused suffering. Today it would be
usual to separate the pain of physical illness from that caused by
exploitation or abuse. The servant was an innocent sufferer who
shared the experience of all those who are 'cut off from the land of the
living' (v.8). In his body and his person, he bore the pain of sinful
humanity and made peace, atonement, between God and humanity.
The faithful servant gave his life for others (v.12). It was inevitable
that these verses would be read from the perspective of Good Friday,
for Jesus certainly took on the role of the suffering servant!

Vicarious suffering is part of the Christian task. Many people
prefer to switch off their radios or television sets when the news
is broadcast. 'There is too much suffering!' or 'The news is so
depressing!' are words that are often spoken. Prayer for others always
involves the use of loving imagination as we attempt to enter into their
suffering in the presence of God who brings healing and wholeness.
We feel helpless and impotent, yet our Good Friday faith is that love
that seeks to bear the pain of others is never wasted.

Hebrews 10.16–25

The 'old' covenant represented God's promise to be faithful and the people's promise to remain obedient. God kept his promise but the people broke theirs, not once but time after time. Jeremiah spoke of a 'new' covenant when the laws would be written not on tablets of stone, as at Sinai, but on people's hearts (Jer. 31.33). In other words, God would give them the will to be obedient. However, something else was necessary: the forgiveness of sin. Once forgiveness became the basis for people's relationship with God, sacrifices offered to atone for sin were no longer necessary. Only on the Day of Atonement did the priest pass beyond the curtain to enter the Holy of Holies, the innermost sanctuary of the Temple, in order to offer sacrifice on behalf of the people. Now Jesus, by his death, had torn away not only the curtain in the Temple, but also the metaphorical curtain that separated people from God. 'Sprinkling' (v.22) is the word used for religious cleansing and may refer to baptism. Jesus has taken the priestly role and made it possible for the people to approach God with confidence because the barrier of sin has been removed. As forgiven people, they must live up to their new position, meeting together for worship and mutual encouragement. 'The Day' (v.25) is the time of final judgement, and for the early church the Christ event must have been seen as the climax of human history leading to the end of the existing order. Although Christians today may not expect 'the end of the world' to come soon, here is a reminder that forgiven people are still accountable for their actions!

Today many who live in a consumer society tend to be more concerned with the gratification of their desires than with a sense of sin! Paradoxically, however, many experience low self-esteem and a sense of being unloved and unworthy that leads to an escalation of stress-related illnesses. Christians too can suffer from depression, and sometimes well-meaning, but misguided people suggest that they should strive for more faith, thus increasing their guilt. Hebrews offers a different model for Christian living. The assurance that we are loved and accepted unconditionally by God provides the imperative for our community relationships. Forgiven and forgiving, accepted and accepting, we are to encourage and urge one another to act in the same way towards others.

Hebrews 4.14–16, 5.7–9

The language of high priesthood is not easily understood by many readers today! The high priest was the one who acted as mediator between God and the people, and, certainly in Protestant circles, Christians feel that they can approach God personally and directly. The writer of Hebrews, however, describes Jesus as the best high priest possible! This is because he understands human weakness. Jesus faced a testing time (v.15). Taken with 5.7–9, this is probably an allusion to his time in Gethsemane and when, like any other human being facing the probability of extreme suffering, he was nearly over-whelmed by the thought of the agony awaiting him and the fear that God had abandoned him. Despite his fear, Jesus obediently accepted arrest, scourging, mocking and death on the cross. The writer of Hebrews offers a picture of Jesus sharing God's 'throne of grace' (v.16). Thus, God and Christ together become the source of grace, that is, the unmerited outpouring of God's loving-kindness: his mercy. People can approach, certain that they will receive the help they need. Jesus' obedience becomes that of all, as Jesus died for all. However, those who follow him take on his obedient response as their own.

To speak of human beings as 'perfect' seems a contradiction in terms! Perhaps it is easier to think of perfection in terms of something we long for and strive after. For example, a person who loves sin-cerely, will long to bring joy to the person loved and will try to do everything possible to ensure that their loved one will grow and flour-ish. This is perfection of will when heartfelt intention seeks the well-being of the other. Inevitably, people fall short of the ideal, but those who follow Jesus will receive help from the one who died that God's people will flourish within the peace (*shalom*) that brings wholeness of life.

John 18.1–19.42

This is the full account of Jesus' death from the time when he and his disciples left the room where they shared the 'Last Supper'. Most congregations welcome the opportunity to 'let the Bible speak for itself' as they listen to an extended passage. It may be that the reading of the Gospel will be followed by a period of silence, an appropriate piece of music, or symbolic action such as candle lighting rather than by the preaching of a sermon. However, for those who wish to preach, a long reading offers many possibilities, some of which will be ex-plored below.

The narrative in John's Gospel differs considerably from the accounts in the other three Gospels. However, it is not the intention here to compare and contrast these, rather to consider some of John's particular themes and emphases. Firstly, Jesus stands over against the world that opposes God, yet despite all appearances to the contrary it is Jesus who is in control. From the moment of the arrest, it is clear that no force could take him, unless he chose to be taken. The number of Roman soldiers envisaged are far more than would have been needed: a whole cohort numbered six hundred men! Alongside the soldiers were temple 'police' sent by the priesthood. All seemed to be confusion until Jesus identifies himself with the words, 'I am he' (v.4). This is Jesus' 'hour' and it is his choice to go to the cross. Secondly, the strength of Jesus is seen as weakness. Standing before Annas, Jesus makes no reply when asked about his disciples. Annas assumes that he has lost their support. When Jesus is struck on the face, he submits. This apparent weakness leads Annas to the conclusion that Jesus will not make any trouble. Thirdly, when brought before Pilate the religious authorities not only place their trust in the power of the Roman state, rather than in the power of God, but also try to manipulate the state for their own ends. The temple priesthood were in an invidious position as Rome allowed them to keep their jobs as long as they prevented insurrection. Nevertheless, they enjoyed a privileged lifestyle and their integrity was compromised. Hence the response 'We have no king but the emperor' (v.15). What amazing words for priests whose religious purity depended upon having no relationship with the pagan world! The irony of Jesus' true identity as 'King of the Jews' is evident. Fourthly, the significance of the crucifixion is spelt out. In John's Gospel the crucifixion of Jesus takes place as the Passover lambs are being slaughtered. Just as God saved the people from slavery in Egypt, so Jesus saves them from sin and death. A death perceived as 'shameful' will be transformed into glory as God raises Jesus to resurrection life. That 'glory' is seen as Jesus obeys the Father and the Father gives honour and authority to the Son. When the inscription, 'Jesus of Nazareth, the King of the Jews' (v.19) was placed on the cross some people objected to the wording. Pilate's response was, 'What I have written I have written.' If Pilate's words cannot be changed, certainly God's words are permanent. In Jesus, God's Word became a human being full of grace and truth (1.14). The story of Jesus' death ends when Jesus' body was taken away for burial by two powerful and influential men who were both secret disciples.

Christians are not called to be 'secret disciples'. Rather, they must proclaim openly that God's Word in Jesus challenges all self-seeking, whether in private and communal life or in international affairs. Jesus died and took to himself the pain of human cruelty and abuse, accepting apparent dishonour and shame willingly for others. This is a lesson the leaders of governments would do well to emulate.

HOLY SATURDAY

Job 14.1–14 or Lamentations 3.1–9, 19–24; 1 Peter 4.1–8;
Matthew 27.57–66 or John 19.38–42

Job 14.1–14

Job believes that God is the author of his suffering and pleads with
God to bring his trials to an end. His argument is that God must be
cruel to cause an individual such anguish especially when it is God
who has made life so short. Lying behind these words seems to be a
conviction that although God seems to be vindictive, this cannot be
true, despite the apparent evidence to the contrary. Job compares the
length of human life to that of a tree. If a tree is cut down it will send
out new shoots, yet death for human beings is final. (Job has no conception of resurrection life.) He shouts at God, 'If mortals die, will
they live again?' (v.14). Job does not think they will! He has no hope
of a future life, yet this is what he longs for. If only! Yet this seems to
be an empty hope. He would like God to hide him in Sheol, the place
of the attenuated, subhuman existence of the dead, until the day when
God would remember him and restore his life.

A life of suffering followed by extinction: this is how life appears
to many. Job's angry words seem hopeless; however, he would not
have shouted at God if he had not believed that God was not as heart-
less as he appeared. Do we get angry enough on behalf of those whose
life is a 'living hell' today? The testimony of many who have suffered
is that their belief in a good, just and loving God has survived despite
their experience. Others have fallen into despair. Many believe death
is the end and consider hope to be misplaced and misguided. As
Easter Day approaches, Christians believe that in Jesus an answer has
been given, but that answer must be lived out as anger is channelled to
oppose injustice.

Lamentations 3.1–9, 19–24

Here, as in the reading from Job, we are faced with human suffering.
The speaker's situation is desperate. God has done nothing to help
him; instead, he feels that God has punished him. He compares his
fate with that of a slave whose master beats him with a rod. Instead of
being led into light he has been driven into darkness as deep as that
found in Sheol, the abode of the dead. His suffering is described in the
language of lament. Whether the description of his wasted flesh and
broken bones are to be taken literally, or to indicate the desperate

nature of his plight and the appalling severity of his suffering, is difficult to determine. One possibility is that the sufferer is a starving man, facing the famine that occurs when a city is under siege. He is 'besieged' by the bitterness generated by his situation and he blames God who could have brought his trial to an end. For the sufferer, being alive is like being in Sheol (v.6). The thought of this passage mirrors that found in Job (above): life for those who suffer is no life; they may as well be with the dead! He feels as if he is imprisoned by his suffering and that God has walled him in and chained him up. The walls are barriers between himself and God, preventing his prayers from being heard. God is the one who has hewn stones out of the rock face that form insurmountable obstacles along his path of life. Verse 19 continues his tirade. His resentment is as bitter as the bitterest of herbs, wormwood and gall. His soul, in other words his whole self, is bent double under his trouble. Yet at his lowest ebb, hope flows again. Despite all evidence to the contrary he remains convinced of God's steadfast love. Without it, how could he have survived so long? God's mercies are 'new every morning' (v.22); in other words, God's faithfulness is constant and no day will ever dawn when God abandons his people. The sufferer's portion, his piece of land, is more than the earthly place promised to Israel, it is the place where God dwells with his people. The sufferer's only true home is with God; in this insight he finds comfort.

Lying at the heart of this reading is the conviction that God does not 'send' suffering. People in this world do suffer, but this is never God's will for them.

1 Peter 4.1–8

The writer is addressing Christians who lived within the Roman world towards the end of the first century. There is little doubt that faithful Christian living resulted in varying degrees of persecution and entailed suffering. However, this is only to be expected, because Christians followed Jesus who not only suffered, but was prepared to die. They may also have to face death! They must arm themselves with a Christ-like attitude and understanding. Jesus trusted God and remained obedient even though he was treated unjustly, and so must they. Their own emotional or physical needs are not to drive their behaviour, only their commitment to living in accordance with God's will. What a change from their pagan past, which encouraged self-indulgence! A list of the kind of vices prevalent in society acts as a reminder of all that they have left behind, for example, the alcohol-fuelled, sexual promiscuity that was linked with idolatry. It is not surprising that their friends were taken aback by their new attitudes, especially as they would no longer be able to participate in pagan festivals. At very least, they would have been taunted and shunned as killjoys! However, they are accountable only to God who is the judge of all people. They need not be concerned about Christians who have died, because they are also the recipients of the gospel and will not be excluded. The belief of the early church in the nearness of the end does not mean that they can abrogate their responsibilities. On the contrary, it is a reminder that accountability before God has to do with a life in community that is concerned for the well-being of every person. The saying 'love covers a multitude of sins' (v.8) may have been proverbial, but what does it mean? It is not that love hides sin, rather that love that forgives unconditionally, does not leave room for any feelings of resentment.

Christians are often portrayed as killjoys whose high moral standards prevent them from partying! In today's society, Christians need a light touch in order to both bring joy to others and to challenge behaviour that damages relationships. Christianity is not to be lived out privately, but publicly and this will sometimes involve taking a stand regardless of the consequences. Although, in the West, Christ's followers are rarely called to put their lives at risk, we are disciples of a crucified Christ and walk in the way of all those 'saints in light' who were prepared to lay down their lives for others.

Matthew 27.57–66

The preacher is invited to choose between Matthew's account of Jesus' burial and that found in John's Gospel. According to Matthew, Joseph of Arimathea took Jesus' body and prepared it for burial. The tomb was new, hewn into the rock face, and had not been contaminated by death. A large wheel-shaped stone was rolled in front of the entrance to seal it. Why did Joseph act with such speed? It has been suggested that he had planned that the body should be stolen or that he was hoping to revive Jesus! However, it is probable that these were the accusations levelled at Christians when the early church split from the synagogue. Certainly, it is highly unlikely that Jesus' enemies would have remembered him talking about the resurrection, saying 'After three days I will rise again' (v.63), or that a detachment of soldiers secured the tomb against theft. Rather, the idea that the tomb was guarded refutes the accusations that the resurrection was a fiction! Readers today might be shocked by the idea that Matthew invented these details; however, that is to apply our own criteria to the text. Matthew's concern was to support his conviction that Jesus had been raised and this is the truth claim he offers.

Faith does not rest on proof that Jesus was raised, but on personal experience of the living Christ. It is rather like swimming! A person can believe that the water will support them, but only by getting into the water and taking one's feet off the bottom is that faith tested. Those who wish to encounter Jesus today must live in the light of their faith, in other words they must take their feet off the bottom. Only then will they discover the truth that lies at the heart of Matthew's words.

John 19.38–42

In John's Gospel two members of the Sanhedrin make provision for Jesus to be buried. Joseph of Arimathea is described as a disciple and Nicodemus was the Pharisee who had come to Jesus 'by night' (3.1). They were Jewish religious leaders and powerful, influential men, who had kept their interest in Jesus' teaching secret. Again, the comment 'for fear of the Jews' (v.38) reflects the later situation when members of the synagogue persecuted Christians whose views they considered heretical. They placed spices, probably in dried form, of myrrh and aloes between the linen cloths as they prepared Jesus' body for burial. The quantity of spices described is extravagant in the extreme and is intended to bring to mind a royal burial, such as that of Herod the Great. Although they acted quickly and expediently, all customs were observed and, as in Matthew's account (above), the body was placed in the new, rock-hewn tomb sealed with a rolling stone. Only in John was the tomb described as being in a garden, possibly an orchard. Joseph and Nicodemus acted out of respect and devotion for Jesus, but there is no indication here that Jesus would be raised. Jesus was dead and these two men had disposed of the body, risking, at the very least, their reputations.

That Joseph and Nicodemus offered Jesus a costly, 'royal' burial is an indication of their devotion. Yet as public figures, they remained 'secret' disciples. Many Christians offer devotion and respect and lead upright lives and, like Joseph and Nicodemus, are prepared to face the cost of that devotion. However, 'daytime' discipleship may be even more costly. Those who allow the Christ who died for others to challenge their values and lifestyle may find themselves making a commitment that is life-changing!

EASTER DAY

Acts 10.34–43 or Isaiah 65.17–25; 1 Corinthians 15.19–26 or
Acts 10.34–43; John 20.1–18 or Luke 24.1–12

Acts 10.34–43

God has already revealed to Peter that those who do not accept the Jewish laws of purity are not prevented from following Christ (Acts 10.9–16). Cornelius, a Roman centurion, was already a 'God-fearer', a Gentile who revered the God of Israel, although he had not converted to Judaism. On his arrival, Peter addresses Cornelius and the members of his household. The speech bears the hallmarks of Luke's style of writing. Peter goes against his religious and cultural heritage when he asserts that God accepts all who revere him and act justly, whether they are Jews or Gentiles. What a change of attitude for the Galilean fisherman, brought up within Judaism! God's message had been sent to the people of Israel in the person of Jesus. Peter's speech includes a brief account of Jesus' baptism, ministry, death and resurrection, which surely provides a mere summary of the conversations that would have taken place. The thrust of Peter's argument is that if there is only one God, he must be the God of all peoples. God, who anointed Jesus with the Holy Spirit and with power (v.38), has given him authority that is universal. His resurrection was witnessed by Jews whose task it is to proclaim this good news. Those who believe their testimony will receive forgiveness, and sin will no longer prevent them drawing close to God. Sin is dealt with not through the Jewish laws of purity, but through belief in Christ. No longer are God's people confined to one race, but include all who respond to the gospel of Christ.

Peter had to face and overcome his own prejudices when he visited Cornelius. His Jewish upbringing would have discouraged any contact with Gentiles, he would not have entered their houses or eaten at their tables. Like Peter, Christians today must recognize their own deep-seated prejudices and overcome them. God's Spirit is not confined to one group of people, but moves wherever people care for each other and follow the way of Christ, whether they acknowledge him or not! Christ is a living Lord and cannot be confined by us!

Isaiah 65.17–25

The prophet looks forward to the time when God will act decisively to transform and renew the whole cosmos. Earth will not be destroyed but changed so that there will no longer be any distinction between heaven and earth. This universal picture of salvation has special relevance for the people of Jerusalem, those whose homecoming from exile has not been the expected idyllic return. They are assured that troubles of the past will be forgotten because God is involved in this new saving act that begins in Jerusalem. (If today's reader feels the universal focus has been lost, it may help to think of Jerusalem as the worship centre for God's people representing an ideal for all cities throughout the ages.) None of the things that mar life will remain: it was usual for people to die young, because of sickness, famine or warfare, but no longer will there be lamenting over premature death, for all people will live the full span of years, the sign of a fulfilled life – to one hundred – or as long as the life of a tree! The work of peacetime will prevail, such as sowing crops and building houses. Verse 25 may have been added by another editor, as transformation extends to the animal world, perhaps reflecting the earlier eighth-century vision in Isaiah 11.6–9.

Is God's renewed world 'a pipe dream' or a vision we are called to share? For a life of peace depends upon people taking responsibility for each other and for the planet itself – then even the animals will be blessed!

1 Corinthians 15.19–26

Paul reminds the Corinthian church about the 'now and not yet' of Christian hope. There is a tension between living faithfully in an imperfect world and keeping a vision of God's ultimate purpose for creation and the promise that we have a place within it. First fruits give a foretaste of the harvest that is to come. This is how Paul understands Jesus' resurrection. He offers a contrast between two ways of being human: Adam's way of disobedience and Jesus' way of obedience. Yet, as history testifies, some human beings have always been corrupted by power and this has resulted in governments that perpetuate unjust regimes where plenty and poverty exist side by side. It is not surprising that Paul uses the word 'enemies' for all who oppose God's rule. Death was seen as the ultimate enemy and so God's raising of Jesus from death heralded the final overthrow of all enemies of life and hope.

At a time when self-gratification is seen as enhancing life, Paul argues that such a view can only lead to corruption and death. A photograph published in a broadsheet newspaper showed a starving woman standing next to a dying tree in a barren land. Here is an image of death brought about by human greed and lust for power and also by the unwillingness of a minority to share from their plenty. The Christian paradox is that God's life is rooted in crucifixion and costly self-giving, yet leads to the joyful resurrection life of Easter.

John 20.1–18

John's Gospel recounts the events at the tomb on the first Easter Day. Three stories, probably independent pieces of tradition, are placed side by side somewhat awkwardly, in order to encourage the reader to respond in faith. Firstly, Mary Magdalene arrived at the tomb only to discover that the stone had been rolled away and the grave was empty. She was horrified and assumed that grave robbers had been at work. (Perhaps this reflects the accusation raised by later opponents of the burgeoning Christian Church.) She ran immediately to Simon Peter and the beloved disciple. Secondly, Peter and the beloved disciple ran to the tomb, the latter outrunning Peter. Does this reflect the rivalry between the two disciples, or between the later church communities they led? (Remember that the beloved disciple represents all faithful disciples. See Wednesday in Holy Week and comments on John 13.21–32.) The beloved disciple stopped at the entrance and peered in, but Peter entered and saw the linen wrappings and the neatly rolled head cloth lying separately. All was tidy and there were no signs of a hurried grave robbery. The beloved disciple saw and believed (v.8). What did he believe? The reader is left to make the connection between this event and all that has led to this moment: Jesus is the one who came from God and will return to God. Thirdly, the scene changes and Mary is seen weeping outside the tomb. Two angels appear marking out the space where the body lay. God is present in the form of his messengers and still Mary mourns. The space left by Jesus' body only increases her sense of loss and her feeling of forsakenness. Even when she meets 'the gardener' she fails to recognize Jesus. It is only when he calls her by name that she understands. 'Do not hold on to me' says Jesus (v.17). He has to return to God in order to send his spirit to those who will continue his ministry.

The time has come for Mary and all Jesus' disciples to continue his work. During Jesus' earthly life they relied on him to preach, teach and heal. He may seem to have left them, but when he 'called them by name' they were commissioned to take the good news to the world. In loving, generous, self-giving they will discover that the space of his seeming absence is filled with the joyful conviction that he is present with them. The living Christ is encountered in the task of ministry, both in those who receive and those who give. This is the good news of Easter Day.

Luke 24.1–12

Luke bypasses the difficulty of how the women were to gain access to anoint Jesus' body as the stone has already been moved away and the tomb is empty. Two supernatural figures appear, their dazzling clothes proclaiming them to be angels, God's messengers, and predictably the women react in terror. Perhaps today, some people find the idea of angelic beings hard to swallow, but this is to miss the point of Luke's picture. Faith in the risen Christ is God-given, through his messengers, and notice the content of the angels' message: that you do not seek the living among the dead (v.5)! They reiterate Jesus' own words that Easter Day's events depended on his willingness to be handed over for crucifixion – it is the way of suffering that leads to new life (9.22,18.33). For Luke, Jesus' ministry began in Galilee, but his disciples will meet the risen Christ in Jerusalem where the first church was established. Jesus is to be found amongst the living Christians of the new community. Whom do the women tell? Luke may have been thinking of two groups of people: the eleven remaining disciples and also the apostles who were the early church leaders. In both cases the men did not believe the women! It is human nature to want to see for ourselves and Peter becomes the representative of disciples then and now who seek first-hand experience. Yet all he sees is linen cloths.

Faith does not depend on an empty tomb; rather Jesus is to be found among the living – those who are open to hearing God's word, whether from heavenly beings, or unlikely human beings! God's word is about a suffering way of love that leads to resurrection life: well-being for all.

SECOND SUNDAY OF EASTER

Acts 5.27–32; Revelation 1.4–8; John 20.19–31

Acts 5.27–32

Tension between the apostles and the Temple authorities comes to a climax with the arrest of the apostles. They have continued Jesus' ministry and crowds had gathered for healing (5.16). Luke portrays a 'head-on collision' that shows the high priest and the Sadducees in the worst possible light: their motive is jealousy. The imprisonment of the apostles ends with angelic deliverance; as none of the usual signs of divine activity are mentioned (cf. 12.7), it is appropriate to ask whether this messenger was a supernatural being or a bribed prison officer! The apostles are not deterred by opposition but return immediately to the Temple and continue preaching. Contrasts are drawn between their courage, the puzzlement of the thwarted temple priesthood and the excitement and support of the crowds who are ready to resort to violence to protect the apostles. The confrontation is highly charged and ready to ignite, but the apostles go quietly to testify at the council. Responsibility for Jesus' death and the apostle's claims lie between the two groups. (The preacher must be careful to recognize the heightened rhetoric of the first century in order to avoid anti-semitism.) The apostles speak with one voice to proclaim that it is Israel's God (v.30) who authorizes them and has been involved in every stage of Jesus' story, culminating in the repentance and forgiveness that characterize salvation. The apostles' courageous preaching, a sign of their obedience, witnesses to the gift of the Holy Spirit.

Christian proclamation often involves a willingness to face conflict. In this passage there is confrontation, yet the apostles prevent crowd violence (v.26), while continuing to speak *with one voice* the message of salvation.

What a difference it makes when Christians from different denominations join together to confront injustice today, whether locally, nationally or on the world map! This is a call to local congregations to support ecumenical events and get to know the names and faces of friends from other churches.

Revelation 1.4–8

Once again, the early Christian church is in a situation of conflict. John (not the author of John's Gospel) writes from exile (v.9), with the authority of God and Jesus (vv. 1–2) to encourage Christians in

Asia Minor. After a conventional greeting he begins with a proclamation that God, who is eternally involved in human history, has through Jesus' death brought forgiveness and holiness, both a gift and a task, to his people – for they are called to share in God's reign. In extravagant, poetic language Jesus returns to earth 'with the clouds'. Clouds both reveal and conceal the divine presence (e.g. Exodus 19.9,16). Jesus comes with God's authority to a world in which sin is rife – then as now. It is not surprising that there is weeping – the word 'wail' is evocative of a fearful response, for Jesus' coming signals both salvation and judgement.

There is always a tension between mercy and judgement. For those who collude with injustice and oppression in this world for their own gain, Revelation offers a note of warning. As forgiven people Christians are called to holiness (the opposite of apathy and complacency?); in other words, to be involved in issues of justice and human welfare.

John 20.19–31

Fear is tangible when the risen Jesus appears to the disciples even though they are meeting behind locked doors. Jesus' first words ease their terror, as his coming brings peace. Speculation about how he came to be in the room is fruitless, as no barrier can be placed between the one who has been raised and his disciples. Jesus, who bears the marks of crucifixion, removes their fear and they are ready to be commissioned to continue his ministry. Just as God breathed life into humanity (Gen. 2.7), so Jesus breathes the Holy Spirit into them. This is the Spirit of truth (14.16) that will help them to make difficult decisions in the life of the early church (v.23). Discerning what forgiveness means in practice is an ongoing difficulty for all Christian communities: at what point does a person's behaviour place them outside the Church? If someone poses a threat to others, how is forgiveness to be balanced with the provision of safeguards for all concerned if offenders are to be reintegrated into the life of the Church?

Thomas, who was not present, found it difficult to believe what had happened. How like many of us! He needed to touch Jesus – and how important touch is to human beings as they seek to discern reality – he needed to touch Jesus' wounds to identify with his suffering. Surely, this is the mark of discipleship, to be willing to feel and to share Jesus' pain in a hurting world and to put our fingers into the marks of the nails!

THIRD SUNDAY OF EASTER

Acts 9.1–6 (7–20); Revelation 5.11–14; John 21.1–19

Acts 9.1–6 (7–20)

This is the first of three accounts of Saul/Paul's life-changing encounter with the risen Jesus found in Acts (9.1–19, 22.3–21, 26.4–23).
It is a moment of both conversion and commissioning: conversion as
Saul changes his allegiance from one Jewish sect to another, and commissioning as he becomes 'apostle to the Gentiles'. Verses 1–6 are
about the moment when Saul 'met' Jesus. With a letter of authoriza-
tion from the high priest, Saul seeks those of 'The Way', the name
used for the new Christian movement, to bring them back to Jerusalem by force. The blinding light, a sign of divine presence, causes
Saul to fall to the ground – the only possible response! 'Why are you
persecuting me?' says Jesus (v.4). Until that moment, Saul thought
that he had been persecuting the group of people who would become
the Church. Here is a timely reminder that Christ is found amongst
and revealed by his people. When Saul realizes that it is Jesus who
speaks to him, all his previous convictions are turned upside down
and he is sent to the city to receive instructions.

Verses 7–20 fill out the details and Saul, through the ministry of
Ananias, receives healing, the gift of the Spirit and baptism. After this
Saul proclaims Jesus as 'Son of God' in the synagogues.

Conversion and commissioning go hand in hand. While some
people encounter Christ in a dramatic 'one-off event', for others it is a
gradual 'getting to know' process. For all Christians, to know Christ
is to be commissioned for the task of proclamation, a task to be performed both by the skilled preacher and through quiet acts of service.
What a responsibility and privilege it is to belong to God's people
through whom others can meet the risen Christ!

Revelation 5.11–14

The writer is allowed a glimpse of the throne room of God in heaven.
The vision painted is poetic and the imagery should not be taken
literally. Its purpose is to portray Jesus sharing the power and majesty
of God, yet Jesus the lamb still bears the marks of slaughter. It is
through his sacrificial self-offering on the cross that rejoicing
becomes possible. The hymn of praise is sung by all creation. However, it is important to contrast the heavenly scene with the unfolding
story of the horror and devastation that takes place on earth. One of

the questions often asked is, 'How can Jesus' death and resurrection be described as the triumph of good over evil when destruction and disorder affect the whole world?' The lamb still bears the marks of sacrificial suffering and fragile human weakness, and in Judaism a dead lamb would have been a source of uncleanness, of exclusion for all contaminated by it. Yet the lamb has a place in heaven because he has borne the brunt of human capacity for cruelty.

The book of Revelation has often been criticized for depicting God as vengeful. However, another approach is to consider its honesty – here in the last writing of the New Testament the reality of the human condition is faced directly. No wonder liberation theologians have turned to these pages to speak a message of hope to oppressed people, as the lamb who bears all the marks of human cruelty bridges the gap between earth and heaven!

John 21.1–19

Chapter 21 is a later addition to John's Gospel, by another hand. It almost certainly reflects the concerns of the early Christian community, in this case Peter's position as the leader of the church. The risen Jesus' appearance to Peter and the disciples who were with him has significance for both Peter and the church. The theme of fishing as a metaphor for the evangelistic task is not new and there are resonances of the feeding miracle (John 6.1–14), for God's provision is superabundant. The significance of the number of fish lies in its sheer quantity! Just as the disciples were fed by Jesus' teaching and by the food he offers, in other words by word and sacrament, so they are to feed others and the net of the church will hold all. These are words of assurance and challenge, as people from different backgrounds join the Christian community.

The imagery moves from that of fisher to shepherd as Peter, who denied Jesus three times, receives a threefold affirmation and commissioning. Peter was hurt by Jesus' need to press him the third time. Yet it is important to remember that the 'shepherd' was the 'leader' and to be a Christian leader inevitably involves hurt. All Christians are called to be 'shepherds' – to speak and act as representatives of Christ in their own time and place. Verses 18–19 refer to Peter's martyrdom, an event that had already taken place by the time of writing.

Leadership can be a lonely task! Sometimes ministers are weighed down by the high expectations of their congregations, while lay people, who seek to represent the Church in the wider world, often feel unsupported by both minister and congregation!

FOURTH SUNDAY OF EASTER

Acts 9.36–43; Revelation 7.9–17; John 10.22–30

Acts 9.36–43

Luke's concern is to show that the apostles stand in the place of Jesus; they are his true successors and act with divine authority and with the power of the Holy Spirit. Now the focus moves from Paul to Peter. Historical details combine with the storyteller's art. Joppa and Lydda are ten miles apart and details about Tabitha's life and death are remembered. However, Luke recounts this healing to demonstrate that Peter has been given the authority of Christ. There are resonances from Scripture: People would remember that Elisha brought the Shunammite woman's child to life (2 Kings 4.32–37) showing that he was true successor to Elijah, who did the same for the widow at Zarephath's son (1 Kings 17.17–24). Jesus followed in the footsteps of these great prophets of old when he raised Jairus' daughter from death (Luke 8.49–56, Mark 5.35–43). Peter performs this miracle in a way reminiscent of Jesus. He too sent the crowds outside and commanded Tabitha by name to get up. Having left the reader in no doubt of Peter's authority, the scene is set for Peter to receive the vision that prepares him to expand his ministry (10.9–16) – for it is while he stays with Simon the tanner that Cornelius, a centurion, sends for him (10.17), the prelude to Peter baptizing Gentiles.

The bringing of healing and wholeness for all people is part of Christian ministry. (Notice the service for healing and wholeness in *The Methodist Worship Book*, p.407.) The Church must also respond globally, as too many people die prematurely in countries where warfare and famine are rife. Healing does not always mean that physical illness is cured; it also has to do with acceptance of infirmity, and sometimes involves preparation for approaching death. The process of healing also includes reconciliation: both the mending of present relationships and the letting go of past hurts.

Revelation 7.9–17

The vision of the heavenly throne room is extended. People from all nations are in God's presence and they carry palm-branches in their hands. A palm was the symbol of Jewish nationalism (much as a daffodil in a buttonhole is a sign of Welsh identity). The new Israel is no longer defined by ethnicity, but by white robes, the sign of the faithful. These are worn by those who have witnessed to God in spite of persecution and so have suffered like Christ. The way of self-giving sacrifice purifies, hence the imagery of 'being washed in the blood of the lamb' (v.14). For the writer of Revelation, Rome like Babylon symbolized all that was opposed to God. It is not surprising that it is in language reminiscent of the promises given to the exiled people that their homecoming from Babylon/Rome will bring an end to physical and emotional suffering. Jesus who reigns with God is their protector (v.17) and so they join in the praise of God sung by all creation.

In the Roman world, Christians would have been eyed with suspicion and suffered at least the petty persecutions of those who were 'different'. Too often today, graffiti and petrol poured through letter-boxes are used to make people's lives miserable. This can lead to escalating abuse both verbal and physical, sometimes leading to greater confrontations. Faithful living is a Christian imperative for both persecuted and protector.

John 10.22–30

The confrontation between Jesus and the religious authorities resumes in the temple precincts. His opponents ask whether he is the Messiah, that is, the anointed deliverer of the people, but did they think the Messiah would be the leader of an uprising against Roman rule? Any rebellion against Rome would threaten their own vulnerable position. Two hundred years previously, the Greek ruler Antiochus IV had desecrated the Temple, and the Feast of Dedication celebrated the rededication of the altar and the resumption of worship. While the readers of the Gospel know that Jesus is the Messiah, his enemies ask the question hoping he will make an admission they believe to be false. Rulers were known as shepherds and their task was to lead and protect their people. Leading the people was the role of the Messiah and Jesus' authority comes from God, the shepherd of all creation. Jesus represents his Father, and his will and purpose are at one with God's (v.30). Those who believe that Jesus is God's agent and follow him share in the divine life, that is, life lived under God; such life has an eternal dimension.

The religious leaders of Jesus' day did not want the temple worship to be banned, or to lose their religious influence; yet, to believe in Jesus and share God's loving purpose may mean risking the loss of cherished traditions. There is more division in local churches and ecumenical groups over small matters than great. For example, a Methodist congregation often wishes to retain small, individual glasses for communion, while Anglican congregations are equally adamant that they wish to use a chalice. How does God react when Christians argue about such matters?

FIFTH SUNDAY OF EASTER

Acts 11.1–18; Revelation 21.1–6; John 13.31–35

Acts 11.1–18

The church in Jerusalem remained part of Judaism and its members continued to keep the Jewish law of which circumcision was the outward sign. It is not surprising that they were horrified when they discovered that Peter had accepted hospitality from Cornelius and had eaten at his table. In their view, Peter had contravened the laws of purity. However, Peter is certain that that he went with the messengers and treated them as if they were Jews (v.12) at the Holy Spirit's insistence. Furthermore, the Holy Spirit fell on the whole household before Peter had an opportunity to present his case (v.15). The emphasis, therefore, is not on baptism but on the gift of the Spirit to those who have faith. Cornelius had believed the word of God's messenger and his faith resulted in the baptism of his entire household – the extended family. What a huge step it was for the Jerusalem church to accept Gentiles, but with what far-reaching consequences!

The Methodist Worship Book places the affirmation of faith before the baptism, but promises come afterwards as a response to God's gift of baptism. Is the faith of the Church, like Cornelius' faith, sufficient for the whole household to be baptized? How do we feel when children of parents who rarely attend church are baptized? Perhaps we do well to remember Peter's words, 'Who was I to hinder God?' The Jerusalem church was silenced – are we?

Revelation 21.1–6

The sandwich boards may read 'The end of the world is nigh!' but the climax in the book of Revelation is not about the end of the world; rather, it is about the end of all that divides God and his people. God's reign is fully realized as earth and heaven become one. In the cosmology of the day, waters of chaos surrounded creation, seeping in to form the sea. The sea is often an image of chaos, perhaps especially when there is a storm, so to say that there will be no more sea is to state that there will be no more chaos, for God's final act of salvation has happened. In the earlier chapters, the seer was permitted a glimpse of the throne room in heaven. Now God is enthroned among his people in the New Jerusalem, decked out in wedding finery – the archetypal beautiful city – symbolizing transformed creation. What a contrast with Babylon/Rome, the symbol of every place where people rebel against God! All citizens of God's city belong amongst the faithful who see God face to face as he dries their tears; no more does human wickedness cause people to weep. From God flows the water of life, not simply an end to death, for now humanity will participate in the joy of the divine life.

Throughout Revelation, people are offered a choice: do they wish to be citizens of Babylon/Rome or of the New Jerusalem? While the final transformation of creation is in the future, God's people already drink from 'the spring of the water of life' when they share the divine task of wiping away the tears of those who suffer today.

John 13.31–35

Judas departs and Jesus speaks of himself as 'the Son of Man', the one who suffers with and for his people as he bridges the gap between heaven and earth. John's Gospel recounts Jesus' final words to the disciples as he speaks about leaving them. The reader, unlike the disciples, knows that Jesus is speaking about his death on the cross and so is able to understand what Jesus is saying. The glorification of Jesus has to do with his loving obedience that honours (glorifies) God and God's honouring (glorifying) of Jesus for his loving obedience. In a culture that valued honour, it is paradoxical that the hour of crucifixion, the moment of greatest shame, was the time when God's glory was revealed fully in the mutual honouring of Son and Father. Last words always have special significance and the commandment to love (v.34) is one of the best-known verses in the New Testament. What is new about this 'new commandment'? The answer lies in the disciples' relationship with Jesus. As yet they do not know the extent of his love – again the reader has privileged information: for Jesus loved them enough to face the cross. This is how his followers should love.

It is good to acknowledge the self-giving of those who serve in quiet ways as well as those whose actions hit the headlines!

Why are the last words we say so important? Think of the words of farewell we use in everyday life: as we wave friends goodbye on the doorstep, as we say goodnight to our children, as we leave the hospital ward when we have been visiting someone ill. Usually, our last words affirm our love and offer comfort and encouragement. What a difference it would make in all our relationships if we always spoke as if our words were the ones people would remember.

SIXTH SUNDAY OF EASTER

Acts 16.9–15; Revelation 21.10, 22–22.5; John 14.23–29 or
John 5.1–9

Acts 16.9–15

At a moment of uncertainty, Paul receives divine guidance in a night-time vision and he and his companions journey to Philippi. The 'place of prayer' (v.13) was where Jews met for worship along with those who were attracted to the Jewish faith. Lydia was a rich woman (perhaps the wealthiest person in the New Testament) as she dealt in purple cloth; purple dye was rare and sold at inordinate prices. Lydia worshipped God but was probably a Gentile rather than a Jew (v.14). Paul's conversation with Lydia led to her baptism and that of her household; and once again, the faith of one is enough for all. Lydia's faithfulness is seen in Paul's acceptance of her hospitality.

Lydia was attracted to the God of Israel before Paul arrived on the scene. Now, as then, many people are ready to respond to the gospel if they can be persuaded of its relevance. Paul was able to engage in conversation – he was sure of his theology! Christians must be prepared to grapple with today's issues with all comers. We can prepare ourselves for that task through Bible study and discussion that relates the gospel message to current affairs.

Revelation 21.10, 22–22.5

Light in the New Jerusalem is provided by God and Christ. God's light has a moral connotation as to 'walk in the light' is a metaphor for the faithful living that is true worship. This is why there is no need for a separate temple. Such light attracts nations and their rulers and the gates are always open. The purity of the city is safeguarded because people who opposed God have excluded themselves – written themselves out of the Lamb's book of life – through their passive or active collusion with the corruption of the old order. The river and tree of life are images reminiscent of the Garden of Eden (Genesis 2). However, this is not simply a restoration of what was, but a moving on characterized by the healing of differences as nations are reconciled. When people see the face of God they will not be destroyed (note Ex. 33.20), instead God's name will be written on their foreheads – their character will reflect God's nature.

Christ reigns with God, and the love that led to a cross will never fail those who seek to live in his way and who share his ministry in this imperfect world.

John 14.23–29

Jesus is answering a question that is asked in every generation: How is it that God doesn't reveal himself to everyone? In John's Gospel, 'the world' is often a euphemism for those who oppose God. When God speaks something happens. God speaks creation into being (Gen. 1) and in Jesus the outpouring of God's creative love is seen in the 'word made flesh' (John 1.14). What is said and done by disciples should reflect the outpouring of God's generous goodness seen in the act of creation – no small task! When people act with loving generosity, they discover the nature of God and Christ within themselves. What a marvellous thought – that God and Jesus can make their home within us! However, those who fail to act lovingly will never have the same insight into the divine nature.

Perhaps a helpful analogy might be that of swimming. Only those people who get into the water and take their feet off the bottom know what it is to swim. Only those who choose to follow Christ discover what God is like.

John 5.1–9

The pool is unlikely to have been like a small lake around which sick people lay. Visitors to Jerusalem today may have seen the area where underground springs bubble up into what looks like an old-fashioned swimming bath with stone sides and steep stone steps. It would have been impossible for a paralysed person to get into the water quickly, except by rolling off the edge which would be to risk drowning! It would be very difficult for friends to carry such a person down the steps into the pool. When Jesus asked the man whether he wanted to get well, he may have been asking, 'Are you prepared to risk your life in order to be made well?' What a question! (Notice the irony – Jesus who asks the question is the one who would be crucified.) The man had been ill for thirty-eight years and in those days life expectancy was about forty. (In Deuteronomy 2.14 a whole generation was wiped out in thirty-eight years.) The faith of the religious leaders who opposed Jesus was virtually dead. Jesus questions both a dying man and his opponents when he asks, 'Do you want to be made well?' Despite the evasive nature of the man's answer Jesus acts decisively and immediately the man is healed.

What risks are we willing to take in order to be made whole? Are we ready to roll off the edge of the pool into the deep water trusting that God will not let us drown?

ASCENSION DAY

Acts 1.1–11; Ephesians 1.15–23; Luke 24.44–53

Acts 1.1–11

This is the second part of Luke's serial story! The Gospel of Luke is linked to Acts by the account of Jesus' ascension (Luke 24.44–53 below). At a time when people believed that the earth was flat, it is not surprising that Jesus' departure is described in terms of his 'ascending' to heaven. Yet the significance of Luke's narrative does not depend on a literal interpretation. Luke includes features from Hebrew Scripture including the angelic messengers and the cloud that both concealed and revealed the divine presence. Great figures of the past had also commissioned their successors who had received God's Spirit, for example Moses (Deut. 34.9) and Elijah (2 Kings 2.11).

Three starting points are offered to preachers: Firstly, Luke places the time of waiting in Jerusalem, the scene of crucifixion and despair but also the place where the first Christian church was established. How important was it for the first Christians to face their fear and 'stay with the pain' in order to discover that the risen Christ had not abandoned them, and continued to call them to follow him? Secondly, the forty-day period of waiting recalls both the time of the wilderness wanderings and the days Jesus spent in the wilderness of Judaea in preparation for his ministry. The desert times were periods of 'testing', but also times when, despite God's seeming absence, he was discovered to be present and constantly faithful. Thirdly, John the Baptist had promised that Jesus would baptize not with water but with the Spirit. Unless Jesus 'departed', they would not receive the Holy Spirit who would enable them to continue his work. When Jesus was with them, they looked to him to solve all the problems they encountered: it was his task to heal and to teach. When he ascended, they took on his healing and teaching ministry in the power of the Holy Spirit.

Jesus had proclaimed 'The kingdom of God' (v.3), but now the risen and ascended Christ would become the content of the proclamation. This was a message for the entire world! We, like the first disciples, are called to proclaim Jesus as we continue his ministry of healing and teaching.

Ephesians 1.15–23

The writer gives thanks that the outworking of the Christians' faith is seen in their loving concern for each other and thankfulness spills over into the prayer that they will grow in wisdom and insight. The lovely and evocative phrase 'with the eyes of your heart enlightened' indicates that their relationships will be illuminated by their perception of God's will for themselves and others. In liturgical language, Jesus is described as the source of that illumination. Jesus, who was prepared to face death, was raised by God and is now the exalted Christ who reigns over everything. Christians, who form Christ's body, the Church, are to continue his ministry. However, the agenda belongs to Christ, who reigns with God the creator, whose sovereignty is over the whole universe! Christ is Jesus who died, who has revealed himself to his followers.

When we thank God for the people we love, our thanksgiving often leads us to pray for them. What better prayer can there be than to ask that they should look at the world through Christ's eyes and that his light might guide their lives? Do we make the same prayer for ourselves? If the 'eyes of our hearts are enlightened' we will begin to perceive the world through the eyes of its creator. Christianity is not a private and personal religion that only affects our domestic lives, for we are caught up in the eternal outpouring of God's generous goodness! As members of 'the body' (v.23), our ministry is part of God's universal mission!

Luke 24.44–53

These verses of Luke's Gospel conclude the first part of his serial story, which will be continued in Acts (see above). Here, resurrection and ascension happen on the same day. Jesus interprets these events for his followers in the light of Hebrew Scripture. Nowadays, Christians are encouraged to interpret these writings, now referred to as 'The Old Testament', within their original context. However, New Testament writers, like Luke, were already using Scripture to underline their conviction that the coming of Jesus, and the events that were still to take place, were a continuation of God's saving purposes. Through Jesus' words, Luke sets out the Church's task: to proclaim repentance and forgiveness of sins for all nations (v.47). By the time Luke wrote his Gospel, churches had been established throughout Asia Minor and already people from both Jewish and pagan backgrounds were present in the congregations. Here is a reminder that the gospel, which began in Jerusalem, is for all who are ready to turn their backs on their old ways of life and follow Luke's congregations, and for all Christians the only appropriate response is that of rejoicing as God is praised!

SEVENTH SUNDAY OF EASTER

Acts 16.16–34; Revelation 22.12–14, 16–17, 20–21; John 17.20–26

Acts 16.16–34

Any church would enjoy retelling such a story about its founding! This is an escape story beginning with a miracle that puts an end to magical practices and exploitation. When the 'heroes' of the tale are flung into prison, nothing less than an earthquake, brought about by divine intervention, opens the doors of the jail. The finale is the conversion of the jailer himself!

These verses are rich in preaching material, but for now comments are restricted to three points. Firstly, when Paul and Silas were dragged before the magistrates the accusation made was not that they had robbed the slave-girl's owners of their livelihood, but that they were advocating Jewish customs – it was prejudice by Romans against the Jewish minority (v.21) that led to mob-violence. The magistrates may have been intimidated or may have shared that prejudice because the sentence imposed was extreme (v.24). The story had begun at the Jewish place of prayer and Paul and Silas were dealt with by the authorities as Jews. Sadly, such prejudice against ethnic minorities is still prevalent today. Secondly, bruised and battered, imprisoned and in stocks, Paul and Silas sang hymns at midnight! The implication is that they were praising God for the opportunity to share Christ's suffering, rather than keeping up their own morale and that of their fellow-prisoners – although it would have had that effect. Thirdly, the task of disciples is to bring the healing and wholeness that is Christ's gift, for they healed the slave-girl in his name (v.18). The jailer's response leads to the baptism of a third household.

The three preaching points offer food for thought today. Firstly, we must proclaim the gospel in a way that does not perpetuate prejudice but enables relationships, based on trust rather than suspicion, to develop between people of different faiths. Secondly, how difficult it is to praise God in times of hardship, yet through praise we are reminded that God does not abandon us even when we feel forsaken. Thirdly, Christ came so that no one would be excluded from his people. Are there people in our own churches who do not feel accepted and welcomed? If so, then how should we respond?

Revelation 22.12–14, 16–17, 20–21

The closing verses of Revelation are a reminder that the book was written to churches who must make a choice – whether to belong to the pagan world of Rome or to Christ. The context is the imminent return of Christ as judge and although not all Christians today share that expectation, it is nevertheless a reminder that we are accountable for our choices. Those who 'wash their robes' are those who keep Christ's commandments whatever the cost (7.13–14) and so are assured a place in God's city. These verses also point to the two Christian sacraments: baptism and the Lord's Supper. Those who 'wash', are those cleansed in the waters of baptism and the words, 'Amen, Come Lord Jesus' (in Aramaic 'Marana tha. Amen.') were used by Christians as part of their celebration of the Eucharist. (They are found in the Didache, a collection of early teaching material.) Participation in both sacraments is about making real in the present the promises of Jesus by sharing his costly self-giving. Yet this is the way to follow Jesus the Messiah (v.16) – through open gates – into the fullness of God's life.

What does it mean for Christians today to affirm that Christ is coming? Surely, Christ comes to all who have eyes to see him – both in those who suffer and those who seek to relieve their suffering – and in every place where people drink the water of life! When we join in the cry, 'Come, Lord Jesus' we affirm that in Christ, who embraces all times and all places (v.13), God's city will be found on earth.

John 17.20–26

These verses are part of Jesus' prayer for his disciples. He prays that they might be one (v.20), but what kind of oneness does he have in mind? We speak about people being 'in it together' when they share a task. The disciples are to share the purpose of God and Jesus – no less than the salvation of the world! For they witness that Jesus was sent by God and therefore affirm his authority and also that his relationship with God is a paradigm for all people. Yet to 'be in it together' also means relying on one another. Just as Jesus was dependent upon God and his trust was not misplaced, so the disciples can rely on Jesus who will keep faith with them. Also to 'be in it together' involves mutual respect. When a relay team is interviewed after winning gold medals they speak highly of the commitment of the whole team – they all share the glory. Once again, glory is about mutual honouring and mutual respect. In John's Gospel the reference to glory is always a reminder that the moment of glory was also the moment of crucifixion – this is the extent of Jesus' loving obedience, required now of the disciples.

PENTECOST

Acts 2.1–21 or Genesis 11.1–9; Romans 8.14–17 or Acts 2.1–21;
John 14.8–17 (25–27)

Acts 2.1–21

Everything starts with the Holy Spirit! When Luke is the narrator it
is not helpful to ask, 'What actually happened?' as Luke blends
historicity and theology together and rather like a cake it is impossible
to distinguish the ingredients once it has been baked! It is more helpful to focus on the significance of the story for the early church.

Pentecost was the festival of the first fruits, when the first sheaf of
the wheat harvest was offered to God in thanksgiving. The festival
also came to be associated with the giving of the law and the renew-
ing of the covenant. It is not surprising that the early church took over
Pentecost as a Christian festival to celebrate the coming of the Spirit
to the first disciples. Here was the promise, the first fruits, that the
Spirit would fall on many more believers. It was also a time to celebrate the new covenant relationship made possible in Christ. The
symbolism of wind and fire would not be lost on the first hearers.
God's breath is life-giving in every way and came to the disciples
powerfully, as the sound of rushing wind testifies. Fire purifies and
cleanses and a tongue of fire rested on each individual, but this was
a shared experience and all were caught up in an event beyond
description! There is no doubt that courage came to a group of
frightened people, who burst onto the streets, and without whom the
gospel message would never have been heard.

The people, depicted as pilgrims from all nations, have come to
Jerusalem for the festival. Perhaps they already seek God? They hear
in their own languages as the Babel division is ended (Genesis 11.1–
9). The crowd acts like the chorus in a Greek play as with humour
Peter refutes their charge that the disciples are drunk (2.15). After
laughing, people's ears are pricked to hear the opening words of
Peter's first sermon as he turns to the prophet Joel and proclaims that
the coming of Jesus has implications for the salvation of all people
and indeed for all creation.

The coming of the Holy Spirit goes hand in hand with the commission and courage to prophesy. The prophetic voice of the Church
needs to be heard above the Babel noises of this world as we dream
God's dreams and share his vision. However, not all Christians agree
concerning the content of God's vision for the world. For example,
congregations will be made up of pacifists and those who believe that

sometimes violence is necessary in the cause of justice. Our commitment to each other and to God must be to listen to one another and to continue to debate the hard questions, in the light of Scripture, as we try to discern God's will for the world. Yet, while that debate continues we must do all we can to bring an end to suffering so that peace will prevail.

Genesis 11.1–9

A wandering people migrate to a plain where they decide to settle. This is their new start and they have great ideas! People who previously lived in tents begin to build a city. It is interesting to remember that the nomadic life, when all families lived in tents, became a symbol for equality. Once people built houses and farmed land some become richer than others and the rich/poor divide began, thus the city became a symbol for injustice and selfish ambition. With the technology at their disposal (using asphalt as mortar), the people built a tower whose top was to be in the heavens. It is often said that they wanted to storm heaven, but the purpose of the tower was more likely to be self-aggrandizement as they sought fame!

In these early narratives, God is portrayed as a 'larger than life' human being. When God saw what the people were doing he 'came down'. The Lord is great and their work was tiny in comparison – even though they had constructed the highest tower ever built! God can see how their concern to 'show off' their skills would lead to greater injustices as some would gain power and fame and others would be left behind. The city with the tower was built at Shinar the site of Babylon. Babylon/Babel became the symbol for all that corrupts and divides humanity from God. This is the last story in a collection of ancient narratives recounting the primeval history, which were written down because they express valuable insights into the relationship between God and humanity. The Tower of Babel is the final stage in a widening gulf between the people and God resulting in punishment as God 'confused their language' and scattered them. This is a tale with no message of hope – fortunately the Bible, the story of God and his people, does not end here!

It is not difficult to make connections between the power-seeking of the ancient world and that of today. In every city in the world wealth and poverty are found side by side. If we listed the different ways in which people are exploited across the cities of the world, we would discover that, all over the globe, the most vulnerable people are being trampled into the dust by those who profit at their expense. Every technological advance can be used for good or ill – and we still build tall towers – but the choice is ours. In our personal lives, in which of our own achievements do we take pride? Are they achievements that benefit ourselves or others?

Romans 8.14–17

Christians in Rome would not have had an easy time! To live as Christians meant disassociating themselves from pagan practices that were the norm in society. If they did not 'belong' in that society, where did they belong? Paul answers that question by saying that they are God's children and so belong to God's family. He explains that the Holy Spirit creates not slaves but sons. The word 'sons' is used rather than 'daughters' because in first-century culture sons were their father's heirs. This is the difference between slaves or servants and sons. Both servants and sons must be obedient, but only sons stand to inherit. A man who did not have sons would often adopt a son, usually in adulthood when the young man had proved himself to be of good character, to become his heir. All Christians become God's 'sons' in this sense as all (men, women and children) are heirs. They belong to God's family and so are able to call God, 'Abba', an Aramaic term that was widely used in Christian circles. 'Abba' was the word used for 'father' in the family circle and was the word Jesus used when addressing God. (While it has been said that Jesus was the first to use this term as a way of addressing God, this is by no means certain.) It is the Holy Spirit who witnesses that Christians are God's children. When the Holy Spirit moves Christians to follow Christ, even when that involves suffering, then like Jesus they are acting with the loving obedience of 'sons'. Yet with God suffering is never the end, for their future in the light and splendour of God's presence is assured.

Both epistle and Gospel suggest that those who are secure in the knowledge that God has their future in his safe-keeping will be able to face difficulties, hardship and even persecution. A rather mundane analogy would be that the one who copes best with the stresses of the day is sure that there is a light in the window at home and a loving welcome awaits.

John 14.8–17(25–27)

Again the reader has privileged information! It is Philip who has failed to recognize the obvious: that in Jesus the nature of God is revealed. Jesus is God's agent because he shares God's purposes and speaks and acts for God. The idea that the disciples will do greater things than Jesus seems almost heretical! Yet, it is Jesus' departure that paves the way for the disciples to take the gospel beyond Judaism to the pagan world. They are the ones who will obey Jesus' instructions and so act in his name. Their love for Jesus must be shown in its outworking. At present, Jesus is with them to offer inspiration and guidance; in the future, that same encouragement will come from the Spirit. Jesus is sending them another comforter – in other words, Jesus is the first comforter. (Notice that the word comforter includes the idea of picking them up, dusting them down and urging them on – rather like a mother dealing with a child who has fallen over!) The second comforter, described as the Spirit of truth, takes Jesus' place. Truth in this context suggests that the guidance of the Spirit is identical with that of God and Christ. They already know this Spirit, because he has been present with them in Jesus. The disciples have already 'taken on board' the teaching of Jesus, so they will be able to speak of the Spirit being within them.

Verses 25–27 are a reminder that the Spirit continues to be their advocate, not like a lawyer pleading their cause, but as the one who is on their side continually reminding them of all they have learned. Jesus' final gift to his friends is peace. Peace (*shalom*) includes the idea of well-being and has a moral content: this is something that cannot be found where God's loving purposes are opposed. For people who know that their sense of wholeness can never be fractured by 'the world', there is no need to be fearful.

After the time of mourning is over, we often discover how a loved one has become part of us. We see with their eyes and share in their response – in laughter and tears. To be Jesus' disciple, is to allow the Spirit to prompt us to see with Christ's eyes and to respond to what we see.

TRINITY SUNDAY

Proverbs 8.1–4, 22–31; Romans 5.1–5; John 16.12–15

Proverbs 8.1–4, 22–31

Wisdom is personified as a beautiful woman. Unlike Folly, the prostitute described in the previous chapter, Wisdom stands out in the open and is found at the town gates. Not all the inhabitants of cities lived within the walls. The religious leaders, administrators and the military would be found within the city, along with the water supply and grain store. Outside the city would be the poorer dwellings of the people of the land. When enemies came, the city gates would be closed and those who were expendable would be excluded from the place of safety. Justice would be meted out at the city gate where the judge would hold court. This was where Wisdom was to be found – at the place of justice! To share Folly's bed would lead to death (7.23) but Wisdom's message is 'to all that live' (8.4).

Verses 22–31 speak about Wisdom's role in creation. Wisdom was present from the beginning and she was God's helper as the universe was formed. Wisdom, although portrayed as a separate being, is part of God's own nature. The climax of this passage is the creation of humanity, and Wisdom shares God's delight in his people.

It is almost certain that these verses were written by men, for men, as Wisdom is compared with the harlot, Folly. Which woman would they choose? In today's world, the lures of the gaudy and garish are often those of instant gratification regardless of the consequences. Wisdom has a lasting beauty, but to seek Wisdom is to seek justice, for the way of justice will bring life to all humanity. The writer of John's Gospel draws on this picture of Wisdom when he speaks of 'the Word' (the *logos*), in the marvellous poetry of his first chapter. It is 'the word made flesh' whom we meet in Jesus. His followers are called to live justly in an unjust world.

Romans 5.1–5

Many readers struggle to agree with Paul when they read that 'endurance produces character' (v.4)! Too often suffering results in depression, illness and even death. However, it is also possible to point to great figures in history and to ordinary men and women – unsung heroes and heroines – who in the face of adversity discovered courage and strength they did not know they possessed.

When Paul speaks about 'justification', he is describing the relationship between God and those who have put their faith in Christ. They can be sure that God's grace, his loving-kindness, surrounds them and that certainty brings peace. While Paul seems to be speaking about human character, it is helpful to realize that hope is possible because it is based on God's character and God is utterly reliable. Once again, it is worth remembering that 'love' is not only about feelings, but also about God's will for wholeness and abundant life for all people. If such love is 'poured' into people's hearts, then in times of adversity this will be their guiding motivation.

Suffering for early Christians was often synonymous with persecution. Those who suffer persecution today include the victims of sectarian maiming and killing. Those who love as God loves will not be destroyed by bitterness and the desire for revenge, and the centre of loving generosity within them will remain unharmed.

John 16.12–15

What are the things Jesus has to say to the disciples that they cannot bear to hear? John invites the reader to participate in the story, showing that he knew about 'interactive communication' before the arrival of the Internet! Only the reader realizes the poignancy of the situation: that Jesus is facing death and the coming of the Spirit of truth will follow the horror of crucifixion. While Jesus was alive, his friends turned to him in a crisis and were guided by his wisdom. It was only when Jesus was no longer physically present that they would discover his Spirit with them and would find that they were equipped for the task of ministry.

Perhaps this is what psychologists speak of as introjection – the taking on of standards, attitudes and beliefs of people who play a significant role in an individual's life. When Jesus is the most significant person then he becomes part of us. In religious language: his Spirit is within us. What is more, that Spirit is also God's Spirit!

God, like any creative artist, is intimately involved in his creation, for God's creation is not static, but relational: people relate to each other and to God. God does not stand outside his creation, for his loving purposes continue and move towards fulfilment. The biblical notion of 'wisdom' as the part of God's nature that moves within his creation, and is linked to the justice that will enable people to live in harmony, is discerned supremely in Jesus, the word made flesh. All three readings encourage us to believe that God's Wisdom, known in Jesus' self-giving love, not only guides us, but can become part of the fabric of our own being leaving us no choice but to seek justice!

SUNDAY BETWEEN 24 AND 28 MAY INCLUSIVE

If after Trinity Sunday

Eighth Sunday in Ordinary Time

Sirach/Ecclesiasticus 27.4–7 or Isaiah 55.10–13;
1 Corinthians 15.51–58; Luke 6.39–49

(Note that these comments can also be found under the Sunday
between 25 and 29 February but have been reproduced here to
facilitate use.)

Sirach/Ecclesiasticus 27.4–7

Jesus Ben Sira was a Jewish Scribe who wrote in about 190 BCE to
encourage Jews to hold fast to their own code of ethics at a time when
Hellenistic (Greek) values were prevalent. His book contains teaching
and a collection of wisdom sayings. In this short poem he considers
the relationship between a person's integrity and the spoken word. He
offers three images by way of illustration: rubbish left in a sieve, flaws
found in a fired pot and the quality of fruit on a tree.

Firstly, he pictures wheat, which after the first threshing is placed in
a sieve so that the grain falls through. What is left behind can be translated as 'refuse' or even 'dung'! Perhaps the oxen have trampled their
own dung into the straw and this remains in the sieve along with husks
and other rubbish. Ben Sira does not 'pull his punches' as he makes
the analogy with the 'filth' (a literal translation) that a person who
speaks with no integrity leaves in the minds of those who listen.
Secondly, he pictures a flawed pot. Just as flaws show up when the
pot is taken out of the kiln, so a person's lack of integrity becomes
obvious during conversation. Thirdly, he pictures a fruit tree. The
quality of fruit will show how well the tree has been cultivated and
tended. In the same way, Ben Sira suggests, a person's words show
how well the mind (literally heart) has been trained and disciplined.
Lack of integrity is a stumbling-block to trusting friendship. The
poem finishes with the suggestion that it is unwise to praise anyone
before hearing them speak.

Today, when integrity is not always highly prized and the actions of
politicians and public figures too rarely match their promises, we
might wonder whether speech is a good indicator of a person's
integrity! Nevertheless, we all know people who will never speak a

bad word about anyone and these people command our respect. Does our speech mirror right actions as we seek to live as God's faithful people?

Isaiah 55.10–13

These verses form the conclusion to Deutero-Isaiah's book (Chapters 40–55). Here, the prophet of the Exile pictures the joyful return of the exiles to Babylon. God's word of promised salvation is certain and can be relied upon absolutely. It is like rain and snow that water the ground and result in a harvest that feeds the people. In the same way, God's purpose will not fail. For God to speak is for God to act and when he speaks something happens! It is no accident that Deutero-Isaiah describes the salvation of the exiled people, the climax of his prophecy, in terms of God's word, the instrument of their rescue. However, this raises a question: 'Would salvation have come about if the people had not listened and responded to God's word?' There is always tension between the conviction that God's loving purposes will not fail and the necessity for people to respond in faith if their salvation is to be assured. In this context the people have already responded to God; the prophecy comes at the end of the story of the Exile when reconciliation brings about the joyful return.

A sense of overwhelming joy pervades the final verses. Creation itself sings as the people set out on their journey home and in a memorable and evocative picture even the trees 'clap their hands'! The return of the exiles has significance for all peoples and also for the whole created order. They left during a time of war and return in peace. The blossoming of the earth is a constant reminder that God's creation will never be cut off from the creator. The song is a shout of praise!

Nowadays there are many displaced people who can hardly dare to dream of a peaceful journey home. Land is laid bare by the destruction and devastation of war and made dangerous by unexploded mines. Where is the joyful return for the exiled people of today? The problem of increasing numbers of asylum seekers raises difficulties for governments and local communities alike. Many of those who flood into our country have experienced hardship beyond our imagining. Do Christians leave the task of the world's salvation to God and sit back in apathy, or are they called to do their part that warfare may end and earth be reclaimed so that land and food may be shared at the time of harvest and wanderers may return home in safety?

1 Corinthians 15.51–58

Paul uses the language of metaphor to speak about the moment of transition from this world to the next, from mortality to immortality. He begins by affirming what everyone knows: that this is a mystery. Nevertheless, Paul tries to 'unfold' that mystery, which becomes an open secret in the light of his belief that the time is coming when Christ will return and God will transform human history. Both those who live and those who have already died will belong to the coming new age. Paul seems to include himself among the living and so expects these events to happen very soon. This poses a difficulty for today's readers who do not share this immediate expectation. Yet, Paul's conviction that those who have already died are not beyond God's reach is one Christians still share. Paul uses conventional images of the day to offer a picture of the moment of transition. He says that all those who belong to Christ's people will be changed and the transformation will happen quickly. Paul uses words which stay in the memory: 'at the sound of a trumpet', 'in the twinkling of an eye' echoing language used in Jewish apocalyptic writings about the end time. Transformation will be like putting on a new garment, that of immortality. Thus, there will be continuity with what has gone before: people who change their clothes are still recognizable, however, the different garment enables personality to be expressed in a new way.

The quotations from Isaiah 25.8 and Hosea 13.14 are linked by the idea of victory over death. Paul picks up the thought from Hosea and equates the sting of death with sin. Obedience to the Jewish law was supposed to prevent sin, but often the law was so detailed that it was virtually impossible to keep it in its entirety and its effect was to highlight people's failure to live obediently. Human sinfulness led to Jesus' death on the cross but was vanquished at the resurrection. In the closing doxology Paul gives thanks that those who believe in Christ share his resurrection life. For Paul, sharing in the resurrection life of Christ must always result in right attitudes and behaviour. The Corinthian Christians who had questioned his authority had failed in a number of ways, but Paul still calls them 'his beloved' (v.58).

When we take issue with people who criticize us and whose ideas we find offensive are we able to address them as 'beloved'? Perhaps, when our feelings are far from loving, it is helpful to remember that those we find hard to like are beloved by God. If our attitudes are to embody those of Christ, then we must treat them lovingly, no matter how difficult that may be. Paul did not turn his back on those who criticized him, but continued to minister to them while continuing to use persuasive argument as he proclaimed the gospel.

Luke 6.39–49

In these verses Luke has collected a number of independent units of teaching and has placed them in an order of associated thoughts. Beginning with the well-known saying about the inevitable outcome when the blind leads the blind, Luke's thought moves to the teacher whose task is also to guide, until students are ready, in their turn, to become teachers. Perhaps the saying about the 'plank in your own eye' is a reminder that those who rate their own learning too highly are at risk of becoming arrogant and judgemental. In ancient thought, the eye was 'the window to the soul'; in other words, the eye reflected the essence of the person, so this saying about clear sight is also about honesty, integrity and the avoidance of prejudice. In contrast, in an image from the theatre, a hypocrite was a person who wore a mask to hide his own personality (actors would be male) and take on another. The only possibility for right relationship is when eyes meet in trusting acceptance.

The saying about trees being known by their fruit is concerned with the nature and essence of goodness. For Luke and his contemporaries the heart was the seat of the will, not the emotions. People's conscious intentions can be turned towards or against goodness and their words will reflect this. (Note the connection with the first lectionary passage above.) The character of the good student (or disciple) should reflect that of the teacher. When Jesus' disciples address him as 'Lord', their relationship with their teacher should be evident, both inwardly in their intentions and outwardly in their behaviour.

Luke concludes this series of sayings with the parable of the house built on rock. It is left to the readers to make connections between this parable, the teaching in the previous verses and their own lives. One way of exploring the connections is to argue that just as a house with firm foundations will not fall in time of flood, so a disciple of Jesus whose character reflects that of his Lord will not flounder, either in terms of character and integrity, or in faithfulness when faced with hardship or persecution. Those who follow Jesus today are also expected to reflect the character and actions of the one they call 'Lord'.

SUNDAY BETWEEN 29 MAY AND 4 JUNE INCLUSIVE

If after Trinity Sunday

Ninth Sunday in Ordinary Time

1 Kings 18.20–21 (22–29) 30–39; 1 Kings 8.22–23, 41–43;
Galatians 1.1–12; Luke 7.1–10

(Note that from this week until the end of the liturgical year two sets
of Old Testament readings are offered: continuous and related.
Further information is offered in the Introduction.)

1 Kings 18.20–21 (22–29) 30–39

Jezebel, wife of King Ahab, came from Phoenicia and insisted that the
god of her homeland, Baal-Melkart, was to be worshipped in Israel.
This dramatic story describes the triumph of Yahweh over Baal. The
contest took place on Mount Carmel, on the Phoenician border, where
Elijah confronts Jezebel's prophets to show that Yahweh alone has
sovereignty over the land. Baal was worshipped as the god of fertility
who controlled the sky and the weather and Elijah's challenge seemed
to 'play to Baal's strengths'! The people had been 'hedging their bets'
by worshipping both Yahweh and Baal. Elijah is aware that they have
been 'limping with two different opinions' (v.21) and it is no accident
that the same description is used for the prophets' limping kind of
ritual dance (v.26). While the prophets rant and rave, dance and cut
themselves with knives to attract Baal's attention, Elijah taunts them
by suggesting Baal has other important business – even suggesting he
is sleeping or has 'wandered away', a euphemism for relieving himself! When his own turn comes Elijah's first act is to reclaim the altar
for Yahweh. The twelve stones would have represented the twelve
tribes. Is Elijah being presented as a new Moses or a new Joshua? By
filling the trench with water he loads the dice against himself and so
proclaims his faith in Yahweh's power and heightens the effect of the
forthcoming miracle; at the same time he shows that he is not about to
cheat! It is impossible to know just what happened on the mountain,
but something extraordinary remained in the folk memory of the
people. We will never know whether a bolt of lightning struck the
altar and coincidence determined that this was the moment when
the rains fell after the prolonged drought. The story affirms that

Yahweh's sovereignty was acclaimed in spectacular style – the flames even 'licking up the water in the trench' (v.38).

Perhaps our first task, like Elijah's, is to 'reclaim the altar' by placing our worship at the centre of our lives. Do we put our faith in God or do we 'hedge our bets' by looking for security elsewhere? When we pray do we believe that God is listening, or do we have a sneaking suspicion that he, like Baal, is too busy? We may not always receive a thunderbolt response, but if we, like Elijah, challenge those who oppose God's ways, we can be certain that God will not forsake us.

1 Kings 8.22–23, 41–43

Solomon, King of Israel, takes a priestly role by officiating at the rededication of the Temple. As was the custom when praying, Solomon stood with hands outstretched to heaven. He prays to the God of Israel who alone keeps covenant relationship with his people. Having prayed for his own subjects, Solomon turns his attention to those from other nations who have heard about Israel's God and will travel as pilgrims to the Temple. These are the people who have heard about God's name; in other words, they have heard about his reputation for constant, steadfast love. Those who 'pray towards God's house' are worthy of God's attention. Solomon asks God to answer their prayers because they will witness to others until all nations come to know and fear God.

The focus of worship is the Temple. While it must be acknowledged that people are more important than buildings, nevertheless visitors to cathedrals, for example, may hope to catch a glimpse of the God who 'dwells in heaven' (v.43), the God who is beyond human understanding. To find oneself in the presence of such a God is to experience awe – the biblical word is 'fear'. Does our worship send shivers down the spine as we become awestruck by God's unceasing faithfulness? Do we enable visitors to our churches to encounter the God to whom Solomon prayed? Perhaps we should consider how our pre-service chatter and friendly greetings move the focus away from God and onto ourselves. In some churches, there is a short period of silence before worship begins, but this is only one way in which we can signal that we come to adore the God who is infinitely greater than we can begin to imagine. Those involved in worship consultations could be encouraged to consider ways in which we can foster the sense of spine-tingling awe as we draw near and are touched by the holiness of God.

Galatians 1.1–12

The key to this passage is in v.6 in which Paul makes it clear that he is writing to oppose those who are leading the Galatian Christians astray. As the letter progresses, it becomes evident that the question dividing the church is: 'Should Christianity remain a sect within Judaism?' If so, Gentile converts should become Jews, committed to observance of the Jewish law, of which the outward sign was male circumcision. Paul is about to argue against this view, as he believes that faith in Jesus is all that is needed. At the beginning of Galatians, he sets out his credentials. Reading Galatians is rather like listening to one side of a telephone conversation – we hear what Paul says, but can only infer what his opponents say. Paul begins by describing himself as an apostle, that is, one sent by Christ himself. Does this mean that his opponents were questioning his authority? Although Paul was not one of the twelve disciples, he encountered Jesus on the Damascus Road and it was Jesus who commissioned him for the task. Paul writes a circular letter to be passed round all the churches and in his greeting he offers them the grace and peace that comes from God and Christ. This is precisely his point: that grace and peace come from Jesus who died for them, so that the barrier of sin should be removed by the power of self-giving love, not by observance of the law. His opinion is that those who consider that the law, or indeed anything other than belief in Christ, is necessary for salvation should be banned from the church (v.9)! Paul could not have used stronger language and it is clear that those who place conditions on Christians, other than that of faith, have no place within the Christian community. Paul will not bow to pressure from influential people who wish to make others take on board their own cultural and religious traditions (v.10), because his only concern is to follow Christ.

Too often Christians try to make others in their own image! Does the Church welcome those with literacy difficulties or do we expect everyone to be able to use a hymn book? Do we welcome people from all backgrounds or does our offer of friendship come with the condition that others should be like us? While all people seek an atmosphere conducive to worship, people from different generations and cultures may choose a variety of styles. One of the challenges facing congregations today is how to cater for everyone so that no one is excluded and all can hear the gospel message.

Luke 7.1–10

The centurion was a 'godfearer', that is, a person from another nation who was attracted to the Jewish religion and the God of Israel, but who had not converted to Judaism (this would include circumcision as the outward sign of entering into the covenant relationship). The centurion had high-placed friends in the local community at Capernaum. In fact, some of the elders approach Jesus on his behalf. This is not surprising, as he had 'built their synagogue'. In Jesus' day, the synagogue would not have been a large edifice, but a small meeting-house. Nevertheless, the centurion has given not only money but support to the people of Capernaum. When his slave fell ill, he turned to Jesus whose reputation as a healer had already been established (4.23, 31–43). The climax of the story is not the healing itself, but the centurion's faith in Jesus' authority – authority that lies in the power of his word. The difficulty of Jesus eating in the house of a Gentile may have been at the back of Luke's mind, but this is not mentioned. The reason given is that the centurion does not believe himself to be worthy to receive a visit from Jesus. That a man of such high status treats Jesus with great respect is noteworthy! In this way, he represents the Gentiles in the early church who have never seen Jesus, but who recognize his authority. How must such converts have felt when hearing this story? Their faith was being commended, along with the faith of the centurion.

Once again in these readings, we are presented with someone who is seeking God. Here the centurion turns to Jesus at a time of crisis. A number of people turn to the Church for help when in difficulty and some of them will have already thought about Christianity. It is often at a time of bereavement, for example, that people return to church or enter its doors for the first time – often as a result of the care offered by the minister. Too often churchgoers care for each other within the family of the church and resent time taken to care for those beyond its doors. Ministers often long to work within the community and are often asked to take on roles such as school governor or hospital chaplain, or to lead school assemblies. Ministers also preside at funerals and weddings for people who rarely if ever attend church. Do congregations wish their ministers to be their own domestic chaplains, or is there a will to reach out to the wider community, not only 'allowing' the minister some latitude, but seeking ways to participate in that wider ministry. Let us remember that acceptance is the first step towards healing and that those for whom we care are likely to ask us questions about our faith. If we are serious about the gospel we must be prepared to enter discussions even when our own preconceptions are challenged. We do not have to come up with all the answers but must be prepared to search for God's truth while holding fast to our faith in Jesus.

SUNDAY BETWEEN 5 AND 11 JUNE

If after Trinity Sunday

Tenth Sunday in Ordinary Time

1 Kings 17.8–16 (17–24); 1 Kings 17.17–24; Galatians 1.11–24;
Luke 7.11–17

1 Kings 17.8–16 (17–24)

Although it is tempting to speak about the sharing of food relieving hunger, the significance of the biblical narrative is that all that takes place is due to God's miraculous provision. It was God who sent Elijah, in a time of famine, to Zarephath, an area outside King Ahab's territory, and commanded the widow to feed him. After the last of the widow's food and drink had been consumed, God filled the jug of oil and jar of meal until the rains came.

Both Elijah and the widow obeyed God's word even though they did not know whether they would live or die. While a 'theology of blessing' makes the assumption that God will always provide for his faithful people, human experience of starvation and suffering show that this is not always the case. Jesus was obedient, but was not spared crucifixion. Those who follow Christ must be prepared to keep God's word, even though self-giving is costly.

Verses 17–24 may be used as part of the same reading, or can stand on their own. The widow's son is either close to death or has already died: 'there was no breath in him' (v.17) is open to both interpretations. In Genesis 2.7, God 'breathes life' into Adam. The Old Testament view of God's breath or spirit, is that one could have more or less of it. Elijah, the 'man of God' (v.24), had a greater share of God's spirit. Death, then, was a weak form of life and the dead led a kind of attenuated existence until there was no more breath left. Like many people of the time, the widow believed that sickness and death were a punishment for sin and so she cast in her mind for a sin she had forgotten! (When faced with illness some people still ask 'What have I done to deserve this?') Elijah took the boy into an upper room and stretched his body across that of the child. This is not about the kiss of life, but about Elijah transferring some of his own share of God's spirit into the child's body by placing his hands on the child's hands, his mouth on the child's mouth, his eyes on the child's eyes, his heart on the child's heart. He repeats this action three times and the child lives and the widow exclaims, 'Now I know that you are a man of God!' (v.24).

Can people seem more or less alive? There are young people who take little pleasure in life and older people whose eyes sparkle with the joy of living – and vice versa.

Galatians 1.11–24

Paul must convince the church that his authority is greater than the authority of his opponents. Although Paul had received instruction from Ananias and the Christians in Jerusalem (Acts 9), it was the risen Christ alone (v.1) who commissioned him to become the apostle to the Gentiles. Paul recalls his leading role in persecuting Christians and the complete change effected by his encounter with Christ on the Damascus Road. Like a number of prophets before him, Paul feels that God had 'set him apart from his birth' (v.15) so that he could bring the gospel to the pagan world. Paul seems to be arguing against those who believed that only the first disciples could be called apostles, but although Paul's meeting with Christ took place later his apostleship is equally valid. What is more the two leading figures in the Jerusalem Church, Peter and James, have both agreed that Paul's work should be with the Gentiles. (Cephas is the Aramaic for Peter or 'rock'.)

Paul had to 'blow his own trumpet' if he was to prevail against his opponents. Preachers too must commend themselves to their congregations. That is why presentation – including such details as appropriate dress, audibility and tone of voice – goes hand in hand with meticulous preparation and study.

Luke 7.11–17

The story of the healing of the Widow of Nain's son echoes that of Elijah's healing of the widow of Zarephath's son (above). Both Elijah and Jesus meet the widows at the gate of the towns (v.12 cf. 1 Kings 10) and after the healings have taken place restore the sons to their widowed mothers (v.15 cf. 1 Kings 17.23). It is worth remembering that there was no social security available for widows and that these two women were dependent on their sons, thus the healings also restore life and hope to them. According to Luke, Jesus was moved by compassion. Unlike Elijah, Jesus does not touch the young man, he heals by commanding him to rise. Jesus is portrayed as one greater than Elijah and so this narrative is a precursor to the following section about John the Baptist, the 'Elijah of Jesus' day'.

True compassion always results in action. Many people in today's world weep but too few are offered the help that restores their quality of life.

SUNDAY BETWEEN 12 AND 18 JUNE INCLUSIVE

If after Trinity Sunday

Eleventh Sunday in Ordinary Time

1 Kings 21.1–10 (11–14) 15–21a; 2 Samuel 11.26–12.10, 13.15;
Galatians 2.15–21; Luke 7.36–8.3

1 Kings 21.1–10 (11–14) 15–21a

The story of Naboth's vineyard is one of greed and treachery that rivals the plot of any soap opera today! King Ahab makes a fair bid for the vineyard that adjoins the palace grounds. However, Naboth does not consider that the land is his to sell, it is his inheritance and he holds it in trust for successive generations. In Israel, it was the king's task to protect his people and the land that was entrusted to them by God and although Ahab sulked, he seems to have accepted Naboth's decision. Jezebel's taunt (v.7) epitomizes the opposing view of kingship as absolute power and sets her on a collision course with Elijah, the representative of God's justice. Naboth seems to have been one of an influential group who moved in royal circles. Jezebel involved some of these powerful men in her nefarious scheme. To 'proclaim a fast' (v.9) may simply mean that usual activities were suspended while the court was in session. The evidence of false witnesses led to the murder of Naboth, his stoning passed off as the execution of a death sentence. Ahab suppressed any doubts he may have had and took the land. Then the cavalry arrives, rather belatedly, in the form of Elijah! King Ahab, protector of his people, has in effect broken two of the covenant commands: not to covet and not to murder! It was the task of the king to protect his people and ensure that they were ruled justly. He has failed as God's representative. In suitably gory language, Ahab's punishment is described. He will die a violent death and the dogs will lick his blood just as they licked the blood of Naboth (v.19)! Ahab's power is at an end.

There is little doubt that 'power often corrupts', especially when land is at stake. The story challenges us at both national and personal levels. If all we possess, including land, belongs to God, then we must use our 'wealth' for the benefit of others. Most of us, no matter how generous we may be, live comfortably and to some extent selfishly. Christian congregations are often possessive about their church premises and many a church council has debated whether to allow groups to use rooms when they have been freshly painted or carpeted for fear that what has been provided will be damaged. Another bone of contention for city churches is about who will be permitted to use the church car park! 'To what extent does a Christian lifestyle involve sharing with others?' may be an interesting question for the church discussion group to tackle!

2 Samuel 11.26–12.10, 13–15

Like the reading above, this is a story about God's prophet challenging the king. King David has become infatuated with Bathsheba and his obsession with her is governing his actions. The opening verse sets out the context: David had arranged for Uriah to be placed in the front line of the battle, so that his death was inevitable. In effect, David is guilty of murder, so that Bathsheba, Uriah's widow, would be free to marry him. Nathan's response is to tell the story of the ewe lamb. While it seems unlikely that David would have failed to recognize that the rich man represented himself, the effect of the narrative is far more compelling when David denounces the rich man's actions and, with what seems like righteous indignation, outlines the punishment he deserves! The climax comes as Nathan wags an accusing finger and declaims, 'You are the man!' If David was in any doubt about his actions the following verses make the despicable nature of his conduct plain.

The idea of God's punishment falls uncomfortably on the ears of today's congregations. In the ancient world, it was often thought that both reward and punishment were transferred through the family line. Every member of the family, across the generations, had responsibility for each other. In today's culture, when people are expected to take individual responsibility for their actions, this is not an easy concept. Nevertheless, the writer shows unequivocally that an all-powerful and just God could not ignore David's reprehensible behaviour. However, this still raises the question for Christians, 'How could the God who is Father of Jesus Christ cause the death of David's future son as punishment?' The same question is often asked by those who struggle to believe in God. Why is it that those who exploit and abuse others prosper? It may help to speak of the way one person's actions have consequences for others and like a pebble thrown into a pool, the ripples spread to subsequent generations. The Church's role, like that of Nathan (and Elijah above), is to challenge and oppose evil in all its forms, trusting in God who is both just and merciful.

Galatians 2.15–21

Paul's central message is that Christians from both Jewish and Gentile backgrounds must realize that their relationship with God is based on faith in Christ alone. It is unlikely that Paul thought that all Gentiles were sinners in a moral sense, rather that they have not had the Torah, the covenant law, to guide them. However, it is faith and not the law that has enabled people both to become and to remain Christians. The term justification refers to 'right relationship' between people and God, exemplified by Christ's obedience and God's faithfulness. Sin can be described as a barrier that prevents such a relationship, but faith in Christ enables all barriers to be broken down. Torah-observing Jews might well have considered that Christians, who put their faith in Christ rather than the law, risked becoming 'sinners' like the Gentiles. Paul refutes this in the strongest possible language: 'certainly not' (v.17) is a polite translation! Sinfulness is about reliance on anything other than faith in Christ, even on the law God gave! To 'die to the law' is to recognize that law-keeping is not the basis for relationship with God. In Paul's own case keeping the law led him to persecute Christians and it was not until he 'died to the law' that he was able to live in right relationship with God. For Paul, to be 'crucified with Christ' could be paraphrased as dying to the authority of Judaism (including the law), even though that was where he had previously found his identity, security and sense of purpose. Paul's 'sense of self' is now inextricably linked with Christ who is at the centre of everything he is and all that he does.

When people are asked to describe their sense of personal identity, they often answer in terms of their roles: 'I am Johnny's mum or Sam's wife, I work as a receptionist in the local hotel', or even, 'I am a church steward!' We all tend to define ourselves in terms of our relationships with other people, especially those closest to us. What does it mean to put Christ at the centre of our lives and to find our identity, security and sense of purpose in him, rather than elsewhere?

Luke 7.36–8.3

Jesus' acceptance and forgiveness of those rejected by society contrasts with the shortcomings of those in high positions whose sense of self-importance replaces compassion. Luke tells the story of the anointing of Jesus' feet in a way that would have shocked his readers as Jesus once again overturns the existing order: the outsider who was rejected by society has the place of honour while the 'honoured' host is shamed. In both Greek and Roman culture honour was highly prized and by exaggerating the failure of the host to offer Jesus the usual courtesies the contrast between the Pharisee and the woman is highlighted. In the Gospels of Matthew and Mark the anointing of Jesus' head takes place during the last week of his life and its purpose is to prepare him for burial (Matt. 26.6–13, Mark 14.3–9), while in Luke's story the emphasis is upon Jesus as the one who is able to offer forgiveness. The setting is formal as the meal is served while people recline at table in Roman style. It is because Jesus reclines to eat that the woman is able to approach from behind in order to anoint his feet. The woman remains an anonymous figure who is described as 'a sinner', although what she has done wrong is left to the readers' imagination. Luke draws contrasts with broad brush strokes: the extravagance of the gift is compared not only with her low status and depth of her repentance but also with the Pharisee's ungracious treatment of Jesus. The irony in the story is that while Simon the Pharisee (identified with Simon the leper in Mark 14.3) suggests that Jesus should have known what kind of woman she was, he was already well aware of the situation as the parable of the two debtors shows. What is not clear is whether the woman anointed Jesus' feet because Jesus had forgiven her sins, or whether her act of love moved Jesus to offer forgiveness. The scene changes as Jesus and his disciples travel on through Galilee meeting women he had previously healed or exorcized. These women would have considered themselves 'outsiders' rejected both by society and by God, yet through Jesus they were restored to God's kingdom life (8.1). Other powerful women of the day are named and help to provide for Jesus' needs, thus enabling his ministry to continue.

The theme of 'reversal of fortunes' offers a challenge to the Church. It is easy to speak about forgiving and accepting those who have made mistakes, but a glance at any newspaper reminds us that crime and violence, often fuelled by drug and alcohol dependency, are features of our society. If we are honest, these are people we would rather not meet and whom we feel deserve to be punished for the pain they cause others. However, we cannot forgive, understand or accept people we do not meet! Amongst our congregations there will be those who have first-hand experience of working with such people. Does the Church offer support to those of its members who work at the forefront in education, the Health Service, in local government and so on, or do we keep church attendance and working life separate?

SUNDAY BETWEEN 19 AND 25 JUNE INCLUSIVE

If after Trinity Sunday

Twelfth Sunday in Ordinary Time

1 Kings 19.1–4 (5–7) 8–15a; Isaiah 65.1–9; Galatians 3.23–29; Luke 8.26–39

1 Kings 19.1–4 (5–7) 8–15a

Elijah, after his triumph over the prophets of Baal on Mount Carmel, gave orders that the prophets should be put to the sword. It is not surprising that Jezebel, who had brought the prophets with her to Israel, sought to kill him and Elijah fled in fear of his life. Elijah who had faced the prophets of Baal with courage and fortitude is now described as fearful and depressed. Perhaps he knew he had behaved badly by arranging the murder of the prophets and wanted to distance himself from his own act. When he reached Beer-sheba, a lonely place in the desert, he rested in the shade of a broom bush (such shrubs grew to a height of three metres), wanting only to die. By considering himself no better than his ancestors (v.4), he may have been thinking of prophets before him and their failure to persuade the people to remain faithful to God. It is when Elijah is at his lowest ebb that he is miraculously nourished as he was once before when ravens fed him (17.4–6). God's messenger keeps him alive and makes sure he is strong enough for the journey. The parallel with Moses' journey through the wilderness would not be lost on the readers. God provided food and the journey took forty days. Here is another echo of Moses' story, although the wilderness wanderings lasted for forty years. Like Moses, Elijah arrived at the holy mountain. In this tradition, the mountain is called Horeb rather than Sinai. At the place where God spoke to Moses, he speaks again, this time to Elijah. The arrival of God on the mountain is associated with wind, earthquake and fire that both announces his presence and conceals him from view. It was only after the storm, when stillness fell, that Elijah heard God's word in a 'sound of sheer silence' (v.12); and the 'sound that silence makes' can be deafening! Elijah could not continue to hide in the cave, but came out, his head wrapped in his mantle so he would not see the face of God, an action once again reminiscent of that of Moses (Exodus 33.20–22). Elijah tried to make excuses for himself, affirming that he had acted out of zealous devotion to God and he blamed the Israelites for turning away from God, destroying altars and killing God's prophets (he doesn't mention that he has treated the prophets of Baal in exactly the same way!). Yet, underlying the words spoken is the knowledge that God has met Elijah at a time of crisis and has reaffirmed his calling. Elijah remained God's prophet and following his encounter with God he was ready to go on.

Perhaps it is encouraging to know that even the great, legendary figures of the Old Testament could suffer what seems to be guilt-induced depression. (After all, Elijah was personally responsible for the massacre of more than eight hundred of Jezebel's prophets and we cannot know what effect that had on his state of mind.) Too often, well-meaning members of churches try to 'cheer up' those who are depressed by telling them that if their faith is strong enough the depression will lift. This simply adds to the problem, as those who already feel dreadful berate themselves for their lack of faith and the more they berate themselves the worse they feel! God's messenger nourished Elijah in his need. Surely, it is our task to stand alongside those who are depressed and anxious without adding to their guilt by suggesting their emotions are incompatible with their faith!

Isaiah 65.1–9

In the years that followed the Exile, there was no obvious change for the better and people continued in their old ways. The opening verse is a reminder of God's unfailing faithfulness and continued presence with them. The repetition of God's words, 'Here I am' (v.1) was a reminder that even in Babylon, where they did not expect to find him, God had not abandoned them, but eventually brought them home. Nevertheless, the people have resumed their idolatrous ways and once again worship other gods: the words 'those who sacrifice in gardens' like the reference to 'offering incense on the mountains' (v.7) refer to the high places. Superstitious practice abounded, such as seeking advice from the dead and participating in initiation ceremonies in caves by night. Food laws that related to cultic purity were flouted and people were in no fit state to approach a holy God. They had left God with no option but to punish them as their reprehensible behaviour mirrored that of preceding generations. Yet there is also recognition that some people had remained faithful: they are like the good grapes among the rotten ones. The message of judgement for the unfaithful is balanced by the message of salvation for the faithful. It is through the faithful that the future of the nation is assured.

When people pick themselves up after a disaster of national pro-portions, there is often a time of optimism during the re-building.

Similarly, when a new government is formed hope and idealism are in the air. However, people soon slip back into their old ways. It is often said that people can worship God privately and do not need to attend church. However, corporate worship that focuses on God's holiness and constant love in the face of human failings, rekindles our awareness of and commitment to God's loving purposes.

Galatians 3.23–29

Paul continues to explain the position held by God's law before the coming of Christ. In Greek culture, boys of wealthy parents often had a 'pedagogue' (disciplinarian vv. 24–25), who was often a well-educated slave, to act as a tutor and guardian. The pedagogue would go with the child when he left the home, and would act as a guide and a mentor. When the child became an adult, he no longer needed a pedagogue to accompany him. Paul suggests that the role of the pedagogue and the role of the law are similar. The law itself was God-given, but is no longer necessary because faith in Christ enables people to live as responsible adults. Entry into the life of faith involved baptism, described as the 'putting on' of Christ like dressing in a new garment. Christ, then, becomes part of the identity of those who are baptized so that they regard others as Christ would have regarded them. This is why the usual divisions in society no longer apply, because all are valued by Christ and by those who think and act like Christ. Although Christians would still have to live in a world where people's status differed within society, their attitude towards others was changed. Together, Christians belong to God's people and so are 'heirs of Abraham'.

Too often, the Church has reflected rather than challenged social divisions in society. Should our decision-making bodies represent ageing, generally 'well-to-do', predominantly white congregations or should they be more representative of those in society at large? It is essential that the churches communicate with people in appropriate ways and that may mean exploring a variety of styles in worship, so that all feel welcome and none are excluded.

Luke 8.26–39

The earliest readers would have realized that this story is set in a non-Jewish region, reflecting the Roman desecration of their country, and this is emphasized by the presence of the pigs. The possessed man had come from the city, where Roman culture predominated and pagan practices were normal. His nakedness would have offended Jewish sensibilities and, even worse, he was living among the tombs, places that were considered unclean and were thought to attract evil spirits. Here was someone who had no place within either pagan or Jewish society. The demons recognize Jesus immediately and the man screams out using the pagan phrase, 'Son of the Most High God' (v.28). In the culture of the day, it was thought that to know someone's name was to have power over the person but here Jesus is faced with the strength of a legion, six thousand soldiers! The abyss is the place of destruction and it is ironic that the demons, who may have thought that they had found another home when they chose to go into the herd of pigs, still ended up in the sea and were destroyed. To ask what the herd's owner must have thought is to miss the point: their destruction is about Jesus bringing purity to a region contaminated by pagan practices. By the time the swineherds fetch the crowd they find the man sitting at Jesus' feet, the position of a disciple. When he pleaded to be allowed to go with Jesus, Jesus refused. Why wouldn't Jesus let him go with him? Presumably because he would not be accepted in Jewish circles. Instead, he is to return to the pagan world from which he has come and speak about Jesus there. Luke's hearers who came from pagan backgrounds would have felt affirmed that Jesus had sent the man he had healed to people like themselves. However, the story ends on a despondent note: the people who lived in the area were terrified when they heard what Jesus had done and their fear did not lead to faith but to their urgent desire for him to leave.

Jesus' power to exorcize both the man and the land itself would have special meaning for Christians living within Roman society. In today's world, 'demonic power' is language used to describe all that pollutes and destroys. Sometimes the extent of the forces to be contended with seems 'legion', yet those who 'sit at Jesus' feet' are still required to go and witness – against all that threatens to damage and mar environmental resources and the dignity of human life. The possessed man did not seek healing, nor do those who exploit others and ravage the land for their own ends. Nevertheless, Jesus acted decisively and swiftly; so should we! Sometimes, the task facing faithful disciples can be frightening and it is tempting to remain cocooned in our own comfortable homes and churches and ask Jesus to go away. Yet our faith is in the one who does not send us out in our own strength, but goes with us as helper and guide.

SUNDAY BETWEEN 26 JUNE AND 2 JULY INCLUSIVE

Thirteenth Sunday in Ordinary Time

2 Kings 2.1–2, 6–14; 1 Kings 19.15–16, 19–21; Galatians 5.1, 13–25; Luke 9.51–62

2 Kings 2.1–2, 6–14

This is a legendary account of how Elisha came to succeed Elijah. Elijah is approaching the end of his life, but no mention is made of his death. Instead, supernatural events will take Elijah into heaven. Two traditions seem to have been combined: one characterized by the appearance of a chariot and horses of fire, the other that Elijah was 'taken up in a whirlwind' (vv. 11–12). Elijah is the archetypal prophet who stands head and shoulders above any other. However, he was not the only prophet as fifty more prophets, from the sanctuary at Gilgal, act as a 'chorus' in the drama. Elisha is portrayed as the loyal disciple who refuses to leave his master. As they travel on together, Elijah takes his mantle and strikes the waters of the Jordan and they part before him, just as the sea parted before Moses as he led the Israelites out of Egypt (Exodus 14.21). Elijah's power was transferred to the mantle through its close contact with his body. Elisha, the would-be successor, asks Elijah for a double share of his spirit. A double share of his father's possessions was the inheritance of the eldest son (Deut. 21.17) who would take on the responsibilities of the father. (This may also shed some light on the parable of the prodigal son and explain the extent of the elder son's resentment.) By asking for the eldest son's portion, Elisha is signalling his willingness to succeed Elijah and perhaps to become the leader of the group of prophets. Elijah, who seems to have supernatural knowledge of the events that are about to unfold, agrees subject to one condition: Elisha must see what happens when God takes him to heaven. In other words, Elisha must demonstrate his ability to 'see' supernatural events. Fire and wind are symbols of theophany, the coming of God. Both the fiery chariot and horses and the whirlwind seem to signal the presence of God. Elisha does indeed see what happens and his response is to rend his garments, a sign of deep mourning. His position as Elijah's successor is assured when he, in his turn, strikes the river with Elijah's mantle and the waters part.

What does it mean to see? Often an awareness of God's presence goes hand in hand with mourning. For to be aware of God is to recognize the gulf between divine love and human failing, and the role of the prophet is to speak out against injustice. Though weeping for his master, Elisha had the courage to put on the prophet's garb and face the challenge ahead.

1 Kings 19.15–16, 19–21

The story of Elisha's call was written down at a later period when Israel was under threat from without and within. Assyria was gaining power and forces were being mustered against Israel and Syria who had formed an alliance. Meanwhile, inside the country many people were turning to foreign cults. The threat of warfare was understood to be a warning that God would punish his people for idolatry. Elijah as God's prophet sets the process of judgement in motion by anointing Hazael as King of Syria (Aram), Jehu as King of Israel and Elisha as his own successor. They were to be instruments of God's punishment, as many people would be slain in the forthcoming conflict. The only good news in this dire situation was the promise that seven thousand who had refused to worship Baal would be saved.

Verses 19–21 recount Elisha's call. His name is symbolic and meant 'God is salvation'. Elisha is from a wealthy family who can afford to plough their fields with two dozen oxen (twelve yokes). One plough would be pulled by a pair of oxen yoked together, each pair with its own driver, and two pairs would work alongside each other. The use of twelve ploughs suggests that Shaphat, Elisha's father, owned a large swathe of arable land. In a symbolic act, Elijah threw his mantle over Elisha (v.19). It has been suggested that prophets wore cloaks made from the skins of sacrificial animals as a sign of their close relationship with God, in which case a hairy mantle might be 'the uniform' of a prophet! Before he finally leaves home, Elisha's family and their neighbours seem to participate in a farewell meal that is both a thanksgiving for his call and a symbolic ending to his former life, signified by the boiling of two oxen with their yoke. Elisha left to become Elijah's pupil and servant teacher.

The summons to become a prophet often came at a time of crisis. This is true now as then. Yet, just as Elisha would not be alone in his task but would be supported by a remnant of faithful Israelites, so today's prophets seek the support of those who share their vision. The Church has to fulfil the dual role – that of Elisha and of the faithful remnant. The Church, like Elisha, must be clothed in close relationship with God and this can only happen when devotional life is placed high on our agendas. At the same time those who belong to decreasing congregations must, like a faithful remnant, continue to trust God, live faithfully and be prepared to speak the prophetic word.

Galatians 5.1, 13–25

What does Paul mean by freedom? Paul explains that Christians are no longer bound ('yoked') to the old securities, such as the law. This is because love of neighbour will be their motivation and lead them to do God's will. Nevertheless, this ideal picture does not seem to match reality; there seems to have been considerable backbiting and friction in the church (v.15). Paul compares the life of 'the flesh' with the life of 'the Spirit'. The terms 'Spirit' and 'flesh' are not about 'spiritual' versus 'physical', rather, they represent two opposing ways of life. The life of the Spirit is life under God's rule, while the life of the flesh looks not to God, but elsewhere as a guide for behaviour. Paul's contention is that those whose lives are not ruled by God run the risk of becoming involved in destructive patterns of behaviour while conversely, those who live under God will reap the benefit. Paul follows a convention of his day by offering lists of virtues and vices. Such lists were not comprehensive, but representative of the kinds of behaviour to avoid or to seek. Sexual imagery was often linked with idolatry, as it included the idea of being unfaithful to God. As the images are heaped one on top of another the adverse effect of self-indulgence on community relationships is evident. Such behaviour prevents people from inheriting the kingdom (v.21). If the 'kingdom life' is life lived under God, this is not surprising! In contrast, the fruit of the Spirit is about those qualities that enable people to live together and build a mutually supportive community. The life of the Spirit is beyond the law's sphere because the law cannot legislate with regard to such qualities as kindness and gentleness. Crucifixion belongs to the past as does the life of the flesh, and the Spirit has become the only possible guide to behaviour.

Paul's emphasis is clearly about life in community. Today people are often encouraged to make their own welfare their first priority. A Christian outlook challenges this view. Most of us belong to more than one community, for example the communities of people where we live, work and spend our leisure time, as well as the community of the Church. Is our behaviour always characterized by the life of the Spirit?

Luke 9.51–62

In words reminiscent of the first of today's passages, Luke speaks about the day when Jesus will be 'taken up'. Those who have already read the Gospel will know that Luke is referring to Jesus' ascension. Yet for the time being crucifixion and resurrection are still in the future and we are reminded once again that suffering and joy belong together. The focus for these forthcoming events is Jerusalem and Jesus 'sets his face' – makes a conscious decision – to continue along the path he has chosen. Samaritans would have been unlikely to welcome a group of Jews, especially those heading for the rival sanctuary at Jerusalem. Jesus, however, does not wish to bring about their destruction (v.54). People are free to accept or reject Jesus, and it is not for Christians to respond in anger when others reject Jesus. Acceptance of Jesus brings its own demands. Jesus as the Son of Man is the one who accepts suffering. (One like a Son of Man in Daniel 7.13, refers to the representative of the suffering righteous who was vindicated by God and shared his rule.) The disciple must be prepared to suffer with Jesus and recognize that the stringent demands of the kingdom have priority over even the most pressing of family ties. In the life of the early church, it was not always possible to follow Christ and retain ties with Jewish or pagan family members: would-be Christians often had to make hard choices.

The idea that following Jesus comes before the needs of family has caused untold suffering for many. Clearly, early Christians had hard choices to make when following Jesus meant being rejected by either pagan or Jewish family members. This kind of dilemma is one that many Christians still face. However, it is also true that when a Christian is more concerned about caring for people beyond the family, resentment grows and family breakdown can result. It is essential that Christians take their family responsibilities seriously and ensure that sufficient time is set aside for marriage partners, children and members of the extended family. Nevertheless, commitment to the family must be balanced with the wider responsibilities of discipleship. It is the task of both the individual Christian and the Church, at local and national levels, to consider the demands of discipleship. Following in the way of suffering love means responding to the needs of others regardless of the cost. It certainly does not involve an angry response that seeks to destroy those who do not choose to follow Christ. What should our relationship be with other faith communities?

SUNDAY BETWEEN 3 AND 9 JULY INCLUSIVE

Fourteenth Sunday in Ordinary Time

2 Kings 5.1–14; Isaiah 66.10–14; Galatians 6.(1–6) 7–16;
Luke 10.1–11, 16–20

2 Kings 5.1–14

Naaman was the commander of the armies of Syria (Aram is another word for Syria). Leprosy was a term used for many skin diseases and it is unlikely that he suffered from a highly contagious disease, such as that known today as leprosy or Hanson's disease, or he would not have had access to the king. The significance of this 'wonder narrative' is to demonstrate Elisha's power to heal 'so that they might know there is a prophet in Israel' (v.8) and to compare the superiority of the Israelite faith with the impotence of Syrian religion.

This tale lends itself to an exploration of the different characters' roles. The servant-girl had been taken captive in a border raid. She had been forcibly removed from her own country and her own family, and might have been filled with bitterness. The biblical narrative does not explore her relationship with her mistress, but we can speculate that she must have been kindly treated, as it is her loyalty to her mistress that leads her to suggest that Naaman should approach Elisha. If events did not turn out well, she must have risked facing severe punishment. Had Naaman been made to look ridiculous, the servants who urged him to bathe in the Jordan would also have been punished. They risked at least a flogging and at worst their lives. It is fascinating to notice that the name, Naaman, means 'charming' or 'pleasant' and it seems as if he must have lived up to his name to merit such loyalty from his servants. Clearly Naaman, as a successful commander, knew how to obtain the respect and devotion of those under him. The kings of the two countries play their parts; and humour and irony abound as the exorbitant amount of silver and gold and the ten sets of garments along with the written request for healing lead the King of Israel to assume that the King of Syria is seeking an excuse for war. The feeling of helplessness in the words, 'Am I God to give death or life?' serves to emphasize the power of the God of Israel. The scene moves to Elisha's house, and the most important character never sets foot on the stage! More laughter ensues when Naaman, the great commander, is left on the doorstep and the prophet does not even put his nose out of the door, but sends his servant to tell Naaman to wash in the River

Jordan. It is no wonder Naaman felt insulted. A dramatic magical act would not only involve some arm waving, but would also have served to emphasize Naaman's plight and the seriousness with which Elisha approached the task of healing. As an example of a pastoral carer, Elisha is hardly a good role model! Yet, it was Nathan's willingness to lose his dignity that enabled him to be healed.

Here is a reminder that God alone is able to bring about healing and wholeness. However, that healing is mediated by those who put their own well-being at risk. The servants in this story have the least status, but it can be assumed that they act from compassion rather than the hope of reward. Today, aid-workers can be found alongside those who suffer. For example, doctors and nurses work in the poorer countries of the world in makeshift hospitals and with inadequate medical supplies; medical aid is provided as people are dug out from under the rubble following an earthquake; and, in our own affluent society, paramedics rush to help those who are trapped and injured in pile-ups on motorways. Not all are Christian, yet wherever self-giving love makes itself known surely God's Spirit is present. Perhaps, part of what it means to be human, to be made 'in the image of God', is the willingness to put ourselves at risk when someone else's life is threatened.

Isaiah 66.10–14

People who love Jerusalem are summoned to rejoice. These are people who have mourned over the shortcomings of city life but have a vision of how different things could be. It is those who are ready to accept God's salvation for the city who will discover the abundance of God's provision. They will be both comforted and nourished like a nursing child in the arms of the mother. The river that brings fertility to the land is a conventional image for salvation. God will make the city prosperous and poverty and injustice will be unknown. Such a city will attract people from other nations who will add to its wealth so that bounty will overflow the river's banks. The feminine imagery is repeated as God holds the people tenderly and carries them into the city where they will be comforted and nurtured. In Jerusalem, they will grow and flourish. Nevertheless, the last line of this passage signals a warning note. Nations have a choice: they can either turn to God and accept his salvation or get their deserts for the way they have treated Israel in the past.

Cities are places where the rich/poor divide is seen at its most stark. The houses of the wealthy compare with the squalid conditions of the poor. Those earning huge salaries live in the same city as those who exist at subsistence level. Jerusalem was no different, yet became the image for a new kind of city. Those who approach in sorrow for the part they have played in perpetuating injustice, whether actively or by passive collusion, will be carried in by the motherly, tender-hearted God. Those who seek entry for personal gain have no place in the city – yet our cities are filled with those who exploit others. Do we share God's indignation? If so, how should such indignation be expressed?

Galatians 6. (1–6) 7–16

Paul reminds the Galatians that it is not possible to be a Christian in isolation, as the life of the Spirit has to be expressed and experienced within community. Paul is not addressing serious offences in this passage; rather, the less serious wrongdoing that is characteristic of the human condition. All people are tempted and sometimes give in to temptation and so there is no place for moral superiority. Mutual support, the carrying of each other's burdens, must be offered with kindly gentleness, as love is the underlying principle that results in right conduct. Christians should not compare themselves with others, rather they should consider what, with God's grace, they are able to become. This way, they would be unlikely to act out of false pride. The allusion to 'sharing in all good things with their teacher' (v.6) may refer to material support, or to learning and acting on all that is taught.

Verse 7 is the beginning of a new line of thought. Paul reminds his hearers that Christians must act responsibly in accordance with the gospel imperative to love. They must not try to make a fool of God by paying lip-service to the gospel, as their actions have consequences for life in this world and for future resurrection life. In other words, Christians were not exempt from God's judgement. At all times Christians were expected to take every opportunity to work for the good of all. How do we hold in tension the needs of the world and those of 'the family of faith'? Should help be offered first to those most in need regardless of their faith or lack of faith? Paul knew that concern for the welfare of each member would help to build a community spirit that would enable effective witness.

In the Church today, it is equally appropriate to ensure that every member of the congregation receives pastoral care, but this is not where the task of caring ends, rather it is where it begins! When people are cared for and supported they are also encouraged to continue the task of caring as they, in their turn, look after others.

Luke 10.1–11, 16–20

Luke describes Jesus' sending out of seventy-two representatives in a way that would have resonated with the readers of his own day. Was Luke trying to portray Jesus as the new Moses, who appointed seventy elders to share his task (Num. 11.1–17, 24–25) and sent out emissaries to facilitate peaceful entry into the Promised Land (Deut. 21.22–25)? Was this a reflection of the missionary enterprise of the early church signalled by the metaphor of harvesting? Harvesting also refers to God's final judgement, and there is a note of urgency about the missionaries' lack of preparation – in matters of life and death there is no time to lose! Their task, like that of future Christians, was to heal the sick and bring the good news of the kingdom (v.9). Healing and wholeness are characteristic features of life lived under God's rule and their ministry reflects and prepares for Jesus' coming. If Luke was thinking about missionaries in his own time, it is not surprising that he mentions the opposition and hostility that they would face only too frequently. The note of judgement sounds continually. Just as the missionaries wipe the dust off their feet, so God will turn his back on them and their destruction will be as inevitable as that of Sodom (Gen. 9.24).

Verse 16 is a reminder that Jesus' representatives were acting with his authority, just as he acted with God's authority, and so the outcome of their missionary enterprise was never in doubt and they return flushed with success. Their triumph over the powers of evil is described in extravagant language. However, Jesus reminds them that their jubilation should not be because of what they have achieved, for this is by God's power alone, but because 'their names are written in heaven' and their place in the coming kingdom is assured.

Those who sought to testify to Christ would have needed courage and determination when taking on the mighty power of Rome! Luke's writing would have encouraged them as they associated themselves with the success of the missionaries in the passage. While history testifies to the inevitable downfall of corrupt regimes, the suffering of those who are treated unjustly is an ongoing reality. Christians must work to bring such suffering to an end, so that God's kingdom life may be experienced by all.

SUNDAY BETWEEN 10 AND 16 JULY INCLUSIVE

Fifteenth Sunday in Ordinary Time

Amos 7.7–17; Deuteronomy 30.9–14; Colossians 1.1–14;
Luke 10.25–37

Amos 7.7–17

Amos lived in the eighth century BCE and prophesied in the northern kingdom although his origins were in the south. This passage begins with his vision of a man building a wall with the help of a plumb-line. He tells Israel that God's plumb-line will test whether they are built securely, in other words, whether or not they remain loyal to God. The implication is that their loyalty has faltered! Amos' message is one of divine retribution. This seems to have caused great resentment. After all, who was he, a foreigner, to speak words of judgement? What is more, Amos was prophesying at the king's own sanctuary, where Amaziah was both priest and prophet by royal appointment, and he was treading very heavily on Amaziah's toes! These verses describe the conflict between Amaziah and Amos concerning who had authority to prophesy at Bethel. Amaziah tells Amos to return to Judah and do his prophesying there. Amos' response seems to be 'shooting himself in the foot' as he denies his status as a prophet, saying in effect that Amaziah is right and that he is a herdsman by trade. However, he goes on to say that God called him to the prophet's task and God's authority is greater than that of any king. The big question is where Amos is to prophesy? He is sure that the word God has given him is for Israel; Amaziah did not agree! By opposing Amos, Amaziah opposes God and his punishment will be to share the fate of Israel. When the attack comes, his children will be slain and his wife forced into prostitution. His land will be shared out between the raiders and his own fate will be deportation followed by death in a foreign land!

The people of the northern kingdom would have found it easier to put their trust in the king and Amaziah than in a so-called prophet from the south. Yet history would prove Amos right. The book of Amos was retained as a reminder to the southern kingdom of Judah that the fate of Israel could be theirs.

When two voices both claim that they are acting for God, the task of discernment is never easy. It is human nature to prefer a message we want to hear over one that unsettles and challenges our complacency. The twofold role of the Church is to be both prophet, ready to speak the unpopular word, and discerner, ready to listen and act in response to God's word regardless of how unpalatable the message may be. Once again, we are faced in this passage with divine punishment that seems entirely at odds with a gospel of grace. Amaziah's fate and the fate of his family does not bear thinking about. However, there is no doubt that many others have discovered that in the midst of warfare human cruelty surfaces and horrific acts are perpetuated. We might take issue with the idea of divine retribution, but we would not dispute that such events occur when people cease to treat each other with respect and generosity.

Deuteronomy 30.9–14

This is the second part of Moses' farewell speech to the Israelites before their entry into the Promised Land. Moses reiterates his conviction that God's loving-kindness is poured out towards them and so they will prosper as people; herds and land will all be fertile. The abundance of God's gifts is his part of the covenant promise; the people's part is to keep God's law. The way to a secure future is through obedience. It is interesting to remember that the Deuteronomic editors were writing during the time of the Exile when the contrast between the future outlined by Moses and the present reality could not have been more starkly drawn. The nation had failed to turn to God wholeheartedly, so Moses' words (v.11) must have made painful reading! God's will was not a secret contained in some inaccessible heavenly realm or far-off country, they already knew it 'by heart' – they could recite it and understood its implications for faithful living. Presented simply, the people have a choice: if they obey God's commands they will receive his covenant blessing, whereas if they disobey God they risk losing what has been promised.

When the chips are down people often realize what matters most. This reading invites us, in our imaginations, to stand shoulder to shoulder with the wandering people looking into the Promised Land and share their hopes and dreams, or to put ourselves in the position of the exiled people who longed to return home. Their choice is ours. Do we choose to 'turn to God' and live faithfully, so that all may share in the abundance of divine love? The imperative is that we make that choice now!

Colossians 1.1–14

Just as Moses prayed for the people in the preceding passage, so Paul prayed for the Christians in Colossae. This is not a 'one-off' prayer, for they are part of Paul's continual prayer-life. Epaphras, their teacher, has given a good report. Faith, hope and love are the three characteristic features of the gospel and find their expression in the Colossians' faithful living. Paul gives thanks that they are part of the fruit of the rapidly spreading gospel and that they in their turn bear fruit – a reminder that the good news of Jesus is for the whole world. Then Paul intercedes for them, praying that they be enabled to discern God's will and be given the strength to live accordingly. Again, the emphasis is upon right conduct and practical ethics. It was not easy to live as a minority group in a city administered by Rome and there would be much to endure. Paul's prayer is not that life should be made easier for Christians in Colossae, rather that they should be given the moral fibre to live according to the gospel in that difficult environment. The language of light and darkness is a reminder that, although they live in a world where darkness is a reality, they have already been rescued from that world and belong to God's realm of light. Paul implies that they must therefore live accordingly because through Christ they have been forgiven and so their 'redemption', their place in the kingdom, is assured.

Few Christians would disagree that faith in Christ and ethical conduct go hand in hand. Paul prayed that the Colossians should be enabled to discern God's will. We need to pray that same prayer as Christians debate today's ethical questions that seem to become ever more complex. Is it ever morally defensible to use force against terrorists? Should gene therapy be used to ensure the health of an unborn infant? When should a life-support machine be switched off? These and many other difficult questions stretch our minds and hearts. Paul's prayer supported those for whom he prayed – and he made sure they knew he prayed for them. Do we take the task of intercessory prayer seriously? To hold people and situations before God is part of Christian ministry, for through prayer we seek to discern God's will for ourselves and for those for whom we pray. Sometimes, our prayers will urge us to take action ourselves, at other times all we can do is hold people and situations within God's love as we seek to align our minds and hearts with God's will. How does intercessory prayer 'work' if we cannot change situations through our own efforts? Perhaps that must remain a mystery, but we are assured that God does want us to pray, for prayer plays a crucial part in our relationship with him, as we share his joy and pain, hope and disappointment.

Luke 10.25–37

The parable of the Good Samaritan is only found in Luke's Gospel. It is Jesus' response to the lawyer's question about how he should inherit eternal life, seemingly asked with the hope of 'tripping Jesus up'. The lawyer, after all, was well able to find his own answer by pointing to the words of the Shema (Deut. 6.5) combined with other words from the 'Holiness Code' in Leviticus (Lev. 19.18), pointing to total commitment to God and its outworking in love for neighbour. Although the 'Holiness Code' is about right treatment of people within the community there is also a commitment to care for resident aliens (e.g. Lev. 19.10), so there is no suggestion that only people within Judaism should be treated as neighbours. Nevertheless, the lawyer presses Jesus to say who is to be treated as neighbour and there is no doubt that he would have found Jesus' parable both shocking and offensive!

Perhaps too many sermons have already been preached on this parable, offering various interpretations as to why the priest and the Levite passed by the man who had been robbed instead of highlighting the comparison between their callousness and the compassion of a rank outsider from a despised group. The comparison would not have been lost on the lawyer, who no doubt counted himself as someone of similar status to the two who passed by! Almost certainly, the lawyer, like Luke's readers, expected Jesus to say that a neighbour could even be someone like a Samaritan – and perhaps the lawyer was ready to argue against that view. To find out that the person despised embodied the ideal of neighbourliness took the wind out of his sails. He could not even bring himself to say 'The Samaritan' when asked who had behaved as neighbour to the person robbed, but muttered, 'The one who showed him mercy' (v.36). For Jesus to suggest he should follow the Samaritan's example was to rub salt into the wound. For Luke's readers, who may have been Christian converts from both Jewish and Gentile backgrounds, this parable would have added force, encouraging the former not to rely on ethical superiority while affirming the latter and challenging both groups to treat each other as neighbours.

We are all capable of callousness, especially when our 'neighbours' are radically different from ourselves. When, for example, they have cultural values that we find alien, or a lifestyle that we cannot begin to comprehend. While we know that when they are injured, like us, they will bleed, it is only too easy to forget that they feel the same emotions and so we ignore their pain. This is by far the easier option, as to acknowledge the pain of others is to recognize that we should act on their behalf.

SUNDAY BETWEEN 17 AND 23 JULY INCLUSIVE

Sixteenth Sunday in Ordinary Time

Amos 8.1–12; Genesis 18.1–10a; Colossians 1.15–28;
Luke 10.38–42

Amos 8.1–12

Amos, either in reality or in his mind's eye, sees a basket of summer fruits. God's revelation may have come in a 'vision' or as the prophet's imagination was stimulated by an everyday object. In Hebrew the word for 'summer fruit' sounds very similar to the word 'end', a pun that is not obvious in the English translation. Amos' realization is that God cannot forgive a people who are determined to keep on sinning, so the end has come for Israel. The prophet's fore-telling would come to pass in the near future with the invasion of the Assyrian army. Then the prophecy of corpses strewn around would become a reality, and there would be no more songs of praise in the Temple but only wailing and lamentation. In what way were people sinning? Rich merchants were exploiting the poor and were so con-cerned to continue trading that they had little patience with the days of rest demanded by law on the Sabbath (weekly) and at the new moon (monthly). They had certainly lost sight of the religious significance of the Sabbath which was to allow people to rest just as God rested on the seventh day of creation and to remember that God rescued them from slavery in Egypt (Exodus 20.8–11, Deut. 5.12–15). They did not even trade fairly, but falsified the scales and added chaff to the wheat! God's punishment would be as certain as their arrogance (v.7). The trembling of the land indicates both God's coming and the extent of the ensuing cosmic disaster. (There may indeed have been an eclipse of the sun at this time and this event would have remained in people's memory.) Amos has no doubt that people's selfishness and greed will mean that even the most joyous of pilgrim feasts will turn into a time of mourning when people will wear sackcloth and shave their heads in sorrow. Famine will come to the land and people will be dispersed as they wander in search of food and water.

Injustice often results in warfare that leads to famine as land is ravaged and people flee. This scenario is as familiar today as it was in Amos' time. The consequences of human greed have far-reaching effects. We are less likely than Amos to speak of God's punishment as direct divine intervention and are more likely to speak of the God who weeps for and with his people. This is because, unlike Amos, we know that Jesus was not sent into the world to become a political Messiah, who would save Israel by leading a rebellion against Rome before being crowned king. Rather Jesus, at his crucifixion, took on the pain of the world to show that God in his love has not abandoned his people. Through Jesus, God calls people to change their ways so that greed and power-seeking cease to be the motivation for their actions. God does not wage war against us and forcibly impose his will, instead God longs for us to turn mourning into joy by rejecting the greed that leads to war.

Genesis 18.1–10a

A visitation narrative describes three divine beings appearing to Abraham. Were all three to be identified with God? Was God accompanied by two angels? Were all three angels? The identity of the strangers will always be clouded in mystery, but the writer is in no doubt that, 'The Lord appeared to Abraham' (v.1). Although later Christian writers identified the visitors as the three persons of the Trinity, this was certainly not in the mind of the Old Testament writer!

Abraham, the nomad, has pitched camp under the terebinths (small trees) of Mamre, near Hebron, a place that would become a sanctuary and a famous site for pilgrimage. Abraham is sitting at the door of his tent at midday, the time of rest, when the strangers 'appear' and Abraham offers them hospitality that goes far beyond his original offer of bread and water. Abraham and Sarah divide the work according to custom. Sarah bakes, while Abraham slaughters a calf for the servant to cook. This is no light repast, but a meal fit for God! The idea of God, or indeed of angelic beings, requiring food, drink and the opportunity for 'refreshment' falls uneasily on modern ears. However, these ancient stories often portrayed God in anthropomorphic (human) terms and in this way the encounter with the divine is both mysterious and accessible. Abraham does not share their meal, but stands and watches, presumably to ensure all their needs are met. Before they leave, the visitors respond to the desire of Abraham's heart by promising that Sarah will have a son. Because Sarah is beyond childbearing age, she laughs in disbelief.

Preachers have often responded to this passage by preaching about the importance of hospitality. Another suggestion might be to explore the mystery of the 'God of Surprises' whom we encounter in unexpected places and through unexpected people. This is the God who already knows our deepest longings.

Colossians 1.15–28

The great 'Hymn to Christ' (vv. 15–20) has been the subject of much scholarly study. It has been suggested that the hymn may be a reworking of earlier pre-Christian material, with language reminiscent of that used in both Greek and Jewish cultures. The hymn is both a song of praise and a statement of belief (like the hymns of Charles Wesley many years later!) and would have been sung during worship. The writer of Colossians was concerned to show how the death of Christ had broken down the barrier of sin, so that all people and indeed the whole cosmos could be 'reconciled' to God. Even though the work of cosmic reconciliation is not yet complete, sin no longer stands between believers and God. It is Christ who shows us the nature of the creator God (vv. 15–17): human beings cannot comprehend the nature of the God who created the cosmos, but God's nature became 'knowable', fully accessible in Christ (v.19) and especially in his death. (It is important not to assume that this hymn points to the pre-existence of Christ. It is God's creative nature, also described as Wisdom (e.g. Proverbs 3.19–20, Sirach 1.1–4) and Word (John 1.1–3), that is present in Christ.) In the words of Graham Kendrick's hymn, the divine Wisdom and Word that 'flung stars into space' can be known in Christ who died. This Christ is the head of the Church. By following him steadfastly, Christians are caught up in a way of life that has cosmic implications! Peace, in this context, refers to the harmony of God's creation, reflected in people's respect for God, for each other and for the universe itself. Christ's death was not an end but the beginning of new life, available to all who, like Paul, lived faithfully. For Paul, faithful living involved suffering, although the nature of Paul's suffering is not spelt out (v.34). Nevertheless, the idea of one person suffering for others is indeed the way of self-giving love seen on the cross, and this is the way of life Paul embraced. His commission was to bring the gospel of Christ to the Gentiles. The 'mystery' (v.27) was that God's people now included not only Jews, but also those from the pagan world who put their faith in Christ. In this way, both Jew and Greek were reconciled and differences were broken down. God's glory is seen in the new respect accorded to each other by people from different ethnic backgrounds who once would have considered each other to be inferior to themselves. In such relationships, people show the wisdom of Christ.

Bishop Desmond Tutu, as a black South African, had experienced the extremes of white racism at first hand. Nevertheless, he knew that reconciliation in South Africa could only take place once people acknowledged the atrocities that had taken place, on both sides, during the years of apartheid. It is only when alienation caused by sin is recognized that forgiveness becomes possible, as only sin that is given a name can be owned. People who care about each other's welfare will not allow the greed of a few to destroy the earth's resources. Ecologists remind us that cutting down forests may deprive others of clean water and therefore of food. Warfare too renders land barren. Reconciliation between people and God does indeed have implications for the created order!

Luke 10.38–42

This is the well-known account of Martha and Mary. It is easy to feel sympathy for Martha; after all, she is doing her best to make sure all the tasks are done, while Mary seems to be shirking! However, this is to misunderstand the force of the story. Martha is distracted by her ministry! Unfortunately, this is true of many Christians, not just those who are ordained. It is only too easy to be caught up in the needs of others. Mary listens to Jesus' word and this is essential, the 'one necessary thing' (v.42). Not only does it lead to wholehearted commitment, but ensures that she remains focused on Jesus.

Those who prepare for visitors may dust the house and prepare food before they come, but what matters most is that time is spent together. Sometimes our busyness and constant activity prevents us spending time with family and friends, let alone with God! To take time to 'sit at Jesus' feet' may help us to realize what matters most and enable us to minister more effectively.

It is interesting that Martha's activity and desire to serve Jesus put a barrier between herself and Mary. Those married to clergy have been heard to complain that the minister is so busy serving God that there is no time left for family life. Some spouses have even been asked if they are also married to the Church! Having time for God also means having time for those nearest to us. There is often tension between making sure the house is dusted and spending time in 'frivolous' ways. Yet, it is when we play games with our children, do the crossword puzzle with our husband or wife, or go for a walk with a friend for pleasure that bonds are formed as we enjoy each other's company. After all, Jesus found time to spend with friends!

SUNDAY BETWEEN 24 AND 30 JULY INCLUSIVE

Seventeenth Sunday in Ordinary Time

Hosea 1.2–10; Genesis 18.20–32; Colossians 2.6–15 (16–19);
Luke 11.1–13

Hosea 1.2–10

Hosea prophesied in the northern kingdom, known as Israel or
Ephraim, in the eighth century BCE. In obedience to God's command,
he married a prostitute as an enacted prophecy signifying God's constant love for an unfaithful people. It is important not to approach this
passage as biography, for its significance lies in symbolic meaning.
God's love had been strained to breaking point: Canaanite religion
was a fertility cult and hill-shrines were places where sexual acts took
place as a kind of 'sympathetic magic' to encourage the gods in their
task of bringing fertility. Men would have sexual relations with
temple prostitutes or women devotees who, in their devotion to Baal,
also made themselves available to male worshippers. God spoke to
Israel through the prophet's marriage to Gomer, who was probably a
temple prostitute, and when Hosea's children were born they were
given symbolic names. The first child was named after Jezreel, a city
set in a fertile valley. Jezreel was the place where King Jehu had
slaughtered those who opposed his kingship. Hosea, by naming his
child Jezreel, is indicating that the people of Israel will be wiped out
in the same way. His prophecy was to be proved correct, as in the near
future Israel would be invaded by Assyrian armies. The second child
was named Lo-ruhamah, which means 'Not pitied'. Such a name was
scandalous as it was the task of parents to care for their children, just
as it was the task of the strong to care for the weak, the rich for the
poor. The people, by failing to care for the weakest and most needy
members of society, were placing themselves beyond God's compassion. The third child was named Lo-ammi, which means 'Not my
people', showing that the covenant relationship had been broken and
judgement was inevitable. Yet as the book unfolds it becomes clear
that Hosea's conviction that God would never abandon his people is
unshaken.

Do we believe in a God who destroys a nation as punishment, or do
unjust regimes sow the seeds of their own destruction? Hosea knew
that the people deserved to be destroyed, yet believed that God's
mercy would prevail. With God, justice and compassion go hand in

hand. There are times when justice demands that those who have committed crimes are tried and punished; for example, persistent burglars cannot be allowed to prey upon other innocent people. Yet compassion would also suggest that those who commit such acts need help to become responsible people whom society will accept. However, not all are willing or able to receive such help and have every intention of continuing to offend. This raises questions about how justice and compassion should be balanced. Clearly, we can be both judgemental and compassionate. Which of these should take precedence and under what circumstances? Perhaps this is a question a house group might like to debate!

Genesis 18.20–32

The three strangers who visited Abraham represent the presence of God, who can be in more than one place at the same time. Thus, God can remain with Abraham, while also travelling on. God tells Abraham that there has been an 'outcry' against Sodom and Gomorrah. The word 'outcry' is a legal term for the cry for help from those who have suffered great injustice. In the ensuing 'courtroom conversation' Abraham acts as defending barrister. Abraham stands on the eastern hillside of Hebron overlooking the city of Sodom, whose people have no idea that he is about to plead for them. Abraham and God are debating the fate of the city and whether it depends upon the majority's wicked actions or upon the innocence of a few. Lying behind this debate is a deeper theological question about God's righteousness and whether God's will to save overrides deserved punishment. Abraham's compassion for the innocent leads him to challenge God's justice (v.25) and he presses his point until God agrees that if only ten innocent people remain the city will be saved. Would God have saved the city for the sake of just one innocent person? It is tempting to suggest that this question was only finally answered in Christ. However, it could be argued that the narrator deliberately leaves the question open-ended to encourage the reader to enter the discussion.

Christians believe that forgiveness lies at the heart of God's justice. However, to speak of forgiveness to innocent sufferers is no easy task. Those whose loved ones have died or been maimed as the result of a terrorist bombing for example, may find the idea of forgiving the perpetrators abhorrent! It is our task to care for them, rather than to press them to forgive while anger and grief are raw. Forgiveness may be a long-term process rather than a 'one-off' act. Those who preach about forgiveness must be careful not to add to people's suffering by making them feel guilty. Nevertheless, forgiveness does overcome destructive emotions such as bitterness and the desire for revenge that can prevent people from letting go of hurts and moving on.

Colossians 2.6–15 (16–19)

Christian faith is rooted in Christ and not in any other teaching, whether Jewish or pagan. It is probable that the 'philosophy' of v.8 refers to a pagan idea: that the created, material world was evil and that the heavenly realm was 'spiritual'. This would explain why the letter emphasizes that in Christ, God 'dwells bodily'. In contrast, circumcision for Jewish males was the outward, bodily sign of belonging to God's people. For Christians, entry into God's people was through baptism, not by initiation into pagan philosophy or through circumcision. Just as Jesus lived and died, identifying himself with sinful humanity, so like him believers are also able to pass through death, signified by the waters of baptism, to the new life God offers. It is sin that separates people from God, and baptized people are forgiven, enabled to strip off all their old ways. Neither pagan initiation, nor Jewish circumcision enabled forgiveness. The record of sin (v.14) was nailed to the cross in the person of Jesus. The spectacle of a man hanging from a cross would have been shameful, but Jesus' death is described as a triumph: he 'disarms', that is 'makes captive', the Roman authorities, representing the power of sin, who had ordered his crucifixion (v.15). The image is of a triumphal procession in which captives were led through the streets as people rejoiced in military victory. Jesus' victory is over sin and as baptized, forgiven people Christians are enabled to live a new life.

Verses 16–19 describe some of the practices in which Colossian Christians were engaged: they may have been blending Jewish and pagan religious practices together in ascetic mysticism. The rites they had been observing must cease, because only by looking to Christ as the head of the Church will the body hold together.

The image of 'stripping off the old self' (v.9) is startling as Christians know that they are as prone to sin as anyone else. Yet baptism is the outward sign both of commitment to Christ, who offers forgiveness, and of God's grace demonstrated in the raising of Jesus. Christians are offered that same grace to enable them to live faithfully. It may sometimes seem like taking two steps forward and one step backwards, but the important thing is that we are part of the procession that triumphs over sin!

Luke 11.1–13

The life of the disciples, like that of Jesus, must be rooted in prayer. 'The Lord's Prayer' has been used in public and private devotions since the time of Jesus and it is always helpful to reflect on its meaning. Luke's version is made up of five short requests. However, while members of a house group might profit from discussing each in turn, this may not be the most stimulating format for a sermon! It may be more profitable to emphasize that the life of prayer begins with the awe and wonder of those who glimpse God's holy nature and who, as they seek to place their own lives under his rule, long that their experience should be universal. God's kingdom life must involve the nourishment of all and 'bread' may refer not only to the sustenance for the body so that famine is ended and all have sufficient for each day (not hoarding more than they need while others starve), but also to eucharistic bread that nourishes a forgiven people who in turn must forgive others. The link between sin and debt has particular relevance in relation to the rich/poor divide. Selfishness and greed are often at the root of sin, so to forgive debt is both to restore people to their rightful place in God's economic order and also to ensure that generosity rather than greed is the motive of God's kingdom people. (We may like to remind ourselves that it is often easier for people to forgive others who have insulted them or treated them badly than to absolve them from paying what they owe. When 'forgiveness' hits our pockets, we discover just how lacking we are in generosity!) For Jesus, the time of trial meant facing the cross, but the cross was the way to kingdom life. It was no easy task for Christians to live faithfully in the Roman world, but 'the time of trial' may also refer to the expectation that cataclysmic events would pre-empt the final breaking-in of God's kingdom rule.

The teaching about prayer is followed by the parable 'The Friend at Midnight'. The imperative for Christians is to offer generous hospitality no matter how inconvenient. However, if we are honest, this is not something we do easily. While we are prepared to open our doors to our friends, few people would take in a homeless person or an asylum seeker. It is easy to say that this is because we would not be prepared to put our families at risk. However, there are agencies that recommend people for placement in people's homes so that risk can be minimized. Even then, we do not want the pattern of our lives to be disrupted by strangers. While human frailty might respond grudgingly to a persistent request, God's generosity is like that of a loving parent, who will never cease to offer nourishment to his children. God's gift is the Holy Spirit, his presence with disciples at all times. What is more, God's gift is freely available to all who ask.

SUNDAY BETWEEN 31 JULY AND 6 AUGUST INCLUSIVE

Eighteenth Sunday in Ordinary Time

Hosea 11.1–11; Ecclesiastes 1.2,12–14, 2.18–23; Colossians 3.1–11;
Luke 12.13–21

Hosea 11.1–11

The infinite tenderness in these verses make it one of the best-loved passages in Scripture. In some cults, the people were thought to be the progeny of the god, but Israel (Ephraim) is portrayed as the child God came to love and chose to be his son. The story of God's fatherly relationship with his rebellious child emphasizes his faithfulness and patience. From the moment God rescued Israel from slavery in Egypt his commitment to Israel never faltered and his love was never exhausted, regardless of his child's wilful disobedience. The tender nurturing of the child (vv. 3–4) is a reminder that when Israel faced starvation in the wilderness, God 'bent down' to feed his people with manna. Now, fully grown, Israel faces peril again as the Assyrian army musters on the borders of the land. Yet, Israel does not turn to the father who can save his child from annihilation, but to another god who is unable to offer salvation. God's agony is immense as he teeters on the brink of destroying his beloved child. In Deuteronomy the punishment for a rebellious son was death by stoning (13.6–11, 20.18–21), although it is by no means certain that such a punishment was ever carried out, but God is not a human father – he is God – and will not abandon Israel!

It may be that this passage reflects later interpretation of earlier material. The Assyrian armies did invade in 733 BCE and the northern kingdom fell. At that time, it would have seemed that God had indeed punished Israel. Perhaps the hope that pervades this passage comes from a later hand as indicated by verses 10 and 11.

People's experience of fatherhood varies and those who have suffered at the hands of authoritarian or abusive fathers may not respond easily to this reading. It is essential that this is stated within the context of worship. Yet God cannot be compared with any human father, for even the most loving of parents will struggle to know when to chastise a child and when to offer comfort and will sometimes make mistakes. Hosea reminds us that God is God (v.9) not a human father and, unlike us, is able to balance justice and loving-kindness. We can be sure that God will nurture all who turn to him and is ready to forgive and help his children to start again. Nevertheless, the reading does remind us that we are accountable to God for our attitudes and actions.

Ecclesiastes 1.2, 12–14, 2.18–23

What a depressing reading! The writer is suggesting that all human enterprises are worthless. The word translated 'vanity' literally means 'breath' or 'breeze', but is always used as a metaphor for what is useless, fleeting or insubstantial. No fruit of human labour is worth the effort! Even a king as great as Solomon, into whose mouth the writer places the words beginning at verse 12, has achieved nothing of any worth. The first readers would have found this a shocking thought for Solomon was revered as one of the greatest of Israel's rulers. After all, God had given Solomon not only wisdom but also great wealth. Yet, Solomon was never contented. What chance do ordinary people have of finding happiness? All people's efforts to achieve satisfaction for themselves seem futile; they are 'chasing after wind'! (v.14)

There is another reason for Solomon's disillusionment: when he dies his wisdom will be forgotten and all his possessions will be frittered away by his heirs. He can do nothing about this, so he resigns himself to a situation he cannot change and simply gives up. Those who have worked hard for their wealth do not like to think of it being wasted when they die. Sometimes, after a death, possessions were appropriated by those in positions of power, leaving family members dispossessed. The king was discovering something his subjects too often had to face. Anyone who is driven by worldly ambition and the pursuit of material goods will be burdened by constant worry and will be unable to sleep at night (v.23).

In our society, many people work long hours, some receiving huge salaries, others the minimum wage. High expectations about lifestyle and possessions create anxiety leading to many stress-related illnesses. Ecclesiastes may indeed make depressing reading, but it also challenges us to take stock and consider whether all our striving is futile, or whether our efforts and our use of our material resources could be better directed.

Colossians 3.1–11

Ethical teaching is offered within the context of baptism. Just as Jesus died and was raised, so believers are called to 'die to sin' and 'rise to new life'. The difficulty is that even those who have been baptized are still subject to temptation and continue to sin. Their sin has to do with long-held prejudices, relating to race, culture and social standing (v.11)! Although they still live on earth – and live within a social framework – they must keep their eyes on heaven (v.2). Their life is rooted in Christ and must reflect 'heavenly life'. Presumably, God's way of life enables people from different backgrounds to live in right relationship both with God and with each other, a way of life that remains 'hidden' and will not become fully accessible until people live in mutual respect and concern for each other's welfare. The list of vices concerns sexual sins that may have been characteristic of pagan practices leading to the exploitation of others. Similarly, the abusive way of speaking to and about others was rooted in anger against those different from themselves. Inevitably, such attitudes were destructive to the forming of good personal relationships.

This passage offers a timely reminder that stripping off the old ways of treating and regarding others is an ongoing task for baptized people. While, in one sense, entering the waters of baptism is a 'dying to sin', in another sense it is a commitment to continue to root out all that runs contrary to the life of Christ. God's longing is that all people should turn to him and this is the hope mirrored by parents and those who bring infants to be baptized. Baptism has to do with a continuing commitment to live in right relationship with God and with other people, it is not simply a 'one-off' event, but has implications for Christian living, and those baptized as infants have the opportunity to confirm the promises made at their baptisms. Confirmation services should be occasions of great joy, as people recognize and share the hopes and dreams of those who brought them to God soon after they were born. Baptized people are called to live within society as those who have their feet on earth and their eyes on heaven as they try to reflect the divine life in an imperfect world! This means that Christians must not collude with the abuse or exploitation of others, even by remaining silent, but must challenge those whose speech or behaviour is governed by prejudice.

Luke 12.13–21

Like the reading from Ecclesiastes, this passage is about the futility of pursuing wealth. Jesus, in his role of respected teacher, was asked to arbitrate in a family dispute over the division of an inheritance. It would seem that one brother's greed had left the others with nothing. People today still argue about the contents of wills, and greed can often destroy relationships between family members who believe they have been treated unfairly. The saying, 'Where there is a will, there is a relative!' may make us smile, but is, unfortunately, all too true. Wrangling over the possessions of a loved one causes untold misery in countless families as items of both material and sentimental value are disbursed. Jesus, however, refuses to take sides by colluding with the questioner. Instead, he responds by echoing Moses' words when he asks, 'Who set me to be a judge over you?' (v.14 cf. Exodus 2.14). Once again, Luke is leaving the reader to answer that Jesus' authority, like that of Moses, came from God.

One of Luke's constant concerns is the proper use of wealth. The wealthy often have more than they need while the poor struggle for survival. Greed must not be the motivation for acquisition of possessions. By ensuring that provisions are stored for the future, the rich man may seem to be acting responsibly and, after all, to enjoy eating and drinking well is to appreciate the good things God provides for his people! However, God arrives on the scene as a character in the unfolding drama and tells the rich man that he is a fool. All his energy has been focused on the accumulation of possessions and his single-mindedness has driven out any thought of God. God's wisdom was a way of describing the outpouring of God's creative energy; and, in creation, God's wisdom has provided enough for everyone. In contrast, the rich man's selfishness has ruled his actions and he has provided only for himself. His death will prevent him from enjoying the fruit of his labours as he has been storing up the wrong kind of treasure! It is implied that the right kind of treasure is generosity of heart that reflects God's own nature and will enable the rich man to participate in the 'heavenly life' described in the passage from Colossians above.

We need only open the gossip page in a tabloid newspaper to realize that many rich 'celebrities' lead unhappy lives. However, it would be simplistic to suggest that money does not matter as those who struggle with debt or find it hard to make ends meet will testify. The parable speaks to people who have more than they need and who are challenged to use their wealth so that others will benefit from their generosity. How many churches have money stored up rather than putting it to good use now? Church councils must be good stewards making sensible provision for the future, but their decision-making about the use of resources must also reflect God's generosity. This reading also challenges individual Christians to consider their relationship to their own wealth. Do we have more than we need? Do we cling to our possessions for comfort and security? Perhaps we need space to reflect prayerfully about those items we hold most dear and consider whether we would be prepared to let them go in Christ's service.

SUNDAY BETWEEN 7 AND 13 AUGUST INCLUSIVE

Nineteenth Sunday in Ordinary Time

Isaiah 1.1,10–20; Genesis 15.1–6; Hebrews 11.1–3, 8–16; Luke 12.32–40

Isaiah 1.1, 10–20

Isaiah prophesied in Jerusalem, the site of the Temple, in the eighth century BCE. This passage has often been used to suggest that the sacrificial system had always been against God's will. However, this is to misunderstand the words of the prophet. The thrust of his message is that devotional acts by those who continue to perpetrate injustice are unacceptable to God. The scene is that of a courtroom with God arguing his own case for the prosecution. Empty worship is an abomination to God, whatever form that worship takes: no matter how expensive their sacrifices, how often they burn incense, how enthusiastically they celebrate at festival times or how often they stretch out their hands in prayer. Those same hands are stained with the blood of the innocent! The removal of sin was the purpose of sacrificial worship, yet the sacrifices described here are peace offerings when the worshipper would host a meal at which the meat would be eaten and the priests would be given a share. Just as the meal would be a social occasion, so were the festivals and both would be characterized by exuberant self-indulgence! Having made the indictment, God demands that they wash away their blood-guilt. This can be done by acting on the realization that the essential sacrifice involves caring for the destitute. Orphans and widows were people who had no property or financial security. They were dependent upon the charity of relations and had no social standing. They were amongst the most oppressed people and suffered because of the structure of a patriarchal society, in which authority and possessions were handed down through the male line.

Few sermons are preached about 'institutional' sin. However, there is no doubt that injustice is perpetuated through the structures of society when those who earn high salaries and are able to indulge themselves refuse to consider structural reforms that would adversely affect their own lifestyles. The Church must be ready to challenge powerful institutions. Conversations with those who work within, for example, business and commerce or local and national government, will enable Christians to become better informed and prepare them to mount a challenge. The reading also confronts us at a personal level. Do we worship solely for our own benefit, or to fit ourselves for the task of ministry?

Genesis 15.1–6

God comes to Abraham in a vision. Any encounter with God would be a terrifying experience as the words, 'Do not be afraid' suggest. However, Abraham is already so overwhelmed by his own trouble that he cannot imagine that even a meeting with God will be able to help him! Abraham seems to be thinking about his own death and is depressed because he has no children and therefore no heir. It was usual for a childless man to adopt a trusted slave, who would inherit. Eliezer's task as adopted son would be to bury Abraham, who is already contemplating his own grave. It is no wonder that he cannot imagine how God will be his shield, after all his death is certain, so he is hardly in need of protection. Nor can he imagine that the conversation with God will profit him in any way. Outside the tent God shows Abraham the stars. He gazes at them and believes God's promise that his descendants, like the stars will be beyond number. Such trust is remarkable as God was asking him to believe the impossible! Abraham's belief was 'reckoned to him as righteousness' (v.6). 'Righteousness' in this context is both about Abraham's conviction that God is faithful and will keep his promises and also about Abraham's willingness to live obediently in accordance with that conviction.

This reading challenges us in a number of ways. Perhaps one of the hardest tasks a person has to face involves preparing for death. Many people find comfort in the thought that their children and grand-children will continue the family line, inheriting some of their genes and therefore some of their own characteristics. This is about 'living on in those we leave behind'. Yet, many people have no children and have to seek meaning for their lives in other ways. In this passage, God answers the prayer of Abraham's heart, but this does not always reflect our own experience and raises questions about how we encounter God and what kind of promises God makes today. Those, who like Abraham are childless, may seek IVF treatment rather than relying solely on prayer! Some may find that, when they reach their lowest ebb, they are ready to meet the God who feels their pain. Others may experience only the seeming absence of God. However, the biblical stories remind us that God remains faithful, does not abandon us and will lead us from despair to hope. Perhaps we discover the true meaning for our lives when we trust in a loving God. It is when we share in God's loving purposes, by treating others with the kindness and faithfulness God shows to us, that we grow to maturity and prepare ourselves to be caught up in his eternal life and love.

Hebrews 11.1–3, 8–16

The writer of Hebrews refers to the story of Abraham in the reading above (Genesis 15.1–6) to speak about faith. Faith is possible because the God who kept his promises to Abraham and Sarah in the past will continue to be faithful in the future. In other words, God can be trusted. The passage is not about what faith is, but about what faith does: it brings hope as there is a good reason to believe that God's promises will be kept. Even though God is unseen, he can be known through his creation because the universe is visible. Abraham becomes the archetypal example of a person of faith. At the time when God promised Abraham and Sarah that they would have countless descendants, they were nomadic people, even though they were already living in the land their children would inhabit. This is how Christians were feeling, like strangers living in a foreign land. They were trying to live as those who had faith in Christ within the alien culture of Roman paganism. Yet, Abraham's real home was not in Canaan, any more than theirs was within the Roman world. Like Abraham, those Christians were citizens of God's city. The foundations of God's building would be permanent, not like the tents of nomads, or any other structure built by human hands. It was through faith that Abraham and Sarah were able to become parents, ancestors of the nation. Those beyond childbearing age were considered to be 'as good as dead', written off because of their inability to conceive. Their descendants show the same faith in God and recognize that even though they may feel like landless nomads on earth, their faith is preparing them to live in God's heavenly city.

It is much easier for human beings to put their trust in what can be seen and touched. The security of a healthy bank balance and the certainty of a roof over people's heads are not to be sneezed at! However, many people in the world have no material security and no home to call their own. The passage from Hebrews does not suggest that these things do not matter! Those who live as 'citizens of heaven' have faith in God whose deepest concern is the welfare of all his children. To prepare for life in God's city is to show that same commitment to others. God did not write off two elderly people and consider them 'as good as dead'. It is unfortunate that 'ageism' is becoming increasingly prevalent in today's society. Skilled, experienced people are being overlooked by employers who prefer to offer jobs to younger colleagues. God's city exists wherever people are nurtured, valued and respected. Attitudes towards the elderly are becoming increasingly disrespectful, as older members of society are considered to have little to contribute, but are thought of as 'burdens' and 'problems' as the difficulty of caring for those who are frail increases. Surely, these are attitudes the Church must challenge.

Luke 12.32–40

Like the others, this reading is about what it means to live in obedient faith. What does it mean to have confidence in God's care? Is it that God will provide for all physical needs, or that God will enable people to take their place within the life of the kingdom? The little flock refers to the small Christian Church. God is the Father and so they belong to him and have a place within his kingdom. This means that they must live out that kingdom life by sharing what they have rather than storing up material security. Those who are wealthy have to work out what this means for them! The two short parables that follow ask what it means to be ready. Those who lived in the early days following Christ's death and resurrection expected his imminent return. By the time Luke writes, that immediate expectation has faded, yet Luke is convinced that Christians should live in the present as those who are prepared for Christ to knock on the door now. They are amongst those who will sit at the wedding banquet of the kingdom as roles are reversed and the master waits on his servants! It is implied that these servants already know what it is to minister to others.

The second story is a reminder that a thief always arrives unexpectedly and similarly the Son of Man's return will be unheralded. Perhaps Christians were beginning to doubt whether Jesus would return at all and two thousand years further on, few Christians share the expectations of the earliest believers.

The Son of Man is the title of Jesus that best expresses his involvement with suffering humanity. To live in obedient faith must mean that Christians must care about, minister to and act as advocates for those who suffer in this life. Readiness to enter God's kingdom is to put our trust in Christ-like attitudes and actions, so that our security lies not in outward possessions but in our inward qualities, in other words the kind of people that with God's help we can become.

SUNDAY BETWEEN 14 AND 20 AUGUST INCLUSIVE

Twentieth Sunday in Ordinary Time

Isaiah 5.1–7; Jeremiah 23.23–29; Hebrews 11.29–12.2;
Luke 12.49–56

Isaiah 5.1–7

'The Song of the Vineyard' is an oracle of judgement written in the style of songs sung at the time of the autumn grape harvest. The vineyard stands for the nation cultivated by God. This may be a reworking of an existing love song as God is described as his beloved. There is poignancy in the disappointment of God who laboured so hard to nurture his people. The farmer did everything possible to care for the vines. He tackled the back-breaking work as ground was prepared, a watch-tower was built to guard against thieves, the wine vat for crushing the grapes was hewn from bedrock and hedges and walls were constructed to keep out wild animals. The cost was great, as the farmer invested money, effort and time, but the vineyard only yielded sour, decaying fruit: 'wild' grapes. God takes over from the prophet in narrating the story, a story that is no longer about a farmer and his vineyard, but refers to God and his disobedient people as he asks, 'What should the farmer do?' This is of course a rhetorical question: the people are being invited to judge themselves! God will not simply walk away from Israel, as a farmer might walk away from an unproductive vineyard. Israel must be punished and so the farmer systematically tears down all he had provided for the cultivation of the grapes and allows the briars and thorns to grow over the vineyard, which is left without even the benefit of the rain. For God is the one who controls the weather and life itself. For any who have failed to understand the metaphor the last verse spells out the meaning of the song: the nation is the vineyard, the people are those who have failed to act justly and so God has had no choice but to act.

To read the song is to share in the bitter disappointment of God who has done everything possible to nurture his people. They have perpetuated social injustice described in terms of rotting, putrid fruit. What then would be the analogy for ripe, luscious fruit? Presumably the commitment to care for every member of society. According to Isaiah, God was left with no choice but to act against an unjust people. Yet, our experience is often that those who perpetuate injustice prosper and God does not seem to act. However, as we read and respond to this passage God is acting by challenging us to be those who work to make a more just society.

Jeremiah 23.23–29

This passage speaks about God and about prophecy. The question raised is whether God is nearby or far off. How are the terms 'far off' and 'nearby' to be understood? Is the God who is 'far off' the creator of the universe, and the God who is 'nearby' the one who is intimately involved in every tiny aspect of creation? These two ways of describing God are not mutually exclusive but complementary! However, the reading is about the integrity of prophets. The one who is 'nearby' can observe the prophets and hear what they are saying. Yet, conversely, the God who is 'far off' sees the big picture and is not blinkered by parochial and maybe petty concerns. It is worth noting that God asks the question. Is God hoping that the people will answer that he is not like other gods who may seem to be more accessible? It was usual for worshippers to try to bargain with local deities to influence their decisions and actions, but it is not possible to bargain with God. Similarly, it was possible to hide from the local deities who were 'nearby', whereas no thought or action could be hidden from God who is always present. The contrast may also be drawn between the ancient God who is 'far off' because he is the God of Israel's past, and the new deities of the local cults. Prophets are those who should speak God's word. However, although God was on the lips of false prophets, their actions belied their words. In salvation and judgement, God is near to those who are unjustly treated and far from those who seek power to oppress the weak. Dreams were one way in which God revealed himself to his prophets. Yet, some prophets seemed to be claiming falsely that they had received divine communication and told lies in order to promote their own social standing and power base. The lies of the false prophets are like chaff that will blow away in the wind. The words of a true prophet have weight that offers nourishment like a bag of wheat. Similarly, God's word is like fire, or like a hammer wielded to break rock: the false prophets will not be able to hide from God's judgement.

It is the preacher's task to help people recognize the 'otherness' or 'hiddenness' of God who is beyond human understanding, while also affirming that God is the one from whom nothing can be hidden, not because God acts as 'big brother', but because God cares about every aspect of creation and every individual. God's word challenges all that is false and self-seeking, and requires people to make a new commitment, to change their ways and be prepared to act.

Hebrews 11.29–12.2

We do not know what opposition this Christian community faced, but the writer of Hebrews pulls out all stops to encourage a frightened group of Christians to have faith in the face of adversity. He reminds them that the Israelites were also fearful when they stood on the shores of the Red Sea and a return to Egypt seemed the safer option. Nevertheless, they managed the crossing and they found their faith as they faced their fear. All the great achievements of the past occurred when people acted in this way. The writer piles up names as he cites great figures from the past as role models. Those who received the reward for their faithfulness in this life are contrasted with the martyrs, for whom resurrection life lay beyond earthly existence. For example, the sons of the widow of Zarephath and the Shunnamite woman were restored to life (1 Kings 17.17–25, 2 Kings 4.18–37), and others faced martyrdom at the time of the Maccabean revolt (v.35). Examples of extreme persecution follow hard on each other's heels. The readers would have understood the allusions. For example, legend suggested that Isaiah was sawn in two by King Manasseh! The long list of sufferings ends with the words, 'The world was not worthy of them' (v.38), and this includes and commends those who follow their example. The wilderness was the place where people met God and were protected by God, but it was not an easy place to be. Not all the 'wilderness people' received the promise of land and justice in this life, but were promised that they would receive 'something better' (v.39) as they would join Jesus in the heavenly realm (12.2). The great figures of the past watch to see how Christians will respond in the present. 'Sin' refers to all that prevents them from standing firm in their faith no matter what opposition they face. Jesus has demonstrated what faith is about! He has gone before them and faced the cross, the most shameful of deaths, but now shares God's reign.

Role models are a feature of society, but who do we choose as our role models? This reading reminds us not only of the great figures from Scriptures, but also of those 'saints in light' whom we have loved and who guided us. It is helpful if preachers allow a period of silence within worship for people to recall and give thanks for those dear to them. When we give thanks for the lives of our loved ones, we recommit ourselves to becoming the people they hoped we would be. In this way, we also recommit ourselves to following in the way of Jesus who faced the cross so that we might share the life God offers.

Luke 12.49–56

Jesus came to earth not to leave everything the same, but to change things! That process involves both the cleansing and the judgement that are described as fire. Fire can burn and destroy rubbish and so is able to purify what was rank and evil-smelling with the potential for spreading disease. In baptism, people are both washed clean and pre-pared for what is to come. The imperative for change inevitably brings division. The Christians of the early church experienced conflict as their commitment to Christ placed them on a collision course within society and often within their own families. When a member of either a Jewish or a Gentile family was converted to Christianity, this would have been greeted with horror and for similar reasons. For Jews who believed in one God, Christianity appeared to be a threat to monotheism, and for Gentiles who believed in many gods, Christianity would have appeared to be atheism! Such conflict was inevitable and Jesus did not turn away from it, but recognized its inevitability (v.50). The crowds who listened to Jesus could read the weather, but not the signs of the times. This is a reference to the apocalyptic expectation that troubles would precede the moment when God would act decisively in human history. For Christians that time had begun with the coming of Jesus. Luke records that Jesus called the people hypocrites. This was a reminder that they knew what God expected of them, but preferred to turn a blind eye, or ignore God's will in the present. Jesus is the one who challenges people to respond immediately, for the time to change is not at some unspeci-fied moment in the future, but straight away.

Christians tend to think of themselves as peacemakers, but we must be prepared to engage in conflict when 'kingdom values' are flouted. The reading is about nothing less than the judgement of the world and its future! Would Jesus call us hypocrites when we fail to confront unjust regimes and ignore the environmental threat caused by life-styles we share? On a smaller scale, are we prepared to face conflict when it affects us personally: in church, at work and in our homes? Conflict can be creative, but it can also be destructive. An interesting topic for discussion groups is, 'Should Christians ever be involved in destructive conflict?'

SUNDAY BETWEEN 21 AND 27 AUGUST INCLUSIVE

Twenty-first Sunday in Ordinary Time

Jeremiah 1.4–10; Isaiah 58.9b–14; Hebrews 12.18–29; Luke 13.10–17

Jeremiah 1.4–10

Jeremiah was 'called' by God to the task of prophecy. We are not told how the Lord's word came to him (v.4) only that it did! Those today, who struggle to determine what God's will is for them, may envy Jeremiah's certainty. Jeremiah was convinced that God was commissioning him to tell the people what God wanted them to hear. He felt that he had been born for this task; it was his reason to exist. This raises questions about whether people are destined to take on particular roles. Some people are fortunate enough to find a role in life that 'feels right', and we have heard comments like, 'She is a born teacher.' In Jeremiah's case, his conviction that he was called to be a prophet did not prevent him from feeling daunted by the task, for he is to become a prophet to the nations. What a mammoth task! Jeremiah lived at a time when foreign nations would exercise control over Israel and its future and Jeremiah would become involved at an international level! It is not surprising that Jeremiah protested that this was beyond his capabilities; after all, he was young, probably still a teenager! In an image that is both tender and reassuring, God stretched out his hand and touched his mouth (v.9) and Jeremiah received his prophetic authority. His commission is spelt out in verse 10: he is the one who will both destroy and rebuild. This is indeed what Jeremiah will do. In the years before the fall of Jerusalem in 586 BCE he became known (unfairly) as a prophet of doom as he warned of the destruction to come, yet once the Exile to Babylon happened he encouraged a despairing people and promised divine forgiveness and restoration.

The Church's role is also a dual one. Christians are called both to challenge injustice at every level in society and to offer reassurance that forgiveness and a new beginning is always possible with God. Jeremiah spoke God's word in his own time and we must do the same. Sometimes it is easy to know God's will, at other times issues are not clear-cut. The Church must face difficult issues, debate them, pray about them and seek to respond. As we try to discern God's will we must not claim, falsely, that we are the special recipients of divine knowledge we do not have!

Isaiah 58.9b–14

The exiled people have returned to Jerusalem, and the prophet responsible for the third part of the book of Isaiah prophesied during the years following Babylonian rule. Economic renewal was a slow process, famine (the result of the land being laid waste during warfare) was fresh in people's memory and some were still short of food. In these verses, the prophet challenges individuals to respond generously to the need of those still afflicted by hunger (v.10). To be hungry is to lose dignity and respect since to be reduced to such dire straits can lead people to beg and perhaps to steal. Instead of pointing the finger at others, you must help them! The promise is that God will reward those who aid others. The prophet illustrates this by metaphors of light and water (v.11), which constitute the language of blessing. There was still much work to be done and those involved in the work would be honoured by God as repairers and restorers. In this post-exilic community it would seem that honouring the Sabbath had become secondary to the revival of the economy, and so business continued as usual. The commandment to keep the Sabbath as a day of rest, because God rested from his work of creation on the seventh day, was being flouted with impunity. People who broke the Sabbath were no longer put to death (Ex. 31.15)! The prophet is concerned that people should treat the Sabbath as a holy day in order to honour God. Once again there is a promise of reward as those who honour God by observing the Sabbath will ride over all obstacles and will live peacefully in the land that is their inheritance from Jacob.

Today's readers may question whether those who care for others (v.10) or those who honour God (vv. 13–14) always receive divine reward, for experience often suggests otherwise. However, although a truism, there is a sense in which right action is its own reward, as people are strengthened morally and blossom as plants that are watered. This is not to suggest that caring for others is not a costly process. To honour God is not a task for one day alone, for it involves bringing dignity to those who are degraded by poverty and hunger. There is also a tension in this passage between time set aside for worship and the need to work in order to ensure economic prosperity. Christians today live within the same tension. Worship is both about honouring and thanking God for his goodness and about responding to God's generosity. Such worship spills over into our everyday business practices ensuring that our motives and methods are in accordance with God's will and not in opposition to it! This is when the division between 'sacred' and 'secular' is dissolved.

Hebrews 12.18–29

A climax is reached as the writer contrasts the coming of God in fire and tempest on Sinai with God's celebratory presence on Zion. At Sinai the people were filled with dread and feared for their lives, in Zion they participated in the festivity and rejoicing that characterizes life in God's city. The two pictures offer a startling contrast. At Sinai any living creature that touched the holiness of God's mountain would die. Perhaps the writer is recalling the worship of the golden calf, a sin so appalling that people under judgement placed their lives in jeopardy, for how could they survive if God abandoned them. Their sense of community as God's people would have been destroyed and each animal and person left to look out for themselves! How different is the second picture as all the family of God's people gather together and join the celebration in heaven! The contrast between the old covenant and the new could not be more striking. This has been made possible through Jesus' sacrifice (v.24). The mention of Abel's blood is a reminder of the jealousy that caused Cain to murder his brother. Jesus' blood does not cry out for vengeance but for forgiveness. The invitation to belong to the worshipping, celebratory community of God's people can be accepted or refused. There is no doubting the ominous note of judgement, for God is not only about to shake the present universe but will replace it! God's universal kingdom, as yet unseen, is unshakeable and eternal. To enter God's presence is like approaching fire, the metaphor for judgement, and fire can either purify or consume. Nevertheless, people who approach God with the right attitude of reverence and awe can enter with confidence for Jesus provides the means of access into God's kingdom.

What a challenging reading! Most people today find the idea of God striking people dead not only abhorrent, but also contrary to the revelation of God in Christ. Perhaps one way of bridging the cultural gap is to recognize that the two pictures reflect contrasting experiences of people today: there are those who are isolated and fearful and those who belong and celebrate life fearlessly. Isolation and fearfulness are caused when people feel that they are not accepted and do not belong. Sometimes their alienation may be partly because of their own behaviour, but often it occurs through no fault of their own, but the effect of isolation is the same, it makes people fearful because they have no support. It is not the Christian's role to judge, but to help. The two pictures are offered so that readers will long to be caught up in the celebration of heaven. Those who celebrate will want the whole world to share their joy. If God's kingdom is already present and unshakeable we must be able to discover it now, especially where God's people care for one another in a spirit of community.

Luke 13.10–17

Once again Jesus heals someone on the Sabbath day. In chapter 6, Luke told of the healing of the man with the withered hand (6.6–11), but now a bent woman with a curved spine is healed. People at the time believed her condition was due to possession by an evil spirit. To understand the implications of Jesus' action, it is essential to enter into the thought-world of the day: she was thought to be under Satan's power (v.16). Jesus both speaks to her and touches her to effect healing, and she responds by praising God. The ruler of the synagogue reprimands Jesus for contravening the regulations that forbid work on the Sabbath. However, saving life was permitted on the Sabbath, and Jesus reminds him that it is permitted for people to release their livestock so that they can eat and drink – and that too is work. If animals are given what is necessary for life, surely the woman has the same right. Of course, she would not have died had Jesus waited until the Sabbath was over to heal her. Jesus' insistence on healing her there and then implies that God's kingdom will not wait: God's rule breaks in on God's day and overthrows the power that binds people and mars their lives! She is described as 'a daughter of Abraham' (v.16), although people failed to treat her as such! A woman who suffered curvature of the spine was doubly disabled, by her physical affliction and by the attitudes of those who shunned her because of the evil spirit they thought possessed her. Now she is restored both physically and socially.

God's kingdom cannot wait. There must be no delay in confronting all that mars the life of God's children. For Jesus this healing involved speaking and touching. His disciples today must be ready both to speak and to touch. To speak to someone is an act of recognition that acknowledges their worth, to touch them is to offer friendship and acceptance.

SUNDAY BETWEEN 28 AUGUST AND 3 SEPTEMBER INCLUSIVE

Twenty-second Sunday in Ordinary Time

Jeremiah 2.4–13; Sirach/Ecclesiasticus 10.12–18 or
Proverbs 25.6–7; Hebrews 13.1–8, 15–16; Luke 14.1, 7–14

Jeremiah 2.4–13

Jeremiah asks 'What has spoiled the relationship between God and his people?' After all, God rescued them from Egypt, led them through the wilderness and provided them with a fertile land that they have ruined (v.7). God has done everything for them and the people's thankless behaviour is inexplicable! Why would people behave in a self-destructive way in the first place let alone continue to make the same mistakes? Jeremiah's questions are ours. How often we see people acting in a way that hurts not only themselves but everyone else. This is true in individuals, society and international relationships. Common sense says that when people realize the dire consequences of their behaviour they should stop before more damage is done. Experience says that people rarely stop once a course of action is set in motion.

Jeremiah takes to task three groups of people. The first group were the priests. Their task was to teach the Torah, the law, yet they were breaking it themselves! Idolatry was rife and many of the priests seem to have been combining worship of God with practices from the local fertility cults. In Jeremiah's eyes, this was both inexcusable and futile as the local gods had no power. The second group were the rulers. Their task was to shepherd the people. In the ancient Near East, rulers were often described as shepherds whose task was to guide, protect and rescue the people. Instead, they have become the predators who exploited those in their care. The third group were the prophets whose task was to proclaim God's word and they too had been seduced by idolatry. In the language of the law court, God will charge them. They are now prisoners in the dock! When Jeremiah speaks of Kedar and Kittim, representing east and west, he is suggesting that nowhere else in the world would such unfaithfulness be found. Other nations, he says, stick to their own gods! Jeremiah is seeing other nations through rose-tinted spectacles, because people often worshipped the gods they thought could do most for them. Nevertheless, his meaning is clear: the people have made the wrong choice in turning away from their God who offers more than any other god ever could! It is as if they have chosen to drink stale water stored in a cracked cistern rather than drinking fresh flowing water from a stream or spring. Who would make such a choice?

Unfortunately, the answer to the last question is, 'Far too many of us'. It is only too easy to turn our backs on the life-giving message of the gospel for immediate gratification and the materialistic rewards that are so highly prized in our society. Jeremiah's words are as relevant now as they were in his own day.

Sirach/Ecclesiasticus 10.12–18

The writer suggests that human pride begins when people forsake God. It is when people have an inflated sense of their own importance and worth that they are more likely to exploit others. On a national or international scale, the result may be anarchy. The writer sees the ensuing chaos as God's punishment of the proud. Perhaps a more helpful way of responding to these verses is to recognize that we bring our punishment on ourselves, because God allows this to happen. God has created human beings and the world we inhabit. We are given a choice about how to behave within God's world. The writer did not believe in life after death and considered that people 'lived on' only in the memory of family and friends, although a few public figures would remain in the nation's memory. Complete extinction occurred when the memory of a person vanished (v.17). The fear of annihilation is perhaps the greatest fear human beings experience.

It is easy to say that Christians are assured that, in Jesus' resurrection, death has been vanquished, but many Christians still feel afraid of death, and guilt may compound that fear if they berate themselves for their lack of faith. Trust in God grows as our relationship with God deepens. As we put our pride aside and learn to love and care for others we will begin to understand that this is how God cares for us – and such a God will never allow us to be annihilated!

Proverbs 25.6–7

The picture is of a procession of notable people coming into the king's presence. The advice given is not to pretend to a dignity or rank you do not possess, because this will lead to rebuttal and loss of face. It is wiser to take a lower place in the order of precedence and be moved to a higher one. The scene here is not that of a banquet, as the people stand before the monarch (v.6), although this is how Luke uses the thought from this passage in the reading below.

Those who swarm around world leaders like bees round the honeypot today are often attracted by joining an influential group and gaining high social status. However, before judging public figures, we need to consider our own motives and why we value the good opinion of others.

Hebrews 13.1–8, 15–16

The advice given relates to relationships between Christians and is not concerned with how Christians should relate to outsiders. To build a community that will please God, members must offer each other mutual love and support. This is why hospitality towards strangers is valued highly. Christians were looked at with suspicion in wider Roman society and the assurance that hospitality would always be offered within the Christian community gave some measure of security to people who felt vulnerable. The writer also reminds them that Abraham 'entertained angels unaware', a way of saying that Christ is to be met in others. Imprisonment is an ever-present threat and some of the community are in prison. Even though they are Christians, they are not immune from the dangers of this world and following Christ means that they must feel the pain of others. Within the context of a close-knit community, unfaithfulness in marriage would affect not only the couple concerned, but everyone. Similarly, the advice about money is a reminder that greed also destroys relationships. When relationships within the community are strained, people are not in a fit state to worship God. While they are to look to their leaders as role models, they must remember that Jesus is the best role model of all! His unfailing faithfulness has been expounded in the body of the letter.

Before the coming of Christ, the means of access to God was through the sacrificial worship offered in the Temple. Now it is through Christian worship and true worship involves faithful living. Both sharing what they have and praising God are described as sacrifice. Faithfulness involves witnessing to Christ through their lifestyle as well as through the spoken word.

This passage acts as a salutary reminder that Christians do not 'go it alone'. Too often today people make decisions that give sole precedence to their own best interests irrespective of the effect those decisions have on the lives of others. That is not to say that anyone should remain in a situation that is damaging to their own well-being, rather that prayerful reflection should take into consideration the consequences for everyone concerned. The early Christians felt each other's pain. Intercessory prayer is a heart-wrenching experience for those who use their loving imaginations to feel with and for those who suffer. Yet, this is how God loves us!

Luke 14.1, 7–14

Jesus has been invited to a meal at the house of an influential Pharisee. Luke implies that the invitation had been issued so that the Pharisee and his associates could 'watch Jesus closely' (v.1). It is worth noting that Jesus was saying the same kind of things Pharisees said. The problem lay not with the content of his teaching, but with his authority. Those at the table would not have disagreed with the advice Jesus gave to guests and hosts. Like Jesus, the Pharisees would have spoken out against Greek and Roman cultural norms about honour and shame. In the Gentile world honour in terms of social status was highly valued. The meal described would have been eaten at a low three-sided table (in the shape of a rectangle with one side missing) at which guests would recline in Roman style. The guests' positions would depend upon their relationship with the host. The advice Jesus gives the guests seems eminently sensible, because it is about courting honour rather than shame! The theme of reversal of fortunes is a central theme in Luke's Gospel. Jesus' advice to hosts is more controversial. Those hosting a meal would invite people of the same social status as themselves and would expect the arrangement to be reciprocal. There would be no point in inviting people who were in no position to invite you in return. In many cases, social life and business life would converge and those in the same circle were interdependent. There would be no reason to invite people who would be in no position to return the favour and it would be suicidal to eat with people you would be ashamed to be seen with! What if your friends heard about it? However, this is not an ordinary meal, it is a wedding banquet (v.8), an analogy often used for the feast that would take place when God inaugurated his kingdom. In the kingdom of God, those who were shunned by society will be assured of their places at God's table. Those who anticipate the kingdom now, by including those at the bottom of the social ladder, will be blessed because they are ensuring their own place at the future banquet. There is still a pragmatic note!

Christian understanding challenged the prevailing views about honour and shame in the Roman world. Two thousand years have gone by, yet social status is still highly valued by many and people still court the favour of those who can help them to climb ladders, whether they seek promotion or are applying for membership of the local golf club! Jesus invites the Church and individual Christians to examine their motives and behaviour. Eating together is a feature of community life. Those who sit at table together are those who belong. Whom do we prefer not to invite into our own homes?

SUNDAY BETWEEN 4 AND 10 SEPTEMBER INCLUSIVE

Twenty-third Sunday in Ordinary Time

Jeremiah 18.1–11; Deuteronomy 30.15–20; Philemon 1–21; Luke 14. 25–33

Jeremiah 18.1–11

This is the story of Jeremiah's visit to the local pottery. The art of creating hand-thrown pots has not changed over the centuries. In Jeremiah's day, potters who worked from home would be found in most villages and their task was to provide the drinking and storage vessels required by the villagers. This prophecy has often been described as an example of 'enacted prophecy' when the prophet dramatized what he wished to say, rather than relying solely on the spoken word. In this case, Jeremiah does not act out the message himself, but offers an illustration by pointing to what the potter does. An ordinary, everyday activity is being used to express something about God, in other words the reshaping of the pot triggers a theological insight. The account begins in the third person, but by the third verse Jeremiah has taken over the narration. There is no need to retell the story because it is self-explanatory. The message is that if the potter is dissatisfied with the pot he has produced he can squash it and start all over again. It is only too clear that God can choose to do the same with a disobedient people!

Here are two suggestions about how to respond to this story. The first is to ask whether we allow God's grace to permeate our understanding through the ordinary experiences of daily life. As the hymn writer suggests, we need to be those 'With minds alert, upheld by grace' (*Hymns and Psalms* 619 v.2). Secondly, what does it mean to be 'squashed' like a lump of clay? Do we believe that God can transform individuals, institutions, society and the world just as a potter can transform a lump of clay into a beautiful pot? However, Jeremiah was thinking not of individuals, but about a nation. Sometimes we need to have both our national and individual pride punctured before we are ready to seek forgiveness and allow God to reshape us. Are people who expect to meet God in and through ordinary everyday experiences those who will be transformed?

Deuteronomy 30.15–20

These words are placed in the mouth of Moses as he gives his farewell speech to the people before they enter the Promised Land and these verses may form the original conclusion to the book. The great themes of Deuteronomy are found here as readers are reminded that the covenant relationship involves obedience to the law and that faithfulness to God leads to blessing. Preachers who like to offer a text may find 'Choose life so that you may live' (v.19) a helpful starting place. Who would not choose prosperity over adversity or indeed life over death? The choice is stark. However, by the time these words were read, the people had entered the land and many, attracted by the fertility cults of the Canaanites, had turned their backs on God. These words reminded them that they had made the wrong choice and had sought death rather than life!

Human nature is often perverse and people are often seduced into destructive courses of action. In Western society today the ways in which human beings destroy their lives are only too easy to see. For example, the increasing rates of marital breakdown, addiction, violence and debt cause untold misery. Yet, none of the people whose lives have been damaged set out to destroy themselves or others. What, then, does it mean to choose life? The question is not as simple as it may seem, as life is more than survival. Deuteronomy offers the answer that to choose life is to live in covenant relationship with God, responding to his faithfulness by reflecting that faithfulness in our own lives. That involves caring for others. However, the individualism that abounds today suggests that quality of life is about cramming in as many exciting experiences as possible, regardless of the consequences, while also enjoying every convenience and leisure activity made available by up-to-the-minute technology. What a contrast with Jesus' way that offered life, but also led to the cross! Too many people in the world barely survive. Surely, the imperative for Christians is to choose life for those who barely live.

Philemon 1–21

Onesimus, who came from Colossae (Col. 4.9) had run away from his master, Philemon, who was a Christian and a leader of the church. The letter offers no hint about why Onesimus had fled, only that he took with him money he had stolen from Philemon. It may be that this abuse of trust had caused considerable hurt. Onesimus could have disappeared into the big city like many others before and since, but instead he had met Paul and become a Christian. Onesimus had served

Paul who was under house arrest. Hiding a runaway slave was not going to enhance Paul's reputation, or help him to regain his own freedom as he hoped (v.22). Paul was faced with a difficult decision! After all, Philemon might choose to punish Onesimus severely or even have him put to death! Philemon and Onesimus were estranged, yet the Christian gospel is about reconciliation. Paul had preached that Christ has broken down the distinctions between slave and free (Col. 3.11, Gal. 3.28) but he must have wondered whether these two people were ready to live out what they believed? It would seem that Paul sent Tychicus and Onesimus to Colossae together (Col. 4.7–9). They probably took with them two letters, the letter we know as Paul's letter to the Colossians and this, the shortest of Paul's letters, to Philemon. Paul made a commitment to pay back the stolen money (v.18) and encouraged Philemon to take Onesimus back as a brother, no small request in the circumstances! What did Paul hope would happen when he urged Philemon to do more than he asked? Perhaps he hoped Philemon would return Onesimus to him, or give Onesimus his freedom. He may have been urging Philemon to offer a more generous welcome than Onesimus deserved (v.17). Certainly, he would have been hoping that the two would be reconciled and that meant Onesimus, no matter how frightened he felt, would have to risk retribution and Philemon would have to abandon his pride and act with immense generosity. This is the relationship that should characterize Christian fellowship.

This letter offers an insight into the culture of the day. Paul did not challenge the institution of slavery that was part of the fabric of society, yet already the gospel was mounting a challenge to established norms in relationships. Both Onesimus and Philemon had to take risks to enable reconciliation to take place. Most readers long to know how the situation was resolved, but the letter is open-ended and we do not know the end of the story! What risks do we need to take to foster reconciliation today whether in our personal lives, in our communities, or between the nations of the world, especially when different faith-perspectives have led to violent rifts? Paul was concerned with the relationship between two Christian people. How do we stay faithful to the gospel while seeking reconciliation with our brothers and sisters of other faiths and those of no faith at all? We do well to remember that many people consider, rightly, that religion has been a divisive force and not a uniting one.

Luke 14.25–33

Jesus stops to speak to the large crowd that are travelling with him. This is a reminder that it is easy to get on the bandwagon, but that people should know just what they are getting themselves into! Discipleship is not an easy option. For early Christians the threat of persecution often involved making difficult choices. It was not always possible to remain loyal to the family and to Jesus. When Christianity split away from Judaism, families were divided and this was equally true for those from pagan backgrounds who became Christian converts. The language of 'hating' family members falls uneasily on the ears of today's readers. However, this is not about emotion, but about the consequences of placing the obligations of discipleship above every other tie. Luke goes one step further than Matthew by including wives in his list (v.26 cf. Matt. 10.37–38), although, in first-century culture, it would have been unthinkable for a wife to reject her husband! By the time the Gospel was written would-be disciples already knew that Jesus had carried his own cross; nevertheless, the idea that discipleship might lead to their own deaths must have been a terrifying thought. The advice Jesus gives in the form of two short parables is not to start what you cannot finish, whether it is a building or a battle! Perhaps the greatest barrier to wholehearted commitment is unwillingness to give up possessions. This is not merely about greed, but about the security that money and material comfort provides. For many people discipleship has involved leaving behind family and possessions. The question for every Christian is whether we would be prepared to make such a commitment.

No preacher should 'water down' the gospel. However, it is clear that not all Christians are asked to make the most extreme gospel sacrifice and for most people commitment to family and commitment to Christ go hand in hand. Nevertheless, our loyalty to Jesus must be wholehearted. To be a disciple is to be ready to respond to others' need. Perhaps our prayer should be that God will give us both resolution and grace so that when we are called to share in the task of ministry we are ready to give ourselves gladly – our time, service and money – no matter what the cost.

SUNDAY BETWEEN 11 AND 17 SEPTEMBER INCLUSIVE

Twenty-fourth Sunday in Ordinary Time

Jeremiah 4.11–12, 22–28; Exodus 32.7–14; 1 Timothy 1.12–17;
Luke 15.1–10

Jeremiah 4.11–12, 22–28

The poem that follows the opening verses speaks of an invasion, but this time the invader will be God! The people are like barley and wheat that is sifted at the threshing floors. Threshing floors were often exposed bedrock high on a hill. When the prevailing westerly wind came, people would take shovels and throw the grain into the air and the wind would blow the chaff away. The good grain represented good people and chaff those who were wicked. However, sometimes the direction of the wind changed and swept across the hot desert from the east. This sirocco wind was strong and would sweep away both the grain and the chaff, both the good and wicked. God as invader would act like the sirocco wind! Although the passage does not make the connection directly, the high places were sites of shrines to foreign gods and threshing floors were often found near such places of worship. The people of Jerusalem, whom Jeremiah addresses, would have been aware that the metaphor he used was a reminder of their idolatry. It comes as a shock in this passage that God will sweep everyone away before him, good and wicked alike. However, this reflected the experience of both innocent and guilty people whose lives were threatened by besieging armies who came from the North (vv. 15–17) portrayed as God's instrument of punishment. Warfare brings devastation and a return to chaos (v.23). In Genesis 1 God created the world by bringing order instead of chaos. Now that order is being systematically destroyed step by step, reversing the act of creation. God's first act was to create light and separate it from darkness, but now the light has gone. The very foundations of the earth shake causing the mountains to topple. This is an apocalyptic disaster of cosmic proportions and a return to the chaos that existed before creation began; such chaos is overwhelming and brings with it the annihilation of all living things, not a bird nor a plant could survive. Everything is barren. The picture is of the end of everything and God will not create it again!

Hearing this passage read may be 'too close for comfort'! The availability of weapons of mass destruction and the possibility of germ warfare are terrifying realities in the twenty-first century. Now, as never before, people have the capacity to destroy themselves and the planet. Is this God's punishment, or the consequence of human greed and hatred? Are these two ways of expressing the same thing? In the face of such a terrifying picture should we freeze like frightened rabbits or do all we can to foster respect, tolerance and mutual care between individuals, communities and nations as we remember Jesus' words, 'Blessed are the peacemakers'?

Exodus 32.7–14

The story of the Golden Calf is well known. The picture is of a people who have just received the law and made their covenant promises at Sinai immediately turning around and creating an idol to worship. Moses' obedience is contrasted with their disobedience and he intercedes on their behalf. There are some interesting points to note. Firstly, Moses' information comes from God who knows everything and tells Moses what the people are getting up to. Already God is tempted to disown them, 'Tell *your* people . . .' says God to Moses! Secondly, even though God has led them to the holy mountain and the covenant has been made, the relationship can still be dissolved. Instead, God suggests that he forms a new nation from Moses' descendants. Moses pleads for the people by arguing that God's reputation is at stake because the Egyptians will wonder why God went to all the trouble of saving them in the first place, let alone bringing them safely through the wilderness only to reject them now. Furthermore, as God cannot be seen to break his promises to the patriarchs, his integrity is at stake!

Yet perhaps the making of the golden calf is not all it appears to be. When the people entered the land the symbol of the bull became associated with God as well as with Baal at a time when cultic practices were blended. The wild scene that met Moses' eyes when he came down the mountain is resonant of the Canaanite worship of a later period. The story here may have been told in a way that would have reminded the landed people that such worship was unacceptable and that God could still reject them.

Moses was concerned about God's standing in the eyes of the neighbours, in this case the Egyptians. While he used that argument to persuade God to be merciful towards the disobedient people, it could be turned on its head: it is the task of the obedient people to show others what God is like by living faithfully. People discover the goodness and grace of God through those of us who act graciously towards others.

1 Timothy 1.12–17

Thanksgivings were a feature of formal letters in the Hellenistic world. Here the thanksgiving is used to introduce the themes of Paul's authority and God's mercy. One of the most highly prized virtues in the Greek world was trustworthiness. Paul was given divine authority and strength for the task precisely because God judged him to be worthy of trust. The picture that is painted of Paul is designed to encourage the Christian community. He is portrayed as a reprehensible character (v.13) but God's mercy was shown because Paul's actions stemmed from ignorance – the implication is that had he acted knowingly that would have been a different story! Faith and love characterized Jesus' relationship with God and this same relationship is offered to Paul as an act of God's grace summarized in the words, 'Christ Jesus came into the world to save sinners' (v.15), words which seem to have already become a short statement of belief. It was sin that estranged people from God and that estrangement could not be put right through their own efforts. It is God who saves the relationship in an act of grace through Jesus. This is what happened to Paul who is the archetypal sinner! If Christ was patient with Paul then there is hope for everyone else. To be in a relationship with God, when sin is no longer a barrier, is to be caught up in the eternal life of God, characterized by grace. This is a matter for praise and rejoicing! The language of worship combines familiar phrases as the only God of Jewish Scriptures is described in phrases from the Greek world as immortal and invisible. The one who is worshipped is king of this age and the coming age, when all creation will acknowledge his reign. It is no wonder that the litany of praise finishes with a liturgical flourish!

These verses are a reminder that both Jews and Greeks became Christians and that God's saving act in Christ was expressed and celebrated in the language of both cultures within the context of worship. This may raise a question about whether we seek to enrich our language of praise by embracing insights from the many different cultures represented in an increasingly multicultural society. Yet, even in multicultural churches, too rarely do people sit down and speak about their own experiences of God and Christ. What enables such conversations to happen? It may be that one way is to ask about people's childhood experiences of how major Christian festivals were celebrated. Reminiscences do not threaten, but open doors and break down estrangement.

Luke 15.1–10

In the previous chapter Jesus was invited to a meal at a Pharisee's house. During the conversation, he told the parable of the banquet when the great and the good refused to attend and the householder sent his slave to collect, from the highways and byways, dinner guests who would appreciate his hospitality. In this new chapter, Luke describes the Pharisees' complaint about Jesus welcoming sinners and eating with them. This is just what Jesus had been teaching in the previous chapter (14.12–24), and the irony would not be lost on Luke's readers! It was bad enough that Jesus ate with sinners, but he did not have to look as if he was enjoying himself! The main complaint here is that Jesus welcomes them. The two parables that follow are about God's welcoming attitude towards those who are lost. There is a contrast between the man and woman in the parables: the man is comparatively wealthy and spends most of his life in the open air, while the woman is poorer and spends her time in her home. Those listening to Luke's Gospel were being invited to identify with each character in turn and to share in both their anxiety and their rejoicing. People do not expend great energy in searching for something that is not dear to them, as to search thoroughly is time-consuming and involves considerable energy. However, the relief and joy of recovering what is lost is worth the effort and the longing to share that gladness with family and friends is a natural human response. This is how God feels too! The picture of the delight in heaven (v.10) is a wonderful way of reminding people who were often shunned by society that they can belong to a community of God's people who value them and are glad to welcome them. It may be worth noting that the emphasis on repentance may reflect Luke's own concern as the analogy is being pressed too far: neither the sheep nor the coin were able to help their owners find them!

We all know the stomach-churning moment when we realize someone we love or something precious to us is missing. There are plenty of illustrations available to the preacher: the child who strays from her mother during a shopping trip; the dog who runs after one squirrel too many in the woods and fails to return to his owner's whistle; the keys lost during a walk in the park – the list is endless. It is easier to think of ourselves as those who search than as those who are lost. Do we believe that God's relief and delight is unbounded when we respond to the divine love that searches for us?

SUNDAY BETWEEN 18 AND 24 SEPTEMBER INCLUSIVE

Twenty-fifth Sunday in Ordinary Time

Jeremiah 8.19–9.1; Amos 8.4–7; 1 Timothy 2.1–7; Luke 16.1–13

Jeremiah 8.19–9.1

In this lament the poet gives Jerusalem a voice as the city expresses profound grief and distress. In 597 BCE the Babylonians sacked Jerusalem and deported many people. They left a descendant of David on the throne as a puppet king, but after the second deportation they put a governor in authority. In this poem the city hears the people crying out from far away, asking 'Is the Lord not in Zion? Is the king not in her?' (v.19). Surely, if God had been in the Temple, he would not have allowed the foreign armies to sack the city! Perhaps God had already left the city and would not return until the city was rebuilt and the exiles returned. For the present, the city and the people felt the absence of God keenly: it was as if God, king over all earthly kings, had been dethroned. The words about idolatry do not seem to be part of the original poem. The NRSV places them in brackets to show that they sit uneasily at this point. However, they serve as a reminder that the people's continuing unfaithfulness, their insistence upon worshipping idols, has played a part in this disaster. It is ironic that the exiled people now live amongst foreigners who worship other gods and are no longer able to visit the Jerusalem Temple. The thread of the poem continues at the time when kingship was celebrated. After the Feast of Tabernacles or Booths when the grapes and olives had been harvested, there was a break for farmers as they waited for the rains to come. This was the time when men left their land and took up arms, either to raid neighbouring countries or to defend their own land from foreign invaders. It was also the time of enthronement ceremonies, when the kingship of those who had led their people safely through another year, was confirmed. On this occasion there would be no festivities, for warfare had ruined the harvest and the people faced a winter of starvation. They had not been saved from their enemies and many had been slaughtered. There was no balm to heal their hurt. Gilead was renowned for its balm, scented resin from the styrax tree. Whether or not the balm helped to heal wounds, or merely disguised the putrid smell of decaying flesh, there was none available. The passage ends with the intense anguish of a city littered with the bodies of the dead.

Whenever people slaughter one another voices cry, 'Where is

God?' In Jeremiah's day, it was conceivable that God had abandoned his people, but not that God did not exist. God's absence was evident because people had experienced God's presence. It is not surprising that people who have never experienced the presence of God find their suspicion that God does not exist confirmed when disasters strike. Yet, even those who sing praises when all is going well can find their faith is undermined when tragedy affects them personally. It is essential that Christians recognize that many people are unprotected when enemies strike, whether the enemy is an army, earthquake, disease or death. It is the Church's task to wrestle with the question, 'Where is God?' There is no easy answer. Yet, the gospel reminds us that Jesus too knew how it felt to be abandoned in his pain as he hung on the cross. The experience of God's seeming absence is devastating, as to be abandoned is a deep-seated human fear. The good news is that Good Friday became Easter Sunday as Jesus discovered that God had never forsaken him. Christians must not ignore the pain of Good Friday, for we live in a suffering world, yet we live with the hope of Easter people, who have already encountered 'God with us', in Jesus.

Amos 8.4–7

Amos' words have lost none of their vitriolic immediacy. The prophet's anger sounds across the centuries as he condemns utterly the injustice of his own society. In these verses, he addresses the merchants who were grinding the poor into the ground, by fraudulent means, for their own gain. They were using false balances so that people paid for less than they received. They even sold the 'sweepings of the wheat', the chaff and dust from the surface of the threshing floor, along with the good grain. This was cheating on a grand scale! Moneymaking was all and everything! There is a play on words in verses 4 and 5 that is lost in translation, as in Hebrew the verb 'to suppress' ('bring to bear' in NRSV) carries the meaning of 'cease to exist' and comes from the same root as the word for 'Sabbath'. The implication is that the merchants' greed was putting the lives of the poor at risk! The merchants had turned their backs on God and had come to resent the holy days of rest because their trading activities had to be suspended. New moon and Sabbath refer to the monthly and weekly holy days that were to be observed as days of rest and this was a statutory commitment in accordance with God's command. Do the words about 'the pride of Jacob' in verse 7 indicate that God's faithfulness is as immovable as the people's arrogance, or is the suggestion that the merchants should take pride in being God's people rather than in their wealth that comes from the exploitation of the poorest? In either case, it is clear that they have behaved so badly that God will not forget what they have done. The words 'never forget' are strong words: they imply that God will punish those who have betrayed the poorest members of society!

Greed has always been the motivation for many acts of injustice and people's lives are still being placed in jeopardy as a result. Amos would certainly have approved of the Church's campaigns regarding the cancellation of debt owed by developing countries. We also need to ask whether we have any 'days of rest' spent reverently as we worship God and reflect on his will for us and for our world.

1 Timothy 2.1–7

Christians living in the Roman world were considered to be atheists because they refused to worship the gods, or the emperor. Groups of Christians who met together were thought to be subversive sects. Those in authority could choose either to prosecute Christians, or to turn a blind eye and tacitly allow them to continue their own religious practice. Their relationships within pagan society could easily be strained to breaking point as they were regarded with suspicion and became subject to the petty persecutions that made life unbearable. The instruction to pray for rulers was so that Christians would be permitted to enjoy a life that could be lived 'in godliness' (v.2) rather than merely a quiet life. In other words, this is about being able to worship without fear. Why was worship so important? It was not only about the Christians' own relationship with God, for worship was the way that other people could be included in God's salvation as they were invited to hear the gospel. The emphasis of the Pastoral Epistles is that all people may come 'to the knowledge of the truth' (v.4). This truth is that through Jesus, the mediator between God and humanity, people may live in right relationship with God and so discover God's purpose for all. Jesus is himself the ransom, the payment that released slaves from captivity; and here it is sin that holds people captive. Is the allusion to the 'right time' made to counter an argument that had Jesus been a significant figure he would have come earlier in human history? In any case, Paul's apostolic task was to act as a herald by announcing the significance of Jesus' coming to the pagan world.

In public worship the Church often prays for rulers. The content of that prayer is usually that they will seek peace and justice for all people. Do we say those words too glibly? As in the passage from Amos (above), we need to do what we can to make the world a more peaceful and more just place for all God's people. It is not enough to say our prayers and then sit back and wait until laws are changed.

Luke 16.1–13

Jesus tells the story of the 'dishonest manager' to his disciples. The dishonest manager has been doing business on his master's behalf. It may be that the master was engaged in some 'shady' practice. The manager, like the prodigal son in the previous chapter, had squandered his master's property and faces dismissal. Like many other administrators, he does not fancy the idea of earning a living as a manual labourer and certainly does not want to be reduced to begging! He decides to play to his strengths and he is good at creative accounting! He still has to 'get the paperwork in order' for his successor. By reducing creditors' payments, he makes sure there are people who will owe him favours in return. Did he do this by reducing or cancelling his own fee, and thus acting honestly, or by continuing to cheat his employer? Unfortunately, we will never know. Yet, it is hard to see how his master would have applauded his actions if he had continued cheating. Both the master and the steward were used to the dishonest ways of this world, but does Jesus really praise them for that? Perhaps the praise is given because someone acts swiftly in a crisis. There may be a clue in the word 'eternal' (v.9) suggesting that the way to eternal salvation involves 'making friends' with those who are poor and that may involve redistribution of dishonestly gained wealth! This is an urgent matter.

The proverbial sayings that follow imply that true wealth is about integrity, that is, living faithfully under the rule of God. The difficulty, then as now, is that people live within a world that necessitates the accumulation of wealth. Society encourages people to behave responsibly, for example by providing for their old age. It is essential that Christians continue to ask questions about the proper use of their wealth and resources. When does behaving responsibly become an excuse for selfishness?

SUNDAY BETWEEN 25 SEPTEMBER AND 1 OCTOBER INCLUSIVE

Twenty-sixth Sunday in Ordinary Time

Jeremiah 32.1–3a, 6–15; Amos 6.1a, 4–7; 1 Timothy 6.6–19;
Luke 16.19–31

Jeremiah 32.1–3a, 6–15

Jeremiah's prophetic task was both to pull down and to build up
(1.10). Before the Babylonians attacked Jerusalem, Jeremiah acted as
'a prophet of doom' who sought to destroy the people's complacency
and unfaithfulness to God. In this passage, Jeremiah fulfils the second
part of his calling as he takes action to build the confidence of the
people during a time of despair. The date is carefully recorded: it is the
time when Babylon is besieging the city of Jerusalem and disaster
seems inevitable. Jeremiah himself is in prison, accused of prophesying defeat. Meanwhile, Jeremiah's cousin, Hanamel, has accrued
debts and will have to sell the land that is his livelihood to pay what he
owes. In Levitical law, it was the task of the nearest relative to act as
'redeemer' (Lev. 25.25–32) and buy the land on behalf of the bank-
rupt. If no redeemer could be found then Hanamel would have to
relinquish his land. He and his family faced starvation unless he could
find a job labouring for another landowner, possibly for the man to
whom he owed money. In peacetime, it would not have been remarkable for Jeremiah to act as redeemer and buy the land, but under the
present circumstances his action was remarkable indeed. Jeremiah
'puts his money where his mouth is' as by his purchase he demonstrates his conviction that land destroyed by Babylonian armies will
once again be farmed and peace will be restored. The odds were that
land would be redistributed amongst the conquering forces, not that it
would be returned to its original owners. What did it cost Jeremiah?
Seventeen shekels of silver would have represented a year's income
for a labourer. The sale is described in detail and there is no doubting
it was a properly witnessed transaction. In accordance with business
practice across the ancient Near East, two copies of the deed of purchase were kept. The unsealed copy was available for anyone to see
but, to ensure no one tried to change the details, a sealed copy was
kept that could be referred to in the case of any later dispute.
Jeremiah's faith is in God who has promised this land to his people
and he is prepared to act upon that faith, at great personal cost, thus

proclaiming by his action that houses, fields and vineyards would once again belong to the people of Israel.

Jeremiah's faith was amazing. He was prepared to risk a huge amount of money gambling on God! Yet he would have said there was no risk, because God's promises were guaranteed. A terrified people who felt that all security was crumbling around them, and who feared that God had abandoned them, must have been comforted and inspired when the news of Jeremiah's action spread. Many people need to hear such words of comfort today, but words must be accompanied by actions and by generous giving.

Amos 6.1a, 4–7

Amos condemns all leaders who live in luxury while their people suffer. He addresses the rulers of both southern and northern kingdoms, those in Judah and those in Samaria. The people in power who should be caring for their people are living at their expense and what a life they are enjoying! The picture of the feast is of people reclining on couches inlaid with ivory. This is an exotic setting of the utmost luxury. What was the occasion of the feast? It may have been a religious festival, possibly the Feast of Tabernacles. They eat the animals used in sacrifice, the lambs from the flock that provided the tenderest meat, and anoint themselves with the oil that is a sign of God's mercy, even though they show no mercy to the people under their protection. Music that should be used to sing God's praise is now idle strumming for their own entertainment. The nation is ruined and faces destruction, yet they seem oblivious and, instead of grieving, continue to over-indulge themselves. The word translated 'revelry' (v.7) is the word used for a funeral gathering. What devastating irony: those who lounge on couches are eating the feast of mourners at the scene of a death!

The leaders of the people held authority under God. The very people whose task it was to protect the nation were exploiting those in their care and thereby dishonouring God. Unfortunately, it has ever been thus! The Church's task is to speak out on behalf of the weak even when it means challenging the leaders of the strongest nations. However, Christians can only speak with integrity when our own house is in order. This means that we must do all we can to perpetuate fair trade and to use our individual wealth, and the wealth of the Church, on behalf of those most in need.

1 Timothy 6.6–19

What is most striking about this passage is the way the writer uses the language and ideas from the Hellenistic (Greek) world, but uses them within the Christian context. The Greek view of contentment is of a life controlled not by emotions and desires but by reason. Such contentment was highly prized and enabled people to be self-sufficient, even when life was hard. For the Christian, contentment goes hand in hand with a faithful lifestyle. Those who look to God will be content with the bare essentials for life and will not seek security in riches. In contrast, those who are rich risk being corrupted by their wealth, hence the saying: 'The love of money is the root of all evil' (v.10). Belonging to the Christian Church was not likely to make people rich! Indeed, Christians must pursue a different lifestyle from those who seek to accumulate wealth.

The pursuit of virtue was a Hellenistic aim, and a list of virtues follows. The first virtue in the list is righteousness. If Timothy is 'a man of God' then he must pursue a just way of life. Justice was a central tenet in the Hellenistic world, but did not seek to challenge established structures, such as slavery. In this passage, the emphasis is on just attitudes and actions within the Christian community and is not about challenging existing institutions within society. The next virtue is 'godliness', a life of worship that spills over into a lifestyle characterized by faith and love. Courage was one of the most highly prized virtues, as in times of war people needed to be courageous. However, persecuted Christians were enjoined not to retaliate physically and so in this list courage is replaced by endurance. The final virtue in the list is gentleness. In the Greek world loss of face was to be avoided at all costs, therefore, gentleness could be seen as failure to stand up for oneself. To include gentleness in such a list was to challenge the norms of the day and to go against the prevailing culture. Yet such gentleness, an expression of the courage that was so highly prized in pagan society, was exhibited by Jesus when he stood before Pontius Pilate.

Christians await the appearing ('manifestation' in NRSV) of Christ (v.14). Again, Hellenistic language is being used in the Christian context. Kings were said to 'appear' to save their people in times of trouble, especially when enemy armies were approaching. The Greek version of the Hebrew Scriptures provides the language to describe Jesus as King of Kings and Lord of Lords, who will be given honour and eternal dominion.

The passage ends with a summary statement about wealth. Christians must trust in God and not in riches. However, this is much easier to say than to do, as we all find security in our bank balances and home comforts! Nevertheless, those who are truly rich are gentle and humble, the opposite of being proud and haughty.

Luke 16.19–31

The story of the rich man and the beggar continues the theme of wealth. Jesus may have been adapting any one of a number of folk tales in which the fortunes of rich and poor are reversed after death. This reflects the idea that after death people found themselves either in Hades, where they would be tormented, or in a place of blessing. In this story, the fortunes of the two men are reversed so that in a post-mortem existence they discover how the other had lived on earth. The contrast between the two lifestyles could not have been greater and the picture is painted in lurid detail: the beggar covered with sores that are licked by dogs, and the rich man, dressed in purple, dining sump-tuously. Purple dye was one of the most expensive commodities in the ancient world. The chasm between Hades and the place of blessing was deep indeed, but no deeper than the gulf that lay between the beggar and the rich man in life, despite their physical proximity. It is easy to assume that this story is about punishment and reward of indi-viduals, but the emphasis is placed firmly on the scandal of such inequality. What is being judged is the life that is lived in luxury despite the abject poverty and misery to be found on the doorstep. The rich man seeks to warn his brothers of the fate that lies in store, yet they already have the advice of Moses and the prophets. These great figures of the past had proclaimed God's word to the people: that to live in right relationship with God involved sharing divine concern for the well-being of every member of the community. It is not surprising that, when this story was retold by the Christian community, a con-nection was made between the people's failure to listen to Moses and the prophets and their present failure to listen to the gospel of Christ. Not even the risen Christ softened the hearts of those who were corrupted by their wealth.

Wealth and poverty often exist side by side in society today. Too many people in the world have no hope that life in this world will ever change for the better; either they despair or trust that God's justice suggests that they will be rich in the life that follows death. How should the Church respond? Is God's kingdom only a future hope, or should we be seeking and building that kingdom on earth?

SUNDAY BETWEEN 2 AND 8 OCTOBER INCLUSIVE

Twenty-seventh Sunday in Ordinary Time

Lamentations 1.1–6; Habbakkuk 1.1–4, 2.1–4; 2 Timothy 1.1–14;
Luke 17.5–10

Lamentations 1.1–6

Jerusalem is described as a woman in mourning. This great city has
suffered much as enemy armies have defeated her and left her desolate. Once she had powerful status amongst the cities of the world and
her strength made her secure from dangers that threatened the weak.
She had been influential in international affairs, but now she has
become a vassal state, forced to labour for others. The reversal of her
fortunes is as devastating as that of a princess who becomes the slave
of her captors. Jerusalem not only suffers because of what has
happened to her, but also mourns for her people who have been
deported. What is more, she laments alone and feels isolated and
abandoned in her grief, believing that even God has forsaken her. Her
experience mirrors that of women in the ancient world: widows who
were left with no means of support at the moment when their loss was
raw and women who were helpless to relieve their children's suffering. All those who loved Jerusalem had gone and she was left without
comfort. Foreigners, once her allies, were now her enemies as it was
no longer in their interest to befriend her. To walk through the streets
of Jerusalem must have been like walking through a ghost town. No
one travelled along her roads or entered her gates. It is worth remembering that in the ancient world the city gate was the seat of justice.
People who lived outside the city would come to the gate to settle their
disputes. The king would meet them at the gate and would judge
between them. Now the gates themselves are in despair! There is no
place for justice in the wake of war; too often anarchy reigns supreme.
It is not surprising that the maidens have been dragged away. The
passage does not speak about rape, but anyone with imagination can
visualize the fate of the young women of the city. As for the princes,
they are like stags who are being hunted. There is no pasture for them
and, weak as they are, their capture is certain. At such a time the
religious life of the city ceased. No one was there to offer praise and
thanks to God. The overwhelming sense of God's absence pervades
this passage. This book is rightly called Lamentations!

The fate of Jerusalem mirrors that of all cities that have fallen before enemies. In the world today, the sound of this same lament is still heard. How can we show those who mourn that God has not forsaken them? Before we offer any practical help, we need to recognize the depth of despair that is so poignantly expressed in these verses from Scripture.

Habbakkuk 1.1–4, 2.1–4

The prophet is struggling with the unanswerable question, 'Why does God allow cruelty, violence and injustice?' The first four verses of the book are a cry for help from a God who does not seem to be listening. God has given him eyes to see the wrongdoing and perversion of justice that goes on around him. This implies that others either do not see or have little difficulty in ignoring what they see. Here, the prophet is wrestling with the problem of having a conscience. Why is it that some people have a clear understanding of right and wrong and feel compelled to do what is right, while others seem to find it only too easy to act in a way that is hurtful and destructive? Psychologists today might choose to look at people's early childhood experiences and upbringing, but perhaps that is only a partial answer. The second chapter finds the prophet taking the role of watchman. Standing at a good vantage point where he can see what is happening, he challenges God to answer his unanswerable question. God tells him not to look at those who are proud, in other words at those who are driven by their own desire for power, but at those who live by faith. God's answer is no answer! What is more, this is the answer that the prophet must inscribe clearly on stone tablets, so that the messenger who carries them can read what is said. However, there is a reminder in v.3 that God has everything under control, there is a time appointed and, presumably, that time is when God will act as righteous judge and the wicked will get their just deserts!

Those whose search for justice in this life is futile find little comfort in the idea of a judgement that lies in the future. Perhaps a better way to respond to this passage is to consider whether we wish to be people who are given eyes to see injustice and wrongdoing despite the pain that brings. For this is what it means to be God's people. We can be sure that, although we feel the anguish of others bitterly, the pain God bears is far greater than ours.

2 Timothy 1.1–14

The letter, by an unknown author, is written as if by Paul to Timothy. Its tone is tender and intimate as befits a letter from the older man to a protégé he seeks to encourage. The writer places himself in the position of Paul during the time of his final imprisonment in Rome. Timothy is the 'beloved child' (v.2) in whom Paul rejoices. Paul gives thanks for Timothy's faith that has been nurtured within his own family, by his grandmother Lois, and mother Eunice. Loyalty within families was valued highly by Hellenistic society. By mentioning Timothy's family, Paul is encouraging him to remain faithful. Paul provides both a role model for Timothy and the means by which his God-given gifts, or charisms, can be fanned into flame. Paul is in prison and cannot lay hands on Timothy literally; however, he holds him in his prayers night and day (v.3). The laying on of hands by the elders of the church was a sign of God's gifting of his people. Timothy was to be given the gifts necessary to maintain his faithfulness in the face of persecution and suffering that was the inevitable consequence of living a Christian life within the pagan society of the day. It would be only too easy for Timothy to feel ashamed of Paul because he was in prison. To be imprisoned was to lose face within society and this was the fate of many members of the church. Yet, Paul is not the prisoner of the state, but of Christ, for whose sake he suffers imprisonment with his head held high. Timothy, as one of Paul's colleagues, might well receive unwelcome attention from the authorities, but God would give him the power to hold on to 'the sound teaching' (v.13) he had received from Paul. When this letter was read out to the church it would have encouraged Christians to remain faithful to the gospel as proclaimed by Paul, rather than by other teachers who may have been adapting the gospel message for their own purposes.

It is easy to understand how a letter written as if by Paul to Timothy would have encouraged a persecuted church. They faced suffering that sometimes ended in death and needed to be reassured that they were part of a saved people for whom death was not an end but a beginning. They also needed to be confirmed in their own calling and receive assurance that God would give them the courage they needed. They also had to contend with the ignominious stigma of imprisonment. In worship today, it is perhaps the more charismatic churches who offer the laying on of hands and affirm that God offers people the gifts they need to live out their calling. Yet, perhaps the 'mainstream' churches should consider ways in which Christians can be affirmed as 'called' and 'gifted by God' for their ministry in the world.

Luke 17.5–10

These verses are about the life of discipleship and refer not only to the first followers of Jesus, but also to Christians in the communities for whom Luke wrote. These are the 'apostles' (v.5) who recognized the difficulties they and their congregations faced. It seems that from the outset people have struggled to find faith and their 'little faith' has never seemed sufficient for the task. Jesus reassures the disciples that even though their faith is as small as a mustard seed it will enable them to do more than they can begin to imagine. It can grow into a mulberry tree (sometimes translated, sycamore tree) that can uproot itself and be planted in the sea! What a strange saying! However, the 'sea' once again represents the waters of chaos that threaten to overwhelm and destroy. The disciples' faith is enough to enable them to face any difficulties or troubles that arise. The overriding characteristic of faithful discipleship is obedience. Slavery was part of the fabric of the society of the day and disciples are reminded that they should compare themselves with the slave rather than with the master. Their task was to serve obediently to the best of their ability. This is not a message that sits easily in today's world. On the one hand, slavery has long since been abolished as an institution and is considered to destroy human dignity, while on the other hand unquestioning obedience is thought to undermine individual autonomy and freedom. However, when the slave's 'master' is God, then the relationship is based on trust. God is always faithful and just and so obedience is based on the conviction that it is the task of disciples to share God's loving purposes. Such obedience is not 'unquestioning' but is always seeking to determine God's will.

When ethical issues become increasingly complex and political issues are by no means clear-cut, obedience requires Christians to debate and discuss matters that affect humanity. However, the hallmark of Christian living is to be certain that we seek to serve God, the one we have come to know in the life, death and resurrection of Jesus Christ. If we trust God, then we will trust also that we have been given sufficient faith to wrestle with the problems of our own time and that, by grace, our faith will be able to overcome all that threatens to overwhelm or destroy God's people today.

SUNDAY BETWEEN 9 AND 15 OCTOBER INCLUSIVE

Twenty-eighth Sunday in Ordinary Time

Jeremiah 29.1, 4–7; 2 Kings 5.1–3, 7–15b; 2 Timothy 2.8–15;
Luke 17.11–19

Jeremiah 29.1, 4–7

Jeremiah sent a letter to the leaders of the people who were amongst
the first to be deported to Babylon. To send a letter such a distance by
messenger was no light undertaking and it is easy to imagine the joy
with which 'news from home' would have been received. The exiles
would have been dispersed and so Jeremiah's letter would have been
passed from one group of people to another. Not only were they many
miles from home, but they were living in a foreign land where people
spoke a strange language, worshipped different gods and everything
was unfamiliar and frightening. The advice Jeremiah offered was both
practical and reassuring. There was no likelihood of an immediate
return home, so rather than succumbing to despair they should make
the best of things! They were to establish themselves afresh, by building houses and planting gardens. These were not flower gardens, but
'allotments' where they would grow fruit and vegetables for the table.
Sheltered and nourished they would survive. They were to give their
sons and daughters in marriage to ensure that there was a new generation. These exiles were the leaders of the Jewish nation, people who
had been influential in government when they had lived in Jerusalem.
Such talent should not be wasted! For this reason, Jeremiah suggests
that they should seek the welfare of the city of Babylon. At first, this
must have seemed to be encouraging treachery, after all the Babylonians were their enemies! However, by demonstrating their good will
the exiled Jews would become accepted, influential and valued
members of society. In this way, their enemies would become friends
and there would be less probability of them suffering the persecutions
that ethnic minorities often face. They would also be able to make
an important contribution towards the welfare of the community. By
following Jeremiah's advice the people did survive and flourish in
exile and the day did come, many years later, when they were able to
return to Jerusalem.

In Babylon, God's people had to decide whether to 'live as
strangers' or participate in the life of pagan society. Christians today
are faced with a similar choice. The Church is part of society and

seeks the good of all, but also stands over against society and challenges its standards and presuppositions whenever that seems necessary.

2 Kings 5.1–3, 7–15b

With the exception of verse 15, comments on this passage can be found under Sunday between 3 and 9 July, Fourteenth Sunday in Ordinary Time (see pp. 130–1).

The climax of the story (v.15) is Naaman's shout of faith in Israel's God. Amongst all the gods on earth only the God of Israel had such power! (The words in v.15 are not pointing to monotheism.) How the Israelites must have enjoyed listening to this tale being told!

2 Timothy 2.8–15

The writer continues to encourage the suffering, persecuted church by describing Paul's advice to Timothy. Paul remains in prison, in chains, yet his hope is in the resurrection of Christ. Suffering does not have the last word, because believers will be vindicated and will share in resurrection life. They must be loyal to Jesus who comes from the kingly line of David. It is inevitable that Timothy, like all Christ's followers will suffer. Yet, just as Paul's physical bonds cannot chain him, Christians cannot be fettered because their salvation is assured. Paul's imprisonment becomes part of his preaching: if he can face his trials with endurance, so can Timothy! Conversely, knowing that Christians remain loyal helps Paul to remain faithful. The saying in verses 11–13 sounds like a liturgical statement that may have been recited in worship. If these words were pronounced in worship they would help to strengthen the people's resolve and their conviction that they would receive a future reward after death. Other people might speak thoughtlessly and irreverently, thus undermining the faith they proclaimed in worship, but Timothy must continue to offer a good example.

Amnesty International often asks people to pray for Christians who are imprisoned for their faith. By focusing on those who still endure for the sake of the gospel, Christians in churches throughout the world are encouraged by their actions. Similarly, those who are imprisoned are upheld by the prayers of others. This passage serves as a reminder that Christianity is not an individual enterprise! Christians belong to the people of God and are bound together by the faith statements we proclaim.

Luke 17.11–19

This is the account of Jesus healing ten lepers. Luke wrote his Gospel outside Israel and has imperfect knowledge both of the geography of the region and of some of the cultural norms of society in Jesus' day. This story takes place near to Samaria and is the only account of Jesus healing a group of people. These lepers were a mixed group of Jews and Samaritans who under normal circumstances would have had nothing to do with each other. The distrust and enmity that existed between Jews and Samaritans is well documented. If Jews and Samaritans were forced to trade it was not unusual for money to be thrown into a bucket of water so that Jews could avoid touching anything that had been in Samaritan hands! Because of their disease, they kept their distance, but this did not prevent Jesus from healing them. His instruction, 'Show yourselves to the priests' serves two purposes: firstly, to fulfil the usual requirement before they could re-enter society and secondly, to witness that they had been cured. However, this shows Luke's lack of understanding, as no Samaritan would have gone to a Jewish priest. Yet, the story is not primarily about the healing miracle, but about the gratitude of one of the lepers, a Samaritan.

One of Luke's concerns was to demonstrate how the gospel of Jesus Christ had relevance for people from both Jewish and Greek backgrounds. The rejection of the gospel message by some Jews was counteracted by the acceptance of the gospel by some Greeks. The story of the healing of the ten lepers would have been a source of great encouragement to pagan members of the early Christian church.

The link with the story of Naaman (above) is not difficult to make. Both Naaman the Syrian and the Samaritan leper received healing from the God of Israel. In both cases, they responded with gratitude. Earlier in the Gospel, Luke recounts Jesus incurring the anger of the synagogue by citing the healing of Naaman in the context of his rejection by his own people (4.27).

Two features of the story are 'inclusivity' and 'gratitude'. The gospel message is not for one group of people ('people like us') but for everyone. It is the nature of gratitude to wish to share. It is not simply social convention that makes us say 'thank you' with flowers or a box of chocolates, it is a natural expression of thanksgiving. If our Christian life was characterized by heartfelt gratitude to God for all that Jesus has done for us, then our response would be to reach out to others wholeheartedly.

SUNDAY BETWEEN 16 AND 22 OCTOBER INCLUSIVE

Twenty-ninth Sunday in Ordinary Time

Jeremiah 31.27–34; Genesis 32.22–31; 2 Timothy 3.14–4.5;
Luke 18.1–8

Jeremiah 31.27–34

Following Babylonia's triumph over Israel the first deportation of prominent people has taken place and many of the nation's leaders have been taken into exile. Yet in this passage reassurance is given that God is the one who sows and his harvest will not fail. The nation will not only survive, but will flourish. The notion that both people and their animals will prosper is an indication that peace and prosperity will return to Israel and Judah in the future. Jeremiah was called to share in both God's judgement and salvation: God breaks down but he also builds and plants. The passage moves on to a well-known proverbial saying of the day. It was as if, through their disobedience, the previous generation had 'eaten sour grapes', but it was the subsequent generation who were being punished, as they were forced to live in exile or under Babylonian domination in their own land. It was their teeth that were 'set on edge' and it wasn't fair! Jeremiah turns the saying on its head by making it clear that people are responsible for their own sins and not those of their parents and grandparents. Those who are faithful in the present have an opportunity to share in the new covenant that God will establish. At Sinai God promised to be faithful to his people and their response was to promise to live obediently by keeping God's commandments. In the past, despite God's saving acts, the people had not keep their part of the bargain. What is 'new' in this 'new covenant' is not the content of the promises. The new element here is the place where the covenant will be written. Today people speak of the heart in relation to feelings and emotion, but in Jeremiah's day the bowels were the seat of the emotions (think of having butterflies in the stomach!) and the heart was the seat of the will. God will write the covenant not on tablets of stone, but on the tablets of their hearts. All people will then 'know' God, in other words they will understand God's nature and be in no doubt about how he wishes them to behave towards him and towards each other. Sins will not only be forgiven but forgotten and there will be a new beginning.

This passage has influenced New Testament writers who have described the Last Supper in terms of 'new covenant'. In services of

Holy Communion these words are often said: 'This is the blood of the new covenant, poured out for all people for the forgiveness of sins.' Christians believe that they have come to 'know' God in the person of Jesus Christ. What is 'new' for Christians is Jesus! Christians are part of the same story as the people of Jeremiah's day. God's faithfulness has never failed, but people have often been disobedient and unfaithful. Yet God has always acted graciously to enable a broken relationship to be restored. This is a matter for rejoicing and recommitment!

Genesis 32.22–31

Jacob was a far from exemplary character! Having cheated his brother out of his inheritance, he was forced to leave home and find work with his kinsman Laban. While working for Laban he continued to act dishonestly until it was clear that he had outstayed his welcome. When he left he took with him more than his fair share of the herds and hoped to appease Esau with a substantial bribe: a gift of animals. With no possibility of returning to Laban and with Esau ahead of him, Jacob camps for the night and in this passage he meets God. At this moment in Jacob's life, caught between his past and his future, recognizing the kind of person he has become involves encountering God.

It was usual for people and animals to travel by night, to avoid the heat of the day, and Jacob's caravan had passed across the Jabbok ford at the foot of a deep gorge. Jacob brought up the rear to ensure all had crossed safely. It was there, alone in the darkness, that he heard someone approaching. The identity of the antagonist remained unknown but the wrestling bout that ensued went on for many hours. The 'magical touching' that resulted in Jacob's hip being put out of joint occurred just as Jacob seemed to be winning the fight. Surely, it would have been unthinkable that Jacob could have prevailed against a divine messenger or even God himself! It seems that this strand of tradition has been hidden in the rewriting of the tale as Jacob, who was easily disabled, was still able to hold on to his opponent and refused to let him go until he blessed Jacob. Jacob's holding on follows more naturally from the idea that he was prevailing in the fight, than from the time he was disabled. During the struggle Jacob must have realized he was fighting a divine opponent, otherwise he would not have tried to extract a blessing from him. His opponent's response is to ask his name. A name signified a person's character. Jacob has to admit who and what he is: a liar and a cheat. It is only when he has acknowledged his own identity as a disgraced, shameful character that his antagonist bestows on him a new honourable name and Jacob, the rogue, becomes Israel. In asking the name of his assailant, Jacob is seeking to discover the nature of God. This is an expression of the longing that lies at the heart of every encounter between humanity and God and it is the desire to know God that elicits the blessing for which he has struggled. To see God 'face to face' had meant facing death (e.g. Exodus 33.20), yet Jacob had not only survived, but he had been blessed!

Many interpretations of this story have been offered and many sermons preached! One suggestion would be the way in which God used a far from exemplary character to become the ancestor of a great nation. Yet Jacob, at a moment of crisis, was willing to enter into the struggle and face himself and God, the person he was and the person who with God's grace he could become. He did not emerge from the struggle unscathed. He was, paradoxically, both broken by the encounter and 'made whole'. Facing who we are in the presence of God is never easy and will always lead to change. Do we want to change, or do we prefer to retreat and avoid the encounter?

2 Timothy 3.14–4.5

From childhood Timothy had been encouraged to listen to Scripture, 'sacred writings' (v.15). The word 'sacred' indicates that in these writings can be found the revelation of God, his wisdom and his will. However, because Timothy is a Christian he is now able to recognize that Scripture points to Christ's work of salvation. Timothy's Scriptures and those of the early church would have included most of the books that we refer to as the Old Testament, although Timothy would probably have had access to them in a Greek translation. The claim that Jewish Scripture was 'inspired by God' (v.16) is tantamount to saying that it is authoritative and is to be used in the ways outlined. Scripture is a tool for teaching, a yardstick against which doctrine can be tested and in this way it guards against error and it provides a model for faithful living against which behaviour can be judged and discipline applied. The study of Scripture, therefore, will enable Timothy and all Christians to 'do every good work' (v.17). This is a salutary reminder that faith must be translated into action that seeks the welfare of all. Chapter 4 begins solemnly and is Paul's final appeal to Timothy. Timothy, like all Christians, remains under the judgement of Christ, which transcends death. There is an expectation that all faithful believers will share in the eternal life of God's kingdom. In the present, Timothy must continue to preach the gospel continually. It is no surprise that there are times when people are particularly receptive to the gospel message, yet Timothy is exhorted to speak out even when people are unlikely to listen! People have 'itching ears' in other words they only prick up their ears when preaching panders to their own selfishness and they do not want to be presented with a hard word! Timothy, however, is to keep his head while continuing to endure whatever trials befall him, while continuing to serve both God and Christ in word and deed.

Luke 18.1–8

This passage, like the story of Jacob (above), involves a disreputable character. The judge is dishonest and secure in his own high position and has no respect either for God or anyone else! A judge's role was to dispense justice and yet throughout history such roles have been open to corruption. The widow represents the very people the judge was supposed to protect, the weakest and most vulnerable members of society. These are the ones God chooses as his own (v.7). The widow's persistence may have paid off, but what of those who were not so persistent! No doubt, the judge would have ignored their pleas. In this case, despite his unwillingness he is forced into right action, even though this goes against the grain! If the dishonest judge responded to the widow's cry for help, how much more quickly will God who is just respond? However, the experience of early Christians, who were waiting for the return of the risen Christ, was that God did not respond as quickly as they expected. This parable encourages them not to lose heart, but to keep praying and calling on God, because he would hear. The Son of Man, the risen Christ who had experienced human suffering, would return and would expect them, like him, to be faithful and obedient.

The unanswered cries of the weak and vulnerable people of the world often remain unheard. Jesus' expected return to earth remains part of Christian faith, but Christians do not agree about when and how this will happen. One way in which Jesus returns is when he comes to the hearts of his people compelling them to speak and act on behalf of those who are most in need.

SUNDAY BETWEEN 23 AND 29 OCTOBER INCLUSIVE

Thirtieth Sunday in Ordinary Time

Joel 2.23–32; Sirach/Ecclesiasticus 35.12–17;
Jeremiah 14.7–10,19–22; 2 Timothy 4.6–8,16–18; Luke 18.9–14

Joel 2.23–32

The prophet looks to the future when present hardships will be reversed. God, who keeps his covenant promise, will rescue them from the time of drought and famine. God will shower the people with blessings and they can look forward to abundant life when there will be grain, wine and oil in plenty. It will be a time of joy when the thanksgiving of the people will be heard in worship and songs of praise will resound. All people will know God who dwells among them and they will no longer look to other gods for help because God alone is the one who will save them. The renewed covenant will last for ever and God's Spirit will be poured out on his covenant people. Sometimes preachers try to universalize the words 'all flesh' (v.28) and suggest that the prophet is looking forward to a time when all people will turn to God; however, this is to misunderstand the context of the passage as the prophet is addressing solely the people of Judah. It is only at the first Christian Pentecost (Acts 2) that the promise is extended to people from all nations. What does the Spirit do? The Spirit enables prophecy and the dreaming of dreams.

This is not the comfortable daydreaming of a people in holiday mode, enjoying a well-earned rest after harvest. Rather, it is a sharing in God's mission and will for the world; it is about understanding God's loving purposes and participating in God's saving work.

Sirach/Ecclesiasticus 35.12–17

God's generosity is not given to some and withheld from others. Such a God requires people to be equally generous in their own dealings with each other. Open-hearted and open-handed giving brings blessings not only to the recipients, but also to the giver. This is often found to be true in practice, as those who give discover in the joy and gratitude of the recipients that they are more than recompensed for their time, effort and kindness. However, in this passage, God is the one who will make sure that they are rewarded. God is like a judge who cannot be bribed. Perhaps this serves as a reminder that kind acts are not a way of 'buying ourselves out of trouble', but must be heartfelt. Those who were most vulnerable in Hebrew society were orphans and widows who were left without support and were wholly reliant on the charity of relatives or neighbours. Our concern, like God's, must always be with those who are most in need and most wronged.

Jeremiah 14.7–10, 19–22

These verses may have been used in worship and take the form of communal laments in times of trouble. Chapter 14 begins with an account of a famine that has devastated the land and left the people in dire straits. The first lament opens with an admission of Judah's sin. Lying behind the confession is the assumption that this disaster would not have happened if the people had done nothing to deserve it. They cry out to God beseeching him not to be like a stranger who travels through the land. After all, he is the one who dwells in their midst in the Holy of Holies in the Jerusalem Temple! The people of Judah bear God's name; they are his to protect. Yet, they have behaved so badly that they believe that they have put themselves beyond God's protection and now face punishment.

Verses 19–22 are part of a second lament following an enemy attack. Nevertheless, the problem of drought remains. The prophet asks why God allows these things to happen. Why are the people struck down? Why are they not healed? Why is there no peace? Why does terror reign supreme? The questions tumble out of the prophet's mouth. Perhaps he cannot bring himself to believe that God could possibly have brought about these terrible events, nor that God is doing nothing to save his stricken people. Verse 20 is an acknowledgement of their wickedness and, once again, these words sound as if they were recited as part of a liturgical refrain. Is the prophet saying what the people themselves should say? God must not despise his people for the sake of his own honour, his name. Everyone knows that Judah looks to God for help; surely God does not want the enemy nations to think he has failed? The people's hope must rest on God; there is nothing else on which they can rely.

In times of famine and drought, in times of warfare and devastation, two recurring questions are asked: 'Where is God?' and 'What have we done to deserve this?' It is worth noting that in the ancient world no distinction was made between 'natural disasters' and 'disasters that are caused by humanity'. Such profound questions can never be answered fully from the pulpit. However there are assertions that the preacher can make: just as the prophet felt the people's pain, we can be sure that God suffered with and for his people just as keenly – as at

Calvary. Famine and drought are often found in the wake of warfare as land is destroyed and water sources are polluted. Humanity must take responsibility for the consequences of greed and war, yet God's spirit continues to work within the 'Jeremiahs' and 'prophets' of this world who intercede for those who suffer, and urge people to live faithfully.

2 Timothy 4.6–8, 16–18

Hellenistic religious practice involved pouring out libations, drink offerings, to the gods. Paul's suffering and forthcoming death is described in terms of this pagan ritual. Paul has continued to struggle in the contest between Christianity and all that opposes God's will. By enduring hardship and remaining faithful, he has reached the goal and will gain the victor's prize. The winner of athletic contests, according to Greek custom, was garlanded (crowned). The present-day equivalent would be the presentation of a gold medal. The risen Christ will present Paul with his reward, for Christ is the one who judges between Paul and those who have opposed him. Paul's Jewish roots would have led him to believe that he would be judged faithful on the last day when Jesus would return. On that day, all who looked forward to Christ's coming (in other words, all who like Paul had remained faithful) would share that same reward, presumably of eternal life in the age to come when all creation would be transformed.

In verses 16–18 Paul asserts that even though no one came to court to support him when his case was first heard, he does not want this to count against the Christian community at the last judgement. He did not stand alone because he was supported and strengthened by Christ and such help enables Christians to remain firm in the face of persecution. This enabled him to proclaim the gospel message within the context of a Roman court. At that time, he was 'saved from the lion's mouth' (v.17). This is not an allusion to Christians being thrown to lions in the arena, but a general statement that Paul was not executed there and then. Paul ends with the ringing affirmation that Christ will save him from every conceivable enemy attack, because Paul's future lies beyond this life, in God's heavenly kingdom!

The early Christian church believed that, when Jesus returned, this world would be completely transformed and there would no longer be a division between heaven and earth. Instead, there would only be one 'heavenly' realm under God's rule. Inevitably, two thousand years later, there is a more 'this worldly' emphasis for present-day Christians whose calling is to share in the task of bringing healing and wholeness to a broken world. Yet that task will often bring Christians into opposition with powerful forces and, like Paul, our faith is in a God who will not forsake his people.

Luke 18.9–14

This is one of a number of parables that only appear in Luke's Gospel. The scene is set in the Temple at Jerusalem. Those listening to the parable for the first time would have expected the Pharisee, not the tax-collector, to be held up as role model and the denouement would have come as a shock! In this story the Pharisee and the tax-collector represent two different responses to Jesus: those who relied on their own righteousness and hardened their hearts to the gospel message and those who recognized their own sinfulness and came seeking forgiveness and help to change their ways. Although the Pharisee's self-righteousness tends to irritate today's readers, people at the time would have honoured him for his undoubted piety. That the Pharisee fasted on days other than those when it was customary for everyone to fast, for example on the Day of Atonement, was a sign of his total commitment to God. Not only did he give a tenth of his herds and crops as the law commanded, but he gave a tenth of all he owned. Standing was the usual attitude for prayer and the Pharisee was amongst those who had gathered at one of the set times of prayer that took place at 9 a.m. and 3 p.m. The Pharisee is being presented as an exemplary character! Again, today's readers tend to respond to his self-righteousness with distaste, but such feeling is not present in the narrative. It was not surprising that the Pharisee gave thanks to God his creator for the nature he had been given. The tax-collector cannot even assume the normal attitude of prayer, his downcast gaze reflecting his lack of self-worth. He is distanced physically both from the Pharisee who prays with the confidence of the self-righteous and from his maker. He is in no doubt that he has sinned. Tax-collectors worked on behalf of the Roman authorities and handled the coins inscribed with the image of the emperor. He made a living out of those who exploited his own people. By acknowledging his own failings, the broken relationship between himself and God is healed. God's mercy is part of the divine nature and reaches out to all who acknowledge their need. There is no suggestion that the Pharisee is brought low. However, the theme of reversal of fortunes constantly recurs in Luke's Gospel: for example in Mary's song of joy (1.52). Nevertheless, the parable did challenge those in the Christian community who tended to be self-righteous and continues to challenge Christians today.

ALL SAINTS

Daniel 7.1–3, 15–18; Ephesians 1.11–23; Luke 6.20–31

Daniel 7.1–3, 15–18

The book of Daniel was written to encourage Jews who were suffering at the hands of Antiochus IV, the ruler of the Greek kingdom, who had invaded Israel. Daniel, a fictional character, was held up as an example of a Jew who had remained faithful during the time of the Exile in Babylon many years earlier. Chapter 7 is written in apocalyptic style, characterized by visions and the use of symbols that would have been understood by the first readers.

While in Babylon, Daniel received a vision from God. The sea refers to the primeval chaos, the 'formless abyss' that threatens to overwhelm humanity, ordered and controlled by God when the world was created (Gen. 1–2). From the waters, four terrifying beasts emerged. What did the vision mean? Daniel turns for help to an angelic being present in God's heavenly court (described in vv. 9–14). The angel explains to Daniel that the beasts represent four kingdoms, described in Daniel 2 as Babylonian, Median, Persian and Greek. The readers were living during the time of the fourth beast, persecuted as they were by the Greek ruler. The angel tells Daniel that earthly rule will pass to the 'Saints of the Most High'. These are the Jews who have remained faithful during the time of trial. They are the ones who will exercise God's power.

The 'saints' in Daniel were a group of people who helped and encouraged each other. Here is a timely reminder that Christianity can never be a solo effort, we are called to belong to God's people and to take joint responsibility as we live out our calling.

Ephesians 1.11–23

It has been suggested that 'the seal of the Holy Spirit' (v.14) is a reference to baptism and the words are part of a sermon addressed to newly baptized Christians. However, this is not necessarily the case. Certainly, what is being celebrated in this reading is the presence of the Holy Spirit in the lives of believers. The writer has begun by including himself amongst the praising community to whom Christ has given hope. In verse 13, he speaks directly to this particular group of Christians. He assures them that the gift of the Holy Spirit, like a down payment or deposit, is a guarantee that they will inherit all that God has prepared for his people. This is the language of financial transaction. God is the one who will take full possession of his property and God's property is all creation! The content of the inheritance is nothing less than the purposes of God and their fulfilment in Christ. Here is assurance that, ultimately, all that contravenes God's rule will be overcome and his people will be part of a new, radically transformed world order. Their hope is certain, because God keeps his promises!

Verses 15–23 are discussed in the lectionary passage for Ascension Day. Here it is enough to reiterate that the outworking of Christian faith is seen when 'all the saints' care for each other.

Christians were 'saints' simply because they belonged to God, not because they were especially good or brave! There is hope for us all! Caring in the early church was focused within the community as Christians stood shoulder to shoulder against the outside world. Nowadays we realize that the church's task is to care not only for each other but also for all who need our help.

Luke 6.20–31

This is part of 'The Sermon on the Plain' which echoes some of the material found in Matthew's 'Sermon on the Mount' (Matt. 5–7). Jesus is speaking to his disciples, including Luke's first readers and those who read the gospel today. This passage begins with beatitudes, each commencing with the words, 'Blessed are you . . .'. Jesus is not suggesting that those who are poor, hungry or abused are blessed while they undergo suffering. Rather, he is speaking about future blessing that will come about because God will act on their behalf. This theme runs throughout Luke's Gospel: those who are wealthy and powerful will change places with those who are poor, exploited and abused. Lying behind these words is the implied imperative that the wealthy and powerful should act on behalf of the weak, rather than for selfish ends. It is probable that many Christian congregations living out their faith in the pagan Roman world would have faced economic pressure. Regarded with suspicion, trading would have been difficult as people could purchase what they needed elsewhere. The woes of verses 24–26 would have reflected their own experience, while reminding them that their condition was temporary. While they were waiting, they were to exemplify the life of the kingdom by treating others with immense generosity, 'doing good' (v.28) and 'praying' (v.29) for their enemies. To be struck on the cheek, or to have a coat or other goods stolen may well have been part of everyday experience, while also mirroring the experiences of Jesus during his passion. The 'golden rule' (v.31) provides a summary of what is required of Christians.

SUNDAY BETWEEN 30 OCTOBER AND 5 NOVEMBER INCLUSIVE

Thirty-first Sunday in Ordinary Time

Habakkuk 1.1–4; 2.1–4; Isaiah 1.10–16;
2 Thessalonians 1.1–4,11–12; Luke 19.1–10

Habakkuk 1.1–4; 2.1–4

These verses present a dialogue between the prophet and God. The prophet is struggling with the question that is often on people's hearts. 'How long will God allow people to suffer as the result of injustice?' The situation being addressed is not known, but it is clear that violence has been perpetrated by the strong and the weak are being destroyed. The judicial system has ceased to function. The prophet's role is to watch out for God's answer. When the answer does come, it is unsatisfactory. The prophet is to act as a messenger. The message will be written on tablets of stone. These words recall the giving of the commandments at Sinai (Ex. 31.18). The implication is that the people have already been given the law and their sole responsibility is to keep it. The tablets of stone that are given to Habakkuk state only that God will act, but that he will act in his own time. There is no doubt at all that the day will come when God will bring judgement to the world and when he does act there will be no escape. People need only to concern themselves with their own faithfulness. The unjust may ignore the commandments, but it is implied that God will catch up with them! Righteous people must continue to live faithfully despite their suffering, for they can be certain that God will act and their hope will not be in vain.

There is an unsatisfactory feeling to these verses. The answer is no answer at all! Yet, throughout human history justice has been perverted and there have been innocent victims. The Church must take on the threefold role of the prophet: that of wrestling with the hard questions, remaining faithful while waiting for God to answer and affirming God's concern for those who suffer. Christians are able to point to the death and resurrection of Jesus to show how God transforms suffering into joy and despair into hope. However, the Christian response must not remain passive, but must be prepared to challenge injustice and bring aid and comfort to those who suffer today.

Isaiah 1.10–16

Sacrificial worship and the observance of the Sabbath and other holy days were an accepted part of Israelite religious practice, so it is extremely unlikely that Isaiah is suggesting that usual ways of worshipping should be abandoned. It has sometimes been suggested that prophets and priests argued about whether sacrifice was an essential part of worship, but there is no evidence to support this idea. Then what was the prophet saying? Sodom and Gomorrah had become euphemisms for any people who were sinful. The particular group of people whom Isaiah singles out as 'sinners' are the rulers, those who were rich, powerful and influential, who were offering expensive sacrifices to boost their own self-esteem. The peace offering of a whole animal was an occasion for a feast. The priest was given a share of the meat, but the rest of the animal was eaten by the worshipper and his friends and such gatherings could become riotous occasions and an excuse for over-indulgence. They were behaving no better than cattle that trample everything under foot! The Hebrew word translated 'abomination' (v.13) is exceptionally strong and usually refers to the worship of Baal. It may well be that the Sabbath and festivals had become occasions when idolatry took place. Of course, God would not listen to the prayers of people who were so busy indulging themselves that they had ceased to care for the poorer people in society. When those in authority failed in their responsibilities, those who had no one to turn to faced extreme hardship and even death. It is not surprising that with the blood of the poor on their hands (v.15) no amount of prayers would be heard by God who expects his representatives to be both just and merciful. It was high time they changed their ways! Perhaps the allusion to 'washing and making themselves clean' (v.16) may refer to a liturgical act of repentance, entered into with integrity, that would mark a new beginning.

How do we approach worship? Do we attend church services for our own benefit, or to worship God? When asked why they do not attend church, people will often say, 'Because I don't get anything out of it'. Others, when asked why they do attend church, will often say, 'Because I enjoy meeting my friends and it is good to belong to a fellowship'. This is not to suggest that it is wrong to enjoy meeting friends or engaging in social activities within the life of the church. Rather, it is a salutary reminder that worship that is acceptable to God does not end with the final note of the hymn, or the 'Amen' at the end of the service, but must be reflected in our lives and in our care for others. Worship is primarily about what we offer and only secondarily about what we receive!

2 Thessalonians 1.1–4, 11–12

During his time in Thessalonica Paul's opponents, who had a different understanding of the gospel message, had tried to undermine his authority. There is no indication who these opponents were, nor how their teaching differed from Paul's. However, it is clear that Paul and his companions won the day. Paul begins by expressing his joy that the Thessalonians are continuing to follow his teaching, even though it was likely that those who opposed him had not left the area. It was usual practice for letters to begin with thanksgiving and Paul uses this conventional opening, within the context of prayer, to recall the church's acceptance of the gospel and so encourages them to remain faithful. As Paul remembers his friends before God, he rejoices that the response of faith is worked out in the obedient lifestyles of Christians. This is the 'labour of love' (v.3) and the word 'labour' emphasizes that the task is hard. Yet, Christians will not fail because their motivation is love. This is the divine love that puts others first and seeks what is best for them. Faith in a loving God leads to actions motivated by love, and this way of life is not a 'one-day wonder' because it is rooted in Jesus Christ. Hope in Jesus will never be disappointed and so Christians will remain steadfast in their commitment. Previously, the Jewish nation had described themselves as God's chosen people. Now Christians from both Jewish and Greek backgrounds are 'brothers and sisters' who belong to the family of faith. ('Brother' (v.4) is an inclusive term that includes all members of the Christian community.)

At the start of the second chapter, Paul contrasts his experience in Philippi, when he and Silas were beaten and thrown into prison, with his visit to Thessalonica. In both places, Paul and his companions had proclaimed the gospel boldly, displaying the courage that itself is a gift from God. From the outset, Paul had his critics and opponents, but the church responded to his message. The implication is that Paul's integrity contrasted favourably with his opponents' methods. Paul was not concerned with his own popularity, but with preaching the good news from God.

It is natural for people to seek approval and the good opinion of others. In today's celebrity culture, it is easy to recognize the attraction of gaining celebrity status. Often a small church community enables some people to become 'big fish in little ponds'! If we look into our hearts, we will recognize our mixed motives. Those who preach enjoy positive comments from the congregation – and there is nothing wrong in that – but the first task of every member of the congregation is to bear witness in word and deed to the gospel of Christ, whether that makes us popular or unpopular. Nevertheless, we are more likely to listen to those we like. Ask the congregation to think of people who have taught them over the years and the subjects they enjoy now and it is probable that there will be a connection between the two. Nine times out of ten, we learned most from those we liked most! The important thing is to maintain an integrity that is rooted in God's will and not our own self-seeking.

Luke 19.1–10

The well-known story of Zacchaeus introduces two themes dear to Luke's heart: Jesus' eating with sinners and the right use of wealth. Zacchaeus is a chief tax-collector and he is rich. Tax-collectors were archetypal sinners because they worked for Rome, handled Roman coins bearing the image of the emperor and had the opportunity to engage in fraudulent practice. It is ironic that the name Zacchaeus means 'upright' or 'righteous'! When Jesus accosted Zacchaeus saying, 'I must stay at your house today' (v.5), this is hardly a request, but rather a demand. Salvation is not in the future; it is a present reality. All that is needed is Zacchaeus' response. Perhaps too many present-day sermons have tried to examine Zacchaeus' state of mind, but that is to miss the point of the story. It is the immediacy of his response that is important. He does not wait but immediately makes reparation, giving half of what he has to the poor and repaying those he has defrauded, four times over, there and then. (Although the English translations often indicate that repayment is something Zacchaeus is intending to do, the original verbs are in the present tense, implying that he acts immediately.) Jesus calls Zacchaeus 'a son of Abraham' because he has accepted the salvation on offer and is restored into the family of God's people. The final verse summarizes Jesus' mission, 'to seek out and to save the lost' (v.10). Jesus refers to himself as 'Son of Man', that is the representative human being who will complete his task only through suffering. To complete his mission Jesus must face the cross.

Salvation is both divine gift and divine command! Like Zacchaeus, we are presented here and now with a choice: to accept God's gift and its responsibilities, or to turn our backs on the gospel of Christ. There is no middle way.

SUNDAY BETWEEN 6 AND 12 NOVEMBER INCLUSIVE

Thirty-second Sunday in Ordinary Time

Haggai 1.15b–2.9; Job 19.23–27a; 2 Thessalonians 2.1–5,13–17;
Luke 20.27–38

Haggai 1.15b–2.9

The year was 520 BCE and the date indicates that the people were participating in the final part of the Feast of Tabernacles (Booths). This was the feast of the year, when the people gathered and the fires were lit for sacrifice (Lev. 23.33–36). The Temple, destroyed by the Babylonians, was now being reconstructed. It seems that the older generation were grumbling, because the new building was only a pale imitation of Solomon's Temple and lacked its splendour. This was the perfect opportunity for Haggai to address the people who were gathered together in festival mode, especially as Joshua the High Priest and Zerubbabel the Governor were also present. Solomon's Temple had been decorated with wood and precious metals and the Temple under reconstruction would not be so ornate even though some of the temple vessels had been returned from Babylon (Ezra 1.8–11). Haggai reminded them that what matters most is that God's indwelling holy presence is with them and that is why they must work on the Temple. Haggai uses words that would have resonated with the older generation, for example the formula 'I am with you'. His 'Exodus' language, reminding them of the mighty acts of God and the glories of the past, would reassure and encourage the die-hards. He includes them by assigning them a task. In a prophetic oracle he reminds the people that when God appears the world is shaken. Now, in their own time, God will shake the earth again to gather the community of his people around a new-built temple. This earth-shaking event will be felt by other nations who will bring their wealth and precious gifts to the Temple. All that had been lost or destroyed when the Babylonians invaded will be restored or replaced. However, Haggai reminds them that this wealth does not belong to the nation, but to God and is a testimony to his glory. Who is the real provider for the Temple? Is it God or his people? The answer is that God provides for his Temple and so building the Temple is what God wants them to do! God's presence in his Temple is the source of 'shalom', peace and well-being for all. The prosperity of the nation depends on this building! Presumably, by this time the older generation are convinced!

These verses from Haggai are a reminder that the Church cannot move forward unless everyone shares a vision for the future. Too often, the generation gap causes division and ill-feeling as older people feel railroaded by those who are younger, and younger people feel that their ideas are not being taken seriously. Haggai used his leadership skills to mend fences and he did so by focusing attention on God rather than on the disappointment or desires of individuals. Haggai enabled the people to become a community gathered around the Temple, the place where God made his presence known. Christians are a community gathered around the cross. That community spans all generations and it is only when tolerance and mutual respect are fostered and all views are heard that we become a gospel people.

Job 19.23–27a

Job stares death in the face. The happy life he had enjoyed is over. The only hope he has left is that he will be vindicated and people will learn that he has done nothing to bring his suffering upon himself. He would feel better if there was a permanent record of his innocence that people could read in the future – preferably letters inscribed in the rock face that could never be erased. The words, 'I know that my redeemer lives' have particular overtones for Christians, but here Job is expressing his certainty that someone must stand up for him and state that he is innocent. If there is any justice at all, Job will be vindicated. The redeemer figure is the last one to speak so his words will carry the day. This is a scene of judgement as God rules on behalf of Job. Is Job still alive, or will Job's vindication take place after his death (v.26)? Either way, the matter of his innocence is so important to Job that he is sure he will know when he is vindicated. It is only then that he will 'see God'. Job's faith is in a God who is just, even though his sufferings may have led him to question God's justice. Only when his innocence is proclaimed will his faith be justified.

Job's situation mirrors the situations of many in the world today, who suffer for no reason. They are the victims of famine, disease and inhumanity. Job's question is ours, 'Why does a loving and just God allow this to happen?' The answer lies with God. Perhaps we should change the question and ask, 'Do those who suffer have to wait until death before someone will speak out for them and work to bring their suffering to an end?'

2 Thessalonians 2.1–5, 13–17

Christians believed that 'the Day of the Lord', referred to the time when Jesus would return to judge the world. It seems that some Thessalonian Christians believed that the Day of the Lord had already arrived and that life as they knew it would end within hours or days! They must have felt shocked, disturbed and excited. Perhaps they wondered whether there was any point continuing with everyday tasks. After all, if the end of the world was going to happen tomorrow there would not be much point cleaning the house or going to work! One response would be to enjoy every moment left and live it up! Apocalyptic thought was that the final judgement would be preceded by a concerted rebellion against God. Such a rebellion would be characterized by words of false prophets and by warfare between nations. The opposition to God's will would be led by 'the lawless one' (v.3) a figure representing evil, in contrast to Christ the divine representative. This evil figure would set himself up in the Temple, in other words he would claim divinity. This had happened in the past, for example, when the Greek ruler Antiochus IV had placed a statue of Zeus in the Temple and when the Roman Emperor, Caligula, had tried to set up a statue of himself for Jewish people to worship. It seems that false teachers were misinterpreting the 'signs of the times' and were proclaiming that the end had come. Paul assures the Christians that the time is not yet, implying that for now they must continue with their daily tasks in a responsible and faithful way.

The importance of faithful living is underlined in verses 13–17. Paul thanks God that the Christians in Thessalonica already belong to God's people and so their future salvation is assured. They are loved by Jesus and will be amongst the first to share in the 'glory' (v.14), the divine life of the new age. These words would have helped to quell any feelings of uncertainty and anxiety. For now, they must remain steadfast, in other words they must reject false teaching and continue to live out their faith as they face the trials and tasks of each day.

Given the availability of weapons of mass destruction combined with the distrust and hatred that characterize many international relationships in today's world, it is not surprising that voices are heard proclaiming that we are living on the brink of destruction. Fear of what tomorrow will bring is always debilitating. Paul's words to the Christian congregation in Thessalonica ring true for us. Christians can be secure in the knowledge that they belong to God and to Christ. Although we are not immune from the dangers and difficulties of life, we are called to live each day faithfully, leaving tomorrow in God's safe-keeping.

Luke 20.27–38

The doctrine of the resurrection of the dead is not present in the Torah, the Jewish law that is found in the first five books of the Old Testament. The Sadducees were the wealthy, influential group often associated with the temple priesthood. Unlike the Pharisees, they rejected later oral traditions and considered the Torah to be authoritative. For this reason, they were conservative thinkers who rejected the notion of resurrection. They believed that God rewarded or punished people in this life. (Sadducees believed that God judged people in this life and propounded a 'theology of blessing', the view that God rewards those who are faithful in material ways during people's lifetime. It is interesting to note that this view is becoming more prevalent in some versions of Christianity today.) A group of Sadducees challenge Jesus by giving an example from Scripture to demonstrate the irrational nature of belief in resurrection. They are attempting both to undermine the belief Jesus seems to share and to test his ability to interpret Scripture. The Torah stated that if a man died without an heir, his brother should marry the widow and the first child of that union would inherit the man's property (Deut. 25.5–10). The Sadducees present Jesus with an absurd picture of a widow becoming the wife of a succession of seven brothers as one after another dies. Jesus' answer seems to imply that marriage is necessary in this life so that there will be children. However, after the resurrection there will be no more death and marriage will become redundant because no more children will be born. He goes on to explain a passage from the Torah. Moses (who for the Sadducees was the ultimate scriptural authority) encountered God at the burning bush (Ex. 3.6). God introduced himself to Moses as the God of Abraham, Isaac and Jacob. Because he is 'God of the living and not of the dead' (v.38), the patriarchs must still live and share in resurrection life! All life is a gift from God and the implication is that the relationship with God prevents death from having the last word.

This passage has generated considerable anxiety amongst bereaved people who long to be reunited with loved ones when they die. Reassurance lies not in the absurdity of the Sadducees' question, but in the bonds of close relationship. If God will not allow death to end a relationship, then we can trust him to lead us, and those whom we love, through death.

SUNDAY BETWEEN 13 AND 19 NOVEMBER INCLUSIVE

Thirty-third Sunday in Ordinary Time

Isaiah 65.17–25; Malachi 4.1–2a; 2 Thessalonians 3.6–13;
Luke 21.5–19

Isaiah 65.17–25

The theme of people's disobedience and the consequences of their sin runs through Isaiah, a book that begins in the eighth century BCE and ends after the return of the exiles from Babylon (though some passages may be as late as the third century BCE). In these closing chapters hope for the future lies in God's decision to deal with human sinfulness by transforming the universe. Those whose worship is reflected in obedient living will take their place within God's new creation. Later apocalyptic thought builds on the ideas present in Isaiah 65, but here there is no suggestion that God's new saving act will begin with destruction, rather that the whole universe, described as heaven and earth, will be renewed. In the past God acted decisively to save his people, not once but many times, but even God's mighty acts will be forgotten because what he is about to do will eclipse anything that has already taken place. Judah and Jerusalem will become the focus of God's renewed act of creation. Today, that focus may seem too narrow, yet the idea that transformation begins with the worship and obedience of God's faithful people is a theme worth exploring. How will this transformation be experienced? In the past Jerusalem was beset from within and from without: injustice and power-seeking within and enemies without threatened the peace of the city. In the future Jerusalem will be blessed and will exemplify God's loving purposes for the world. Those who live in the city will have long lives and the sound of mourning for those who died prematurely will no longer be heard. In Hebrew thought, longevity was a sign of God's blessing and shortness of life was the result of sin. Because of people's faithfulness, they will receive divine protection. The relationship between God and his people will be reciprocal: just as the people will delight in God, so God will delight in them and will be ready to answer their prayers even before they are asked! Yet the picture drawn is not of an 'otherworldly' lifestyle. The people will continue their everyday work, they will build houses and plant and harvest crops, but their labour will not be fruitless. They will live a peaceful existence not marred by warfare or famine, and they and their children will enjoy a life of plenty. Verse 25 looks back to 11.6–9 and the idea that this new peaceful existence will extend even to the animal world. The serpent was a sinister presence in Eden and a reminder of the way that sin crept into the world, but in the transformed creation sin will have no place.

One of the difficulties faced by those who preach on this passage today is that the renewal of the world has not yet taken place. Although Christians point to the Christ event as God's decisive transforming act, they cannot deny that human sin is still endemic. People still die prematurely because of warfare and want, cruelty and neglect. Lions and lambs do not lie down together and the serpent still slithers through the garden. Perhaps the most productive way of responding to the passage is to affirm that the picture we are being offered represents God's will for his creation and that transformation begins with God's faithful people.

Malachi 4.1–2a

The 'day that is coming' (v.1) is the time when evildoers will be judged. These are the arrogant, whose high opinion of their own worth has led them to act unjustly towards the weaker members of society. Their wickedness leads inexorably to the day when they will be burned like the stubble left in the field. This contrasts with the fate of the righteous on whom God's warmth and light will fall like the rays of the sun. The term the 'sun of righteousness' is unusual in Hebrew Scripture, possibly because the sun was worshipped by many of Israel's neighbours. Perhaps Malachi was appropriating this language from Persian culture, but this remains a matter for speculation. In the Aaronic blessing are the words, 'The Lord make his face to shine upon you' and this phrase conjures the image of the sun's warming light-giving rays. The people will be like calves that have been kept in a stall and, when let out into the pasture, kick up their heels and sport in the sunshine.

What a joyful image! Let us hold on to this picture of exuberant freedom from all that oppresses and restrains. One of the criticisms of Christians is that they are perceived as killjoys and Christianity a religion of 'thou shalt nots'! Yet the overriding characteristic of Christians should be that of a joyful people.

2 Thessalonians 3.6–13

Once again Paul offers a practical solution to a pastoral problem. It seems that some members of the Christian church were failing to pull their weight and had slipped into lazy, idle ways. Perhaps the problem stemmed from the same misconception as that discussed in last Sunday's passage (2 Thess. 2.1–5,13–17) as the idlers could see no point in continuing with their usual tasks if Jesus was about to return within hours or days and bring life as they knew it to an end. Paul counters this argument by pointing to his own actions. When he and his companions stayed in Thessalonica with Jason (Acts 17.7) they did not sponge on him but worked to pay their way. This, Paul asserts, is how all Christians should behave. Perhaps some people in the church and in wider society looked down on manual work and thought it was beneath them. If so, Paul counters this view by the uncompromising statement that those who do not work do not eat! Perhaps Paul was quoting a well-known maxim, possibly the kind of words a master might have used towards a lazy slave. It is assumed that work is available and everyone has the opportunity to earn a living. The translation in the NIV picks up the play on words 'they are not busy, they are busybodies'. The implication seems to be that the idlers were spending their time gossiping, minding other people's business rather than their own. Christians should do their work quietly. In other words, they should not be a nuisance to other people, for example, by living on the charity of others rather than providing for themselves. Paul's advice is that persistent idlers are to be shunned; other members of the congregation must not mix with them. After all, it is better to avoid those who cause trouble rather than be caught up in it! When people exercise discipline, it is difficult not to let personal antagonism show. Paul makes it clear that offenders should not be treated as enemies and this remains good advice to any congregation! Paul closes with a blessing. Having offered them advice, he hopes that the situation will be resolved. He prays firstly that there will be peace amongst them, in other words that relationships will be mended, and secondly that the Lord will be with them all. No one is left out of Paul's prayer.

What sensible advice! Paul's theology was often thought out in relation to practical problems that arose in the early Christian church. Sometimes we assume that if only we could return to the early days of Christianity our present problems would be resolved. What a misconception! From the beginning, Christians had differences of opinion and churches were fraught with tension and misunderstandings. Our task, now as then, is to seek to resolve our differences and to explore together what it means to follow Christ in today's world and to continue his work by providing materially and spiritually for those in need.

Luke 21.5–19

The apocalyptic thought-world of the day is represented in this passage. Apocalyptic thinking was characterized by the expectation of a time of cosmic upheaval that would affect both heavenly and earthly realms. There would be a period of immense suffering followed by ultimate victory for those who remained faithful during the time of trial. Visionaries often made prophecies about the manner and time of these events. The ultimate victory would be the end of the present phase of world history inaugurating a new age of peace and plenty under God's rule. These ideas gained ground between 200 BCE and 200 CE, the centuries that included the Christ event and the founding of the early Christian church. Luke, like Matthew, is dependent on Mark 13, but rewrites this passage in the light of his own understanding. Luke was writing to encourage Christians who lived outside Palestine to remain faithful within the pagan Roman world.

Jesus begins by telling those who were praising the beauty of the Temple that its days were numbered. Indeed, the Jewish Revolt (66–70 CE) culminated in the destruction of the Temple by the Romans. For those Christians who lived to see its destruction it must have seemed as if God was being vanquished by his enemies. These words serve to remind them that the troubles they experience are part of God's greater plan. In the years leading up to the Temple's destruction there were a number of 'would-be Messiahs' whose claims were false and misleading. While Christianity remained under the umbrella of Judaism, Christians were allowed the same privileges as Jews who were allowed freedom of worship within the Roman Empire. Eventually the time came when the church and synagogue separated and Christians lost the protection of the parent-body. Divisions sprang up within families and Christians were brought before the civic authorities to explain themselves (21.12–17). While this was an opportunity to testify, it was also a risky business and there is no doubt that some were martyred. The assertion that 'not one hair of your head will perish' (v.18) was over-optimistic as many lost their lives, unless as implied by v.19, Luke is asserting his faith in life beyond death.

Few people today hold an apocalyptic world-view and one of the hardest problems for Christians is to explain why God does not act immediately to prevent suffering. However, our faith remains in a God whose constant love for the world is seen in Christ. In the midst of a suffering world, Christians are called to be faithful. In other parts of the globe, many Christian people are called both to endure and to remain steadfast. How can we speak and act for them?

SUNDAY BETWEEN 20 AND 26 NOVEMBER INCLUSIVE

Sunday before Advent

Jeremiah 23.1–6; Colossians 1.11–20; Luke 23.33–43

Jeremiah 23.1–6

Shepherds are the leaders of the nation. In the ancient Near East, the sign of office for Pharaohs and kings was a shepherd's crook. The people's leaders had failed them. Now God will both do the shepherding and appoint new shepherds who will do the job properly. Scattered people will return to Jerusalem where they will multiply and prosper under a just leader. Jeremiah looks to the restoration of the Davidic monarchy and the coming of the one he calls 'The Righteous Branch'. The word 'righteous' may refer both to the legitimacy of the new ruler, who will be a descendent of David, and to his moral authority. 'Branch' was a word used of a forthcoming Messiah (Zech. 3.8) and Davidic kings were 'shoots' from the tree of Jesse. When Jehoiakin the king had been deported, the Babylonians placed a 'puppet king' Zedekiah on the throne. Jeremiah had nothing good to say about Zedekiah and this oracle implicitly compares Zedekiah with the 'righteous branch' who will save the people.

Christians speak of Jesus as 'the good shepherd' and the 'Branch' from the line of Jesse. Next week the Church will enter the season of advent. The expected Messiah is the one we know already, for Christians follow Jesus in whom we see God's constant love for his people.

Colossians 1.11–20

The writer prays for the Colossian Christians who need God's power to enable them to maintain right conduct. They share the inheritance of God's people. The language echoes the promise made to Abraham and, like him, Christians will enter their own 'Promised Land'. This is the kingdom of Christ, a place of light where there is no more darkness because they have left their old ways behind and now live under Christ's lordship as forgiven people.

Verses 15–20 are an early Christian hymn and statement of faith. Firstly, it is because God's creative power is present in Jesus that he has authority. God is revealed in Jesus who both represents God and shares God's character. This idea is present in Jewish thought that speaks of God's 'wisdom' as the agent of creation and is found in

John 1.1–3, where it is God's 'word' that becomes a human being (John 1.14). Secondly, Jesus 'holds all things together' (v.17). In other words, only in Jesus can we see the divine purpose for humanity and the created order. Christians acknowledge Jesus to be the 'head of the body' who leads them through death to new life. Thirdly, it is through Christ's death that humanity and the universe are rescued from all that opposes God's will for creation and are brought into harmony within God's loving purpose.

It is only through Christ's death on the cross that the extent of God's love is revealed. Such love invites a wholehearted response: to care for all humanity and all creation. This is what it means to experience life under Christ now.

Luke 23.33–43

This is Luke's account of Jesus' crucifixion. Two criminals are to be crucified along with Jesus. The words 'Father forgive them, for they know not what they do' are only found in a few manuscripts of Luke's Gospel, but reflect Luke's constant concern with forgiveness. Although it was the Romans who crucified Jesus, Luke writes for Christians who lived within the Roman world, and he does not want to show the Romans in a bad light. For this reason it is the Jewish authorities who need and receive forgiveness. The crowds watch quietly, but the rulers mock Jesus and by calling him 'chosen' echo the account of the transfiguration. The irony is obvious: the Messiah is the one who saves others and those who mock Jesus have not realized that they are witnessing God's ultimate saving act or that the 'King of the Jews' signalled Jesus' true identity. Both the criminals, unlike Jesus, deserved punishment. However, only one asked Jesus to 'remember' him. To remember is the opposite of forgetting, and to be remembered by God is to be saved from annihilation. The criminal does not express remorse or ask forgiveness, rather he acknowledges Jesus' kingship. Paradise, a Persian expression for the place where those blessed by God went after death, was thought to be like the Garden of Eden before the fall. The surprising emphasis is that the criminal will join Jesus in paradise that very day. Throughout his ministry, Jesus brought the healing and wholeness that enabled outcasts to take their place within the people of God. Yet, ultimately, the opportunity for salvation is the moment of Jesus' death.

We are assured, through the cross, that we are 'remembered'. To be remembered by God is to belong to him and to be assured that he will never abandon us. We are included within the company of God's people.